Also by Ha Jin

THE BANISHED IMMORTAL

HA JIN

THE BANISHED IMMORTAL

A Life of Li Bai (Li Po)

PANTHEON BOOKS, NEW YORK

Grateful acknowledgment is made to The Permissions Company, Inc. on behalf of Copper Canyon Press for permission to reprint an excerpt of "Tu Fu to Li Po" from *Cool, Calm and Collected: Poems 1960–2000* by Carolyn Kizer. Copyright © Carolyn Kizer. Reprinted permission of The Permissions Company, Inc. on behalf of Copper Canyon Press (www.coppercanyonpresss.org).

Library of Congress Cataloging-in-Publication Data
Name: Jin, Ha, [date] author.
Title: The banished immortal : a life of Li Bai (Li Po) / Ha Jin.
Other titles: Life of Li Bai (Li Po)
Description: New York : Pantheon, 2019. Chinese versions of his poetry will be included. Includes bibliographical references.
Identifiers: LCCN 2018024328. ISBN 9781524747411 (hardback).
ISBN 9781524747428 (ebook).
Subjects: LCSH: Li Bai, 701–762. Poets, Chinese—Biography.
Li Bai, 701–762—Criticism and interpretation. BISAC: BIOGRAPHY & AUTOBIOGRAPHY/Literary. LITERARY CRITICISM/Poetry. HISTORY/Asia/China.
Classification: LCC PL2671 .J554 2019 | DDC 895.11/3 [B] —dc23 |
LC record available at lccn.loc.gov/2018024328

www.pantheonbooks.com

CONTENTS

v

PRELUDE

He has many names. In the West, people call him Li Po, as most of his poems translated into English bear that name. Sometimes it is also spelled Li Bo. But in China, he is known as Li Bai. During his lifetime (701–762 AD), he had other names—Li Taibai, Green Lotus Scholar, Li Twelve. The last one is a kind of familial term of endearment, as Bai was twelfth among his brothers and male cousins on the paternal side. It was often used by his friends and fellow poets when they addressed him—some even dedicated poems to him titled "For Li Twelve." By the time of his death, he had become known as a great poet and was called *zhexian,* or Banished Immortal, by his admirers. Such a moniker implies that he had been sent down to earth as punishment for his misbehavior in heaven. Over the twelve centuries since his death, he has been revered as *shixian,* Poet Immortal. Because he was an excessive drinker, he was also called *jiuxian,* Wine Immortal. Today it is still common for devotees of his poetry to trek hundreds of miles, following some of the routes of his wanderings as a kind of pilgrimage. Numerous liquors and wines bear his name. Indeed, his name is a ubiquitous brand, flaunted by hotels, restaurants, temples, and even factories.

In English, in addition to "Li Po," he once had another pair of names, Li T'ai Po and Rihaku. The first is a phonetic transcription of his original Chinese name, Li Taibai, the name his parents gave him. And Ezra Pound, in his *Cathay*—his collected translations of classical Chinese poetry—called Li Bai *Rihaku* because Pound had translated those poems from the notes left by the American scholar Ernest Fenollosa, who had originally studied Li Bai's poetry in Japanese when he was in Japan. Pound's loose translation of Li Bai's "The River-Merchant's Wife: A Letter" has been included in many textbooks and anthologies as a masterpiece of modern poetry. It is also one of Pound's signature poems—arguably his best known. For the sake of consistency and clarity, in the following pages let us stay with the name Li Bai.

He also has several deaths ascribed to him. For hundreds of years, some people even maintained that he had never died at all, claiming to encounter him now and then.[1] In truth, we are uncertain about the exact date and cause of his death. In January 764, the newly enthroned Emperor Daizong issued a decree summoning Li Bai to serve as a counselor at court. It was a post without actual power in spite of its high-sounding title. Yet to any man of learning and ambition such an appointment was a great favor, a demonstration of the emperor's benevolence and magnanimity—and in Li Bai's case, a partial restoration of the high status he had once held in the court. When the royal decree reached Dangtu County, Anhui, where Li Bai was supposed to be located, the local officials were thrown into confusion and could not find him. Soon it was discovered that he had died more than a year before. Of what cause and on what day, no one could tell. So we can only say that Li Bai, despite his renown, passed away in 762 without notice.

However, such an obscure death was not acceptable to those who cherished his poetry. They began to give different versions of his death, stories spun either to suit the romantic image of his poetic personality or to provide a fitting conclusion to his turbulent life. In one version, he died of alcohol poisoning; this was in keeping with his lifelong indulgence in drink. Another claims that he died of an illness known as chronic thoracic suppuration—pus universal and ever reliable—"Raising my head, I see the bright moon, / And lowering it, I think of home" ("Reflection in a Quiet Night"). The legend of his attempt to embrace the moon suggests an ultimate fulfillment of his wish and vision—a reversed spiritual ascent. Some of his contemporaries believed him to have been a star in his previous life, and so by joining the moon in the water, he returned to the heavenly space where he had once dwelled. The brief "Li Bai Biography" in the eleventh-century book *New Tang History* reads, "When giving birth to Li Bai, his mother dreamed of the star Venus, so he was named Taibai (Venus)."

The poets who came after him have continued to celebrate his moonlit death: even though they know it may not be true, across the centuries they have eulogized the shining moment in their verses. Even today, lovers of Li Bai's poetry indulge in the myth. One contemporary scholar writes that Li Bai "rode a whale, floating away with the waves, toward the moon."[2] This heaven-ward journey is presented from the distraught, drunken poet's point of view so that Li Bai appears to be returning to his original, divine position. Such romanticization shows the nature of scholarship around Li Bai, which is partly based on legends and myths. Because people want him to have a glorious end, they have been eager to perpetuate the moon-chasing legend.

However, for all the imaginative attempts to glorify him, a single clear voice spoke about his situation presciently when the poet was still alive and in exile. His staunch friend Du Fu laments in his poem "Dreaming of Li Bai":

冠蓋滿京華　　斯人獨憔悴
孰云網恢恢　　將老身反累
千秋萬歲名　　寂寞身後事

《夢李白》

penetrating his chest and lungs. The first mention of this comes from Pi Rixiu (838–883) in his poem "Seven Loves": "He was brought down by rotted ribs, / Which sent his drunken soul to the other world." Although there is no way we can verify this claim, it sounds credible—such a chest problem could have been caused by his abuse of alcohol. In his final years, Li Bai's drinking and poverty would have aggravated his pulmonary condition. But the third version of his death is far more fantastic: in this version, he drowns while drunkenly chasing the moon's reflection on a river, jumping from a boat to catch the ever-shifting orb.

Even though this scene smacks of suicide and is perhaps too romantic to be believed, it is the version that has been embraced by the public—in part because Li Bai, as his poetry shows, loved the moon. Even in his early childhood he was fixated on it. In his poem "Night Trip in Gulang," he writes, "As a young child, I had no idea what the moon was / And I called it a white jade plate. / Then I wondered if it was a mirror at the Jasper Terrace / That flew away and landed on top of green clouds." In Chinese poetry, Li Bai was the first to use the image of the moon abundantly, celebrating its loftiness, purity, and constancy. He imagined the moon as a serene landscape with sublime dwellings for *xian,* or immortals, who are often surrounded by divine fauna and flora and their personal pets. The beliefs of the ancient Chinese did not separate divinity from humanity, and their imagined heavenly space resembled the human world, with similar (but more fantastic) landscapes and architecture and creatures. If cultivated enough, any human being could rise to the order of divinity, becoming a *xian*—many temples in China worshiped these kinds of local deities. Heaven was inhabited by these beings, who were somewhat like superhumans, powerful and carefree and immortal.

The moon in Li Bai's poetry is also associated with one's home or native place, and as a beacon shared by people everywhere,

The capital is full of gorgeous carriages and gowns,
But you are alone gaunt and sallow despite your gift.
Who is to say that the way of heaven is always fair?
At your old age you can't stay clear of harm.
Your fame that's to last ten thousand years
Will become a quiet affair after you are gone.

THE BANISHED IMMORTAL

ORIGINS

When we talk about Li Bai, we should keep in mind that there are three of him: the actual Li Bai, the self-created Li Bai, and the Li Bai produced by historical and cultural imagination. Ideally, our ambition here should be to present the actual Li Bai as much as we can while also trying to understand the motivations and consequences of his self-creation. But we should also bear in mind that such an ambition is necessarily tempered by the relative scarcity of verifiable information on Li Bai's life.

Several chronologies of his life have been produced in recent decades. They are very similar in content and approach, listing the major biographical events mainly based on the information provided in his writings, the principal source of his self-creation. Every one of his biographers writing in Chinese has fleshed out Li Bai's life according to these events, and these biographies have themselves built on each other over time. Three of the most prominent and most useful have served as my main sources: *A Critical Biography of Li Bai*, by Zhou Xunchu; *A Biography of Li Bai*, by Li Changzhi; and *Li Bai: A Biography*, by An Qi. In English, Arthur Waley published his *The Poetry and Career of Li Po* nearly seventy years ago; though the information in his slender book is incomplete and somewhat outdated, the monograph still shows solid scholarship and sound judgments, and I have sourced from it as well. In recent decades, the Li Bai Institute in the city of

Ma'anshan has regularly published volumes of academic papers, some of which have also helped me construct my narrative. Like the writers of the chronologies, these scholars rely foremost on the original poetry—over the centuries people have created stories and episodes of his life based on the references provided in his verses. Still, according to Li Bai's uncle, Li Yangbing, "nine out of ten of his poems" are lost. His writings that are available to us now are based on two collections of his works compiled by his disciple Wei Hao and Li Yangbing—about a thousand poems and essays—and they are only a small part of his total output.

Although Li Bai's own poems are our most important sources, a few of his friends also wrote about him. We have from them a handful of poems and short pieces of prose that depict his personality as well as his physical appearance. According to his contemporaries, he had striking features and an insouciant personality. Wei Hao describes him with flashing eyes and a powerful, energetic mouth: "His eyes were piercingly bright while his mouth opened like a hungry tiger's. He often tied a sash around him, which gave him a casual but elegant manner. Because he had been inducted into the Daoist society in Qi [modern northeastern Shandong], he wore a black embroidered hat."[1] Such hats were characteristic of Daoist masters at the time. Throughout the centuries that followed this writing, some portraits of Li Bai have resembled Wei Hao's description. Gao Shi's verses evoke a tall, broad man with a commanding presence: "Duke Li has an innate grandeur. / He's strapping with a straight back. / His mind wanders through different worlds / While his robe and hat fit the current fashion here."[2] Li Bai was cheerful and stylish; in fact, he often described himself as "a carefree spirit," someone who could never truly fit the mold of the government official he had been expected to become. The stories of his legendary drinking also reveal a free-spirited nature. Du Fu praised him as an unshakable drinker, saying, "Even summoned by the Son of Heaven, / He won't get on the boat." In another poem, Du Fu writes that Li Bai had "a divine bone structure," which matches Gao Shi's line: "strapping with a straight back."

There is also a rare piece of material evidence that offers more direct insight into Li Bai's personality and skill: we still have a small scroll of calligraphy inscribed by him, containing twenty-four words. This is the only extant calligraphy of his. It was loved by Mao Zedong, who kept it for years before surrendering it to the Forbidden City's museum in 1958. In China, calligraphy has long been a common way of displaying one's literary cultivation and artistic spirit, and handwriting is traditionally read as an index of sorts to one's character and even physique. Bai's small scroll states, "The mountain is high and the water long; only a vigorous brush can portray the beauty and grandeur. Inscribed by Taibai at Shangyang Terrace, on the 18th Day." It is evidently an occasional piece, whose context is unclear. Yet the lettering is extraordinarily robust and beautiful and floating, displaying the writer's innate radiance. These characters show the work of a master calligrapher with a striking, unique style. Judging by the bold beauty of his calligraphy, Li Bai must have been spiritually free and physically strong.

There is scant information on Bai's childhood and family background. What we have is largely from the accumulated scholarship around him, which has striven to flesh out his life. In his writings, he almost never mentions his parents or siblings. Strikingly, he doesn't say a word about his mother. It is believed that ethnically she was not a Han Chinese but from a minority tribe, probably a Turk. Mixed marriages were common in the far-flung land of China's western frontier, where the Li family lived for two or three generations, and from where they later migrated back inland to Sichuan. China's border was not clearly defined at the time, and the vast western region was inhabited by Mongols, Persians, Turks, and Uighurs. The borders continually shifted among those western kingdoms as well, some of which were formed by allied tribes.

Wars were often fought, and states appeared and disappeared. As a result, people of different ethnicities mingled, and interracial marriages were inevitable. It's believed that Li Bai was half Han and had foreign features—this has not been proved conclusively, though we do know that people of his time could tell that he was partially *hu,* barbarian. The Tang dynasty was a relatively tolerant regime—much more open than the China of our time—and foreigners could find suitable roles in society and government. Even some top marshals in the Chinese army were foreigners.

Although Bai never speaks of her directly, it's safe to say that his mother was a remarkably strong woman, full of vitality and endurance. She gave her husband several children, and Bai, despite having numerous older brothers ahead of him, was wild with energy and spirit. It is hard to fathom how strong the older sons must have been. We know that Bai had a younger sister, named Round Moon, who either came back to Sichuan with their family or was born inland, and who later married a local man. Her grave, which lies in the family's Sichuan hometown of Jiangyou, is still well kept and surrounded by flowers and plants. Bai also had a younger brother, who might have been born in Sichuan. Before returning inland, the Li family had lived in the area of Suyab (modern Tokmok in Kyrgyzstan), which in the Tang dynasty was under the control of Anxi Circuit, a regional government, as well as a military command.[3] Li Bai's father was a successful merchant dealing in grains, fabrics, wines, dried foods, utensils, and paper. Paper was widely available in China at the time, and there were many kinds made from various materials, such as hemp, straw, and bark. Bamboo paper, durable and glossy, was by far the most precious. Through the Silk Road, the famous network of trade routes begun in the Han dynasty (206 BC–AD 220) connecting China, India, Central Asia, Arabia, Africa, and Europe, paper was introduced to Arabia and then to Europe. Li Bai's father was one of those traders whose caravans of camels carried westward commodities produced in China. They also trekked inland with goods from the outlying western regions—mostly pelts, medicinal herbs, and dried fruits. The man often took his older sons on his trading trips inland and taught them how to conduct business. Along the Yangtze River the Lis had several trading stations and their enterprise continually expanded. The evidence suggests that they amassed a considerable amount of wealth.

Li Bai's father is called Li Ke, a name that to Chinese ears sounds unusual and exotic. *Ke* in Chinese means "guest," and very few people of that time and place would have gone by a name that connoted "stranger" and "outsider." In fact, we are not even sure if his family name, Li, was genuine. It has been argued that such a surname might have been invented by Bai's father when he came back inland. Self-invented surnames were common at that time—people often associated themselves with powerful clans as a way of self-promotion and protection. Throughout his life, Li Bai asserted that he belonged to the royal clan, because the emperors and princes had the same family name. Although the emperors of the Tang dynasty did all have the name Li, the royal family had also altered their history to make their pedigree appear more authentically Chinese. The first Tang emperor, Taizu, had had foreign blood through his mother, a Sien-pi, a Tartar from southern Hebei. But later, the emperor and the court historians claimed that the royal family was originally from Guanlong, an area in between Gansu and Shanxi provinces—for in Hebei the Lis were a minority clan, whereas the Lis of Guanlong were prestigious and powerful, authentic Chinese from the central land. This might partly explain why the royal family never denied that Li Bai was one of them—their genealogy seemed to allow room for self-invention.

Li Ke was an astute and calculating man. According to Li Bai's own account in a preface to a poem,[4] his father was well learned (most likely self-taught) and familiar with the classics, which he taught to his children. Li Ke told others that his family had lost its genealogy book on their journey back inland, but that they were nonetheless descended from the great general Li Guang (184–119 BC), who had been garrisoned in the western lands more than eight centuries before. Li Guang was a legendary figure who had guarded the outlying region against the aggression of the foreign forces—mainly the Huns—from Central Asia. Many poems and stories celebrate his bravery and deeds. One poem declares, "So long as the Flying General is here, / The barbarians' horses dare not cross Mount Yin." Mount Yin was a passageway from the western lands to inland China, and "the Flying General" was the name that the Huns had given Li Guang because of the swift, unpredictable movement of his troops. A story, recorded by the historian Sima Qian, relates that Li Guang and his bodyguards once caught sight of a tiger in a forest. The general shot an arrow at the beast. The next day, when his men went over to fetch the kill, they found it was not an animal but a brown rock in which the weapon was lodged—the general's strength was capable of embedding an entire arrowhead in rock. Try as they might, they couldn't pull the arrow out. Despite Li Guang's victories and loyalty to the Han court, he was never properly rewarded by the central government, nor was he allowed to return inland. He was so disillusioned by the mistreatment he suffered at the hands of his superiors that he eventually cut his own throat.

Li Ke's claim of blood relation with the renowned forebear, as one of the sixteenth generation of Li Guang's line, could not be refuted, since it was known that the general had indeed left behind a branch in the western reaches of China. There was more to be said about Li Ke's claim, however. The Tang royal clan's revised genealogy indicated that its members and General Li Guang shared the same ancestors who had once lived in Guanlong in the central plain, so Li Ke's family, by his own claim, must have also been related to the Tang rulers by blood. Moreover, by this lineage, Li Ke in fact was descended from an earlier generation of this family tree, well ahead of the royal family. This is why Li Bai later implied that Xuanzong, the current emperor, was by genealogy a grandnephew of his.

Self-inventions of this kind could be confusing. What is more complicated is that Li was a widely used name, reputable and made prestigious by the association with the royal family. (Today there are approximately one hundred million Lis in the world.) Whenever Li Bai traveled, he would encounter people with the same surname. Out of habit and courtesy he would acknowledge a blood relationship with them, especially powerful officials, and would call them "cousin" or "nephew" or "uncle" and even dedicate poems to some of them. As a result, he had "relatives" everywhere, and there is no telling who was actually connected by blood.

Li Bai was five years old when his father uprooted the family from Suyab and moved them back inland. They crossed a chain of the Tianshan Mountains and then deserts, and reached Sichuan more than half a year later. Li Bai must have remembered the arduous trek, as his poetry often displays an immense wilderness uniquely his own. "The Mountain Moon," one of his most celebrated frontier poems, begins with a description of such a vast landscape:

明月出天山　蒼茫云海間
長風幾萬里　吹度玉門關

《關山月》

The moon rises from Tianshan Mountain,
Sailing in an ocean of clouds.
The wind, tens of thousands of miles long,
Is blowing through the Yumen Pass.

Having entered Sichuan, the Lis settled in Changming County (modern Jiangyou) and set up their homestead in Qinglian Village. The village was about twenty miles north of the county seat, and the landscape there had a mystic air to it. Yellow flowers hung on trees, interspersed with bamboo bushes, and the area was enclosed on the south by the Fu and Jian rivers, their waters sending up steam and mist that obscured the land and sky.[5] It was a remote, isolated place, and the entire county had no more than a few thousand households. Why would Li Ke relocate his family to such a distant village? Surely this would not have been convenient for his business or wholesome for his children's upbringing. The answer remains a mystery. Some scholars speculate that the move might have been a way to avoid dangerous fallout from a feud or some serious trouble with local officials.[6] Jiangyou was the starting point of the Silk Road, so Li Ke must have been to this area before on his business travels and would have been familiar with its surroundings and the local people. In other words, his choice of location—far-off but still connected with the outside world—seems to have been carefully made.

Li Ke and his sons resumed trading in Sichuan and along the Yangtze. Wealthy and shrewd, he also loaned money to others. Soon he began to work on behalf of Daming Temple, a well-known Buddhist site of the time, perhaps clandestinely serving as its front man to lend money and collect interests and debts, because temples were not supposed to be overtly active in trade and business. He continued to prosper and gradually became a local power of sorts.

It was conventional wisdom that a large, affluent household should send its sons into varying professions. This was a way to expand the family's influence, to ensure its prosperity, and to secure protection for its members and property. Such diversification could also help a family weather setbacks and social upheavals. Li Ke followed this course with his sons: some joined him in the trade down the river, but he wanted Bai to become a government official—the boy had an energetic mind and a powerful memory and could excel in an official career. To achieve that goal, Li Bai needed to study books and acquire extensive schooling. This also meant that Li Ke had to spend much more on Bai's education than on his other sons'.

At the time, businesspeople belonged to the lower strata of Chinese society. At any moment the state could—and still can—seize people's personal wealth and even turn them into criminals, regardless of whether any crime had been committed. Whenever the government lacked funds, it would fleece businesspeople and property owners, leaving them no space for safety or growth. As a result, wealth was not viewed as an effective means of self-protection. For millennia, the best way to safeguard one's interests in China has been to affiliate oneself with political power—to befriend high officials and even join their occupation. The Li family's arrangement for Bai's career seems to have followed such a convention. His father must have had other purposes in mind as well—to enhance the family reputation and to put Li Bai in a position to accomplish significant deeds that could give him a lasting name.

Although the civil-service examination system had been in place for more than a century, the way to join officialdom was still narrow and extremely competitive. As a merchant's son, Li Bai was not allowed to enter for the exam. Businesspeople were viewed as dishonorable elements of society, so their sons were not eligible for civil service. Only young men from official and aristocratic families or from an agricultural background could take the exam. At that time, China had slightly more than ten thousand officials, but each year only around thirty were actually appointed through the examination. Worse still, a candidate was not judged by the results of the tests alone. He also had to have an advocate, usually an official of considerable rank, to support his candidacy. Because of this, many scholars, though intelligent and erudite, never could find a way to an official career.

However, there was another, older way of becoming an official: *zhiju,* which meant through recommendations and interviews. Ever since the Qin dynasty (221–206 BC), high officials had been obliged to recommend capable talents to court. The emperor would interview them individually to assess their abilities. If the ruler was impressed and satisfied, the candidate would be granted a significant post. (This method continues today in state programs like "The Plan for a Hundred People" and "The Plan for a Thousand People," which have been designed to recruit experts in various fields from all over the world.) The Tang government needed to secure as many talented men as possible to consolidate its power and strengthen its rule. A candidate undergoing the process of recommendation and interview had to be extraordinarily well learned and acute—ideally, a successful candidate would go on to become a linchpin of the country. Having no access to the civil-service examination, Li Bai would pursue this older path to officialdom, which required mastery of several key areas of knowledge: statecraft, philosophy, classics, writing, swordsmanship.

By age ten he had studied most of the classics available; he was mainly taught by his father and at tutorial schools, each of which had four or five pupils. Sichuan was far from the central land and had not yet been penetrated by the prevailing bureaucratic culture that reflected the imperial order of the time. As a result, education lagged in the region, placing more emphasis on older books written in the era of the Warring States (475–221 BC), when seven states fought over the control of the central land so as to unify China under a single government. Li Bai did not find the Confucian classics appealing—his recalcitrant character was at odds with the rules and rites associated with governance. One of these classics, the *Book of Rites,* describes the ancient rites and social forms and court ceremonies; another, *Spring and Autumn,* is a volume of historical records of the State of Lu. The classics also teach official manners and decorum, as shown in the *Book of Documents,* and together the Confucian texts—the Four Books and Five

Classics—provide an education in the official culture. Bai found them boring. He did not like historical books either, especially those written by court historians. He preferred the Daoist texts, particularly *Chuang Tzu,* a book of writings by the philosopher Zhuang Zhou (369–286 BC).

Bai was inspired by Zhuang's boundless imagination, and would indulge in his own wild reveries. He often alluded to the beginning passage in *Chuang Tzu,* in "Xiaoyao you" ("Free Wandering"), which reads, "There was once a fish in the north sea, named Kun. Its size was so immense that it stretched a thousand miles. Later the fish changed into a bird, which was named Peng. Peng's back was so vast that it was a thousand miles long. When it soared, its wings moved like clouds over the horizon. This bird followed the swells of the ocean to the south sea, which is a big natural pool." The bird, Peng, refers to a legendary roc—an enormous bird of prey—to which Li Bai compares himself in one of his early rhapsodies, "The Great Peng." In the poetic essay he expresses his aspiration, like the roc in flight, "to make heaven tilt with the bird's soaring while the mountains are quaking and the oceans churning and surging below." Later, in another rhapsody, he again identifies himself as a mystical roc, dreaming of flying and scanning the human world from above. It was Zhuang Zhou that first fired his imagination.

The genre of rhapsody, or *fu,* is an ancient kind of prose poetry that, thanks to its structure and unlimited length, has more room for dramatization, description, and exposition. Li Bai loved the rhapsody: in one of his poems, he extolls his own talent in the form, saying, "At fifteen I began to read rare books / And surpassed Xiang-ru in writing rhapsodies" ("For Zhang Xianggao"). "Xiang-ru" refers to Sima Xiang-ru (179–117 BC), a court official and a man of letters who is regarded as one of China's greatest writers of rhapsody. (Although Li Bai loved the form, rhapsodies are a minor part of his literary output. He was much more at home with verse poetry and displayed extraordinary talent in poetic composition at an early age.) Throughout his youth, Li Bai viewed Sima as an exemplary model to follow—a man who was also from Sichuan and had excelled in both his official career and his literary accomplishments.

Like most pupils at the time, Li Bai memorized many ancient poems and essays and went on to emulate them. One of the texts he studied was an old anthology titled *Zhaoming Selected Masterpieces* compiled in 526, comprising more than seven hundred canonical poems and essays. Li Bai is said to have imitated every piece in the book three times. He often threw away attempts that he believed were not good enough, and grew impatient with his slow progress. One day he came upon an old woman on the side of a brook in his hometown. She was grinding an iron bar on a rock, and he asked her what she was doing. She replied that she was making a needle out of the iron bar. How could that be possible? he wondered aloud. As long as she went on grinding, she said, she would one day reduce the bar to a needle with which she could make embroidery. He was so struck by her answer and her will to persevere that from then on he studied harder and more patiently. Today in Qinglian Town, Jiangyou County, there still flows a creek named the Needle Grinding Brook.

Li Bai's father encouraged him to compose poems. Although poetry was not a skill required of officials, it could enhance one's career to be adept in the art. There were great examples of poets from modest family backgrounds who became significant officials without passing the civil-service examination. Chen Zi'ang (661–702), another Sichuan poet just a generation prior to Li Bai, had been appointed a court counselor not through the exam but through the sponsorship of Empress Wu (624–705), the current emperor's grandmother. Chen's poems were known everywhere, and people would chant his lines: "The sky is green and the wilderness endless. / When the wind blows, the grass dips revealing herds of cattle and sheep" ("Song of Ascending Youzhou Terrace").

Poetry had been a major source of entertainment for more than a millennium, both in palaces and in cities and towns. Poems were composed orally or in writing on many kinds of occasions. Court officials were usually vain and proud of their ability to produce poetry, and their sovereigns often invited them to improvise verses at festive gatherings. A particularly outstanding poem would be set to music, and the new song would then be added to the court's repertoire. Over the centuries, however, poetry composed at court had become hackneyed and routine, though occasionally a genuinely well-crafted poem still emerged. Two centuries before Bai's time, in the Kingdom of Liang (present-day Henan Province), a general named Cao Jingzong (457–508) had led troops to war and defeated the army of Wei, an enemy kingdom. At the court's celebratory banquet, King Liangwu had pairs of rhyming words distributed among the courtiers for them to compose poems. Cao was not given any words because he was a warrior and thought unlikely to know how to make verse. He requested a pair of words from King Liangwu three times, and finally was granted the last two: *jing* ("compete") and *bing* ("illness"). This was a very odd pair, nearly impossible to rhyme due to their semantic disconnection, and people were ready to laugh at Cao. After thinking a moment, he wielded a brush and wrote out this poem:

去時女兒悲　歸來笳鼓競
借問行路人　何如霍去病

When we were departing, our children grieved.
Now we are back, flutes and drums are competing.
My soldiers, tell me
Were you as brave as Huo Qubing?

Huo Qubing (140–117 BC) had been a valorous general centuries before, famous for his victorious battles against the Huns. Cao's poem amazed the entire banquet hall, and King Liangwu was so impressed that he promoted him to duke. Afterward the poem was set to music and became a classic. How many poets since have envied Cao for the permanent mark he left on Chinese letters by happenstance.

The Tang court had an official, known as the Harmonious Regulator (*Xie lü lang*), who was in charge of studying and refining versification. Just as social rules and official rites had been strictly standardized by then (the process had accelerated after the centralized government was established in the Qin dynasty of 221–207 BC), poetics had also become regulated—so much so that poetry began to grow overly tight and formal, enervated by strict metrical prescriptions. Many practitioners of this standardized poetry focused on technical skill and rules instead of human spirit and experience. However, this was about to change because Li Bai would soon burst onto the scene, and genius always revises the status quo.

From the very beginning Li Bai was not fond of regulated verse—although he could produce it with virtuosity—because he was not someone who liked to be hemmed in by requirements. What he admired most were three poetic traditions: *gufeng,* or ancient folk poems, a kind of poetry written before the Tang dynasty without specific metric patterns or rhymes; *yuefu,* or folk songs, which Bai composed throughout his life; and *Chuci, Songs of Chu,* a body of poems composed mainly by Qu Yuan (340–278 BC).

Gufeng is rather loose and spacious; a poem of this kind can be of any length and can express drama at its fullest and most vivid. Folk songs in the *yuefu* tradition had a long history prior to Bai's time. He loved their liveliness and vitality, rooted in immediate human experience; throughout his life, he also learned from the contemporary folk songs performed in inns, taverns, and teahouses. *Chuci* suited Li Bai's natural disposition and, later, his vision of the universe shaped by Daoism.

Qu Yuan, the author of *Chuci*, had once been a court official in the State of Chu in charge of religious worship, but because of his dissenting political views, particularly his fervent opposition to Chu's alliance with the aggressive Qin State, he had resigned, self-banished, and wandered the wilderness. Two decades later, his country was conquered by the State of Qin, the same enemy to which Qu Yuan had been vehemently opposed. At the news of the loss of his country, he drowned himself in the Liluo River. Ever since, people in China have observed the date of his death, May 5, as a holiday in memory of the great poet. Because *zongzi*, steamed glutinous rice dumplings wrapped with reed leaves, are eaten on this day, the holiday is also called Zongzi Day. Originally people believed that the dumplings would satiate the fish in the Liluo River so that the body of the drowned poet would be spared. Several other countries in East Asia also celebrate May 5 as a holiday, eating *zongzi*, holding dragon boat races, and putting on festive shows, although by now its origin is almost forgotten.

What attracted Li Bai to Qu Yuan's poetry was the celestial space in it, and he would carry on this tradition in his own work. Unlike poetry in the West, which traditionally is rooted in divine inspiration from a poetic Muse, Chinese culture has no concept of Muses, and so the poetry on the whole is chthonian by nature. Poems tend to stay within the worldly domain, focusing on human drama and experience. They do not evoke the divinity for auspices—Qu Yuan's are a striking exception. A poem in *Chuci* describes his meeting with an imagined deity this way:

浴蘭湯兮沐芳　　華采衣兮若英
靈連蜷兮既留　　爛昭昭兮未央
蹇將憺兮壽宮　　與日月兮齊光
龍駕兮帝服　　　聊翱遊兮周章

靈皇皇兮既降　猋遠舉兮雲中
覽冀洲兮有餘　橫四海兮焉窮
思夫君兮太息　極勞心兮忡忡

《雲中君》

In fragrant water I bathe myself and wash my hair
And put on clothes that shine like jade.
I see the cloud goddess lingering as if reluctant to leave,
Her full splendor radiating endlessly.
Above us the Longevity Palace stands aloft,
As glorious as the sun and the moon.
She wears a colored gown and rides a dragon carriage
Going back and forth through the vast sky.
See, she is about to descend, then
Swiftly she flies away and disappears in the clouds.
She scans the whole of the central land below,
Beyond which spreads the ocean in every direction.
I am thinking of you, my goddess,
And can't stop sighing, laden with worries.

"THE ONE IN CLOUDS"

Through his imagination, the poet travels freely between heaven and earth; his poetry presents an entire celestial sphere where he longs to reside. This space is superior to the mundane order of the secular world and signifies another kind of existence. Li Bai was fascinated by such a space and would ultimately inhabit it in his poetry. Considering the three poetic traditions from which he drew inspiration, Bai was very selective in forming his own poetic heritage.

In addition to the private tutorials and his father's home-schooling, Li Bai in his midteens also stayed in Daming Temple on Kuang Mountain, studying with the Buddhist monks there.

He not only studied books but also learned the art of the sword from an older monk named Master Kong-ling. Swordsmanship would become a lifelong passion. Bai's stay in the temple seems odd—he did not practice Buddhism and later would become a staunch Daoist. Though he dabbled in Buddhism throughout his life, he was never a serious believer, because while Buddhists were supposed to be detached from politics, his ambitions centered on a government position.

Daoism and Confucianism have each served as the state religion in different dynasties throughout Chinese history; in Li Bai's time, the Tang rulers held Daoism as the religion of the royal family and therefore of the country. Although Daoism has little to say about governance (it advocates joining the natural course, the way things exist, waxing and waning), the Tang rulers found prestige in associating themselves with Lao Tzu, the author of the *Tao Te Ching,* claiming him as their ancestor since his personal surname—Li Dan—was the same as theirs. In other eras, Confucianism—with its emphasis on the rites and decorum of officialdom and the ethical order of families and society—has been strongly linked to the state, forming the underpinnings of the bureaucratic culture. Both faiths were more secular than Buddhism, which has never been associated with a governing power, never having become a state religion.

Li Bai's incongruous taking of refuge in the Buddhist monastery gave rise to a myth meant to explain it. The story goes that he often ran into trouble in his teens and even killed people, so his father hid him away in the temple from time to time.[7] Bai might indeed have been a problematic youth, as he later wrote in his poems that he had often fought with others. But the story of his manslaughter is written with such hyperbole that it has the ring of a fanciful boast. In several of his poems, he mentions manslaughter as a way to display his bravery and swordsmanship (attributes valued by the society at large). Lines like these are often cited as evidence: "After three cups I began to play with my sword, / Cutting down people like weeds" ("Song of a White Horse"); "Surrounded by white blades / I killed men in red dust" ("For Brother Hao, Magistrate of Xiangyang County"); and "Walking every ten steps, I cut down a man / And I didn't stop for a thousand *li*" ("Song of a Knight"). One *li* is five hundred meters, and so here his boast of killing for "a thousand *li*" is an impossibility, a wild poetic exaggeration, similar to analogies in his other poems, such as "In the Yan area snowflakes fall as large as mats" and "My hair grows white, thirty thousand feet long."

Undoubtedly Li Bai was a hothead, impulsive and intolerant of injustice, and he might have wounded people with his sword, which he carried wherever he went, but it is unlikely that he could have continued his life with impunity if he had committed manslaughter, an extremely serious crime in the Tang dynasty. Its law states unequivocally that capital punishment is to be meted out for such an offender: "Intended manslaughter committed in a fight—to be hanged; manslaughter with a blade—to be beheaded; manslaughter with a weapon in a fight, even though by accident—to be treated the same as intended manslaughter."[8] A Buddhist monastery like Daming was unlikely to harbor a murderer, and Li Bai would later travel through the central land without fear of punishment.

Bai's boast does seem to reflect his impulse toward destruction and crime, which is often inseparable from artistic creation. He bragged about this impulse even as he might not have been clear about how it was rooted in his being and was a source of his creative energy. Many great writers share this fascination with the dark, violent force in the human soul—Goethe in his *Faust* and Dostoyevsky in his great psychological novels.[9] And Bai's poetic exaggeration also reflects a broader tendency of the Chinese language in general to use wild analogies. Some of its expressions are based upon very large gestures: to describe pain, for instance, one can say that "my heart is pierced by ten thousand arrows." In English, a more restrictive and precise language, such an analogy sounds hyperbolic, but to the Chinese ear it sounds proper and even credible. To praise a man's capacity for alcohol, Du Fu writes that "he drinks like a long whale sucking a hundred rivers"—an impossible image, but Chinese readers take it as natural and wonderful. To describe a woman's beauty, people will say that her looks make fish dive deeper and geese drop to the ground (as if out of shame). Li Bai's boasts about his murderous deeds fall into this same tradition: they are not meant to reflect literal truth, but rather to impress others by highlighting his extraordinariness.

2

AWAY FROM HOME

Li Bai's father was impressed by his son's imaginative poems. Many visitors to their home praised the poems as well, but Li Ke could see that Bai lacked the life experience necessary to produce truly original work: his verses were derivative, more like exceptional exercises. Without original experience, he would not be able to develop his poetic singularity, so his father gave him a generous allowance and allowed him to travel locally to see the landscapes and the people and customs of the region. Traditionally, for one's education, travel was regarded as equally important as the study of books. An ancient adage says that one must read ten thousand books and travel ten thousand miles to become an educated man. So in his late teens Li Bai began to roam the neighboring counties and towns.

Most Li Bai chronologies, such as the ones compiled by An Qi and Yu Xianhao, specify 718 as the first time he left home. One day in the spring he took a boat down the Fu River and reached Zi Prefecture, whose administrative center was in the seat of Chang County, a commercial hub in northern Sichuan. The town's marketplace stretched along the riverside. But Bai did not stay in Chang County for long, because his interests lay elsewhere. He had heard of an extraordinary man living in Changping Mountain, just north of the town, and he wanted to pay him a visit. The man, Zhao Rui (659?–742?), was to play a major role in Li Bai's development. Zhao was widely known as an erudite recluse; he lived in a cave on a cliff with his wife and children. He came from a renowned family and was well versed in classics. In his youth, he had studied hard for the civil-service examination, only to fail it time and again. Finally he gave up and returned home to write his own work, titled *Long and Short Scriptures,* a minor classic of pragmatic philosophy that is also called *The Reversed Scriptures.* He despised the canon of Confucian classics, on which he had wasted many years studying for the civil-service examination, so he positioned his own book as an antithetical text. He lived and thought like someone who had existed a millennium prior, in the time of the Warring States (475–221 BC). Most of his views were derived from the Legalist thinkers of the violent period, such as Han Feizi, Shang Yang, and others. Zhao was also an expert in swordsmanship. As his reputation grew, he was repeatedly invited by the central government to serve in the capital, but he refused to leave Changping Mountain.

When Li Bai arrived, the Zhaos received him with caution, unsure of his intentions. But Bai was greatly impressed by Zhao Rui's ability to be at home in the wilderness. According to Bai's own words,[1] Zhao had befriended more than a thousand birds of various kinds, and called many of them by the names he had given them. When he beckoned them, stretching out his hands, the birds would land on his arms. They flew around him and ate from his palms without hesitation. His connection with the birds indicated that he was extraordinarily accomplished in Daoism, which stresses being one with nature.

Zhao Rui gave Bai a volume of *Long and Short Scriptures,* hand-copied by his wife, the bound paper still in the form of a manuscript. Li Bai was struck by the views and the eloquence of the writing and implored the recluse to accept him as his student. Zhao and his wife were in turn impressed with Bai's sincerity and enthusiasm. For a seventeen-year-old, he also had a commanding physical presence: from Bai's writings, we know that he was nearly six feet tall[2] and had strong bone structure, fierce eyes, and a stout nose. He spoke in a clear, deep voice. His thoughts were bold and his mind quick in responding to questions.

So Zhao Rui took him on as a student, and Li Bai began to study under the master's guidance. The focus of the lessons was largely political. Zhao's *Long and Short Scriptures* is a book of stratagems, tactics, and practices in the political arena, containing such chapters as "The Ruler's Virtues," "The Courtier's Behavior," "Ways of Dominance," "The Imperial Reign," "Army Training," "Failure and Success," "War Strategies," even "Physiognomy." It is not concerned with right and wrong or good and evil. It teaches how to persuade, to conquer, to govern, and to rule.

In ancient Chinese politics, there is a term for this kind of thinker and practitioner: *zongheng jia* (strategists). Some of those ancient men were top advisers to state rulers, and their efforts shaped the fates of the countries they served. Yet unlike most other classical texts of this sort, *Long and Short Scriptures* has never been put into practice. On the whole it is anachronistic and derivative—its views reveal their origins in the works of the master statesmen of the Warring States period. Zhao's ideas emphasize the absolute power of the sovereign and the need for effective force. Such theories apply only to a society in chaos that needs a powerful ruler to restore order and hold a country together. But by the eighth century, the Tang dynasty had reached its peak, the political order was firmly established, and there was no need for the application of Zhao's outdated ideas.

Nonetheless, Li Bai embraced Zhao Rui's ideas unconditionally and began to view himself as an aspiring master statesman whose position should ultimately be next to the emperor. By studying with Zhao Rui, he wandered in his mind back to the time of a millennium before, dreaming of ancient heroes and their glorious deeds. For both men, the greatest course in life was to perform important political acts and then return home or simply to nature, living out a quiet, reclusive life. Despite the forty-year gap between them, they were similar in many ways.

Zhao taught Li Bai practical subjects too—military tactics, agriculture, medicine. Together they practiced swordsmanship, calligraphy, and musical instruments. Sometimes Zhao assigned Li Bai arithmetic problems, so that he could learn some of the basic skills needed in the organizing and managing of government affairs. Of course, poetry was a major subject for them as well. In this Li Bai excelled. In response to the topics assigned by his teacher, he would compose poems in his mind rapidly and with ease. Unlike other poets, some of whom would spend days on a line, Bai could create poems effortlessly, his lines full of verve and exuberance. Usually he would recite his compositions and later commit some of them to paper. On occasion he wrote them out directly. There was always an improvisational air to his poetry. Every so often his compositions would take on such momentum that he couldn't stop, allowing a poem to run into a second and even a third. Later he would have to undo the entangled piece and divide it into individual poems.

Both Zhao Rui and his wife were accomplished Daoists, and their practice reinforced Bai's. As a religion, Daoism emphasizes the Dao as the primal force or principle of the universe. It exists everywhere and permeates everything and every life. From this force emanates the process, Yun, which can be roughly defined as vicissitudes of fortune. Everything has its Yun: rising and falling, waxing and waning, existence and disappearance. Daoists believe that life is limited and there is no afterlife. What humans, Daoist practitioners, can do is try to prolong the life they have. From this concept arises the pursuit of longevity. One must expend the body and the mind as little as possible so that their vitality can be conserved and stretched to the maximum. This is why Daoism stresses the way of nature, which is something the Daoist must follow and strive to join.

From the need for longevity came the art of making immortality pills, which many accomplished Daoists have attempted to master. But because there was no set formula or standard process of producing the pills in ancient times, practitioners would travel in search of Daoist masters to learn the secret from them directly. In a dark irony, such pills were often poisonous and many people ruined their health by consuming them. Now Bai was here to study the religion and its practice with Zhao Rui, including the preparation of the immortality pills.

Soon birds would land on Bai's arms too, and he also would feed them directly from his hands. Some locals, after witnessing the teacher's and student's acts of communing with birds, volunteered to recommend them to the regional government so that they might be given official posts. The governor of the prefecture came to visit them, and after seeing their ornithological feat and conversing with them, he decided to recommend them to his superiors for civil service. Zhao Rui and Li Bai declined the offer. Their precise reasons aren't known, but most likely they believed it wasn't yet time to leave the mountain. They had an eye on more consequential positions and were reluctant to strive among petty officials for the rest of their lives. A prefecture, consisting of a handful of counties, was too small for their vision of serving and shaping an entire country.

Throughout his life, Li Bai often presented his magic with birds as evidence of his Daoist cultivation—he was capable of identifying with wild animals and plants and becoming one with the Dao. He was also learning from Zhao Rui the pursuit of longevity. Teacher and student would go deep into the nearby mountains to pick herbs, with which they tried to make the pills of immortality. Li Bai learned some basic alchemic techniques from his teacher and would continue to produce the elixirs for the rest of his life. The years he spent with Zhao Rui, from age seventeen to nineteen, were a happy period for him.

Because it was understood that Li Bai could not pursue the civil-service examination, the next practical step for him to take was *ganye*—meeting with officials for patronage and opportunities. One day, Zhao, who occasionally descended the mountain to practice medicine in local communities, told Li Bai of the news he'd heard on one of his trips: the emperor had decreed that officials higher than the fifth rank could recommend talented men directly to court. In the Tang dynasty, there were roughly nine ranks in the official echelon; those who held the first rank were court chancellors and prime ministers, and at the bottom were magistrates of small counties. The fifth-rank holders were usually prefects and adjutant generals who had no commanding power. What Zhao said could be good news for Li Bai—an opportunity for him to seek office. But how could he get to know a high official?

Zhao explained that there was a common practice called *xingjuan:* presenting one's writings, essays or poems to an official. If the man was impressed by a youth's work and took a liking to him, he might be willing to recommend him. If this happened, the door to the official world would be opened. But Zi Prefecture was such a small place that few important officials would pass through. Li Bai would have to go to a city where there were more opportunities to approach influential men. Following his teacher's advice, he soon bid Zhao Rui and his wife a tearful farewell and set out for Chengdu, the metropolis of Sichuan at that time.

In the fall of 719, as most sources suggest, Li Bai began to travel extensively within Sichuan. His destination was Chengdu, but he was unhurried and took a meandering route whenever he could. At the time, Chengdu was the capital of Yi Prefecture and served as the political and cultural center of the region. It was also the home base of Jiannan Circuit, a regional government that controlled a vast territory of more than thirty prefectures in southwestern China. The city had stood for more than four hundred years. Its layout was modeled after Chang'an (modern Xi'an), the capital of the Tang dynasty. Like Chang'an, it consisted of a South City and a North City and more than a hundred alleys. Chengdu was also a commercial center, where merchants from different lands flocked and mingled. Businesspeople from inland China would go there to purchase brocade and embroideries, both of which were well-known products of central Sichuan, and to acquire goods from Central Asia and the Indian subcontinent.

Li Bai's father had provided him with a deep trove of funds to see him through his journey, and so he was able to travel at leisure. He would wander to a town or a famous site along the way whenever a fancy struck him. He meant to visit noted men and see what the land was like. One day he and his pageboy, Dansha, arrived at Mount Emei, which had picturesque, breathtaking views. Bai was enchanted by the tranquil scenery, sensing that this must be a sacred place inhabited by *xian*. Deep in the mountain was a Buddhist temple called White Water (modern Wannian Temple). Bai immediately took to the peaceful surroundings—deer appeared then disappeared in the woods, monkeys howled here and there, birdcalls rose and fell, and hunters roamed with dogs in tow. Then from the temple came music that sounded like a stream falling on rocks. The wind mingled with the notes, rustling through the pinewoods, but Bai was unsure if it was the music or the wind that was stirring the branches. Perhaps both. He went over to the temple, where under an ancient cypress a monk sat, playing a lute. The monk stopped to greet Bai and introduced himself as Guang Jun, nicknamed Monk Jun. Bai sat down and started to converse with the man. The more they chatted, the more Bai took a liking to him.

Li Bai decided to stay at White Water Temple. For a period of months, he would read books and listen to Monk Jun play his instrument every day. Life went on peacefully, and sometimes, between different pieces of music, Jun would talk to him about Buddhism, which Bai, instead of objecting as he had in the past, now found fascinating and enlightening. According to legend, which is probably inspired by Li Bai's poem on Guang Jun, one night when the two of them sat on a pond, Bai asked Monk Jun, "Does the music you play on the lute also contain the sound of your preaching?" The monk replied, "Buddha's words are everywhere, in every sound of the universe." Bai was about to dismiss this as a stock answer, but then, as if on cue, frogs in the water burst out croaking. Monk Jun threw back his head and laughed, and Bai was amazed.

He stayed at the temple for three or four months, and then resumed his journey toward Chengdu. The time he spent with Monk Jun left him with fond memories. More than three decades later, when Li Bai heard that Guang Jun had passed away, he recalled the holy man and composed this poem in memory of him:

蜀僧抱綠綺　西下峨眉峰
為我一揮手　如聽萬壑松
客心洗流水　餘響入霜鐘
不覺碧山暮　秋雲暗幾重

《聽蜀僧浚彈琴》

The monk in Shu holds his lute,
Sitting below the peak of Emei Mountain.
For me, he plucks away while I hear
The wind shaking the pines in the valley.
My soul is again cleansed afresh
As the lingering sound is still touching

The bell glazed with autumn frost.
I haven't noticed the green mountain
Cloaked in the sunset as the clouds
Turn darker than a moment ago.

"LISTENING TO MONK JUN PLAY THE LUTE"

Li Bai arrived in Chengdu in early spring. He had heard that the new royal inspector, Su Ting, a revered minister at the central government, had come to the city to take charge of Jiannan Circuit. Most people viewed Su Ting's departure from the capital as a kind of demotion or even banishment, but the man himself believed that his new appointment embodied the emperor's utmost trust in him, because he now governed a vast southwestern territory that was vital to the safety of the country. Before Su Ting left the capital, the emperor had told him to watch for standout talents in Sichuan, a region known for having produced numerous historical figures.

After arriving in Chengdu, Su Ting worked diligently to increase the government's revenue and to improve people's livelihoods by promoting the production of salt, iron, porcelain, fabrics, tea, and other local goods. He also tried to reduce the government's administrative expenses and avoid starting construction projects. He was practicing the old way of governance—"ruling without action"—based on the Daoist principle that advocates peace and laissez-faire as the way of nurturing and fulfilling the potential of the populace. His wise policies earned him the respect of the locals. He was also known as a writer. Writers were rather common among the Tang officials, some of whom were highly literary. Li Bai knew Su Ting's writings, especially his essays, which were masterly, though Bai didn't have a high opinion of the man's poetry. Now that Su Ting governed the whole of southwestern China, Bai by any means should try to seek this man's favor first.

Although it would be difficult for Li Bai to get access to the highest official in Chengdu, he was determined to present a piece of his writing to him. Bai had recently written two rhapsodies, "The Bright Hall" and "The Great Hunt," and he picked the latter to show to Su Ting.

"The Great Hunt" is a rhapsody, a lengthy poetic essay. In lyrical language, it expresses the young author's political ambition and his views on the art of writing. Indulging in hyperbole, Bai declares at the outset, "Rhapsodies are a branch of ancient poetry. The more splendid their words are, the further their meanings can reach. Otherwise, how could they be magnificent enough to move heaven and gods?" The essay goes on to cite examples of great rhapsodies and to speak about Bai's own political principles and aspirations. He uses hunting as a metaphor for managing a country, which, he writes, is like a hunting ground wherein the emperor is the supreme hunter. But his language is so excessively poetic that the meanings become opaque and detached from the actual affairs of the dynasty. As the rhapsody progresses, the poet's mind travels around the whole of the universe and through ancient times, and finally ends with these sentences: "The emperor then has the banners furled and returns to the royal carriage. On his way back, he visits immortals to find the Dao and searches for gods in their mystic caves. He tries to uncover precious pearls in the Chi River, though nobody in the world knows what he has been doing." Here Li Bai casts his own Daoist ideal onto the emperor, portraying His Majesty as a supreme hero who can give up all worldly attachments and return to the wilderness in search of the True Way.

I have simplified the quoted sentences to make them comprehensible, because most of the language in the essay is so laden with allusions that a word-for-word translation would be too convoluted to elaborate on clearly. In brief, the entire rhapsody reads like a flight of poetic indulgence, though the power of imagination and the linguistic strength are fantastically original. It shows

Li Bai's singular talent, but contains little meaningful discussion of politics.

Li Bai went to Su Ting's residence and announced himself. To avoid being turned away at the door, he asked a servant to take his writing in to his master first. A few moments later, the man came back and led Bai into the main hall, where Su Ting received him. The governor, in his early fifties, had a heavyset square face and wore a long, sparse gray beard. He was courteous, clearly impressed by Bai's rhapsody, and over tea they talked about the art of writing and ancient literary masters. Bai said that for him writing was secondary and that his ambition was to serve the country and make it safe, strong, and prosperous. He believed that one should earn one's name through accomplishing great deeds in the political arena or the battlefield, not just with a writing brush. Su Ting was pleased and said he would consider recommending Bai to a post, but that Bai must be patient for now. Before the visit was over, a group of local officials arrived. Su Ting introduced Li Bai to them, saying, "This young man is exceptionally talented and can write effortlessly without stop." The officials were curious about the young visitor and began to ask him questions, but on hearing that Bai's father was a businessman from the backwaters, they turned so contemptuous that they secretly had Bai dismissed.

Nonetheless, for days Li Bai was hopeful. He believed that Su Ting would keep his promise. Good news might come at any time, so he decided to stay and wait. It was mid-spring: Chengdu was warm and filled with white pear blossoms, and the mild climate enabled him to go sightseeing during the day. Accompanied by his pageboy, he visited the terrace where the rhapsodist Sima Xiang-ru had often played the zither eight centuries before, and to the marketplaces, not to shop but to experience the energy of the setting. He ascended many towers and pavilions on hill slopes, and from them he scanned the cityscape and watched salt wells spitting out white steam in the distance. He also paid a visit to the shrine of Zhuge Liang (181–234).

To Li Bai, Zhuge was the ideal political figure, a hero whom he and his teacher Zhao Rui had often discussed. Zhuge had been a great statesman in the period of Three Kingdoms (220–280), a chaotic era ravaged by wars and peasant uprisings, and as the prime chancellor of Shu State, Zhuge helped its king, Liu Bei, establish his kingdom in Sichuan. His devotion to his master and his brilliance in statecraft earned him a reputation as the most loyal and foresighted chancellor in Chinese history. In China, he has been revered and lionized as a model statesman and military strategist who was virtuous and erudite and prescient. He meant even more to Li Bai personally, because Zhuge Liang was also a local figure, a great son of the kingdom he'd helped establish in Sichuan.

Then Li Bai went to the Tower of Scattered Flowers on the city wall and lingered there. He gazed at the limpid Mohe Lake, the cityscape—the waves of rooftops, the distant wooded mountains and rivers. Moved by the scene, he composed a poem in pentasyllabic verse with strictly regulated metrics and rhymes. In it he begins with the sight that struck him when he came to ascend the city wall in the morning, then jumps to the afternoon as if he had been up on the tower for many hours:

日照錦城頭　　朝光散花樓
金窗夾繡戶　　珠箔懸銀鉤
飛梯綠雲中　　極目散我憂
暮雨向三峽　　春江繞雙流
今來一登望　　如上九天遊

《登錦城散花樓》

The morning sun is shining on the city wall,
Light splashed on the Tower of Scattered Flowers.

Golden windows embrace pretty doors
And pearl curtains are held aside by jade hooks.
The soaring steps stretch into the green clouds
And I climb up to gaze afar to dispel my worries.
The afternoon rain is moving away to the Three Gorges
While the two rivers curve around Shuang-liu Town.
Today I have come up to get a distant view
As if I am touring nine heavens.

"ASCENDING CHENGDU'S TOWER OF SCATTERED FLOWERS"

This is a typical example of Li Bai's early poems, lacking in the fresh suppleness, the overflowing energy, and the spontaneity that characterize his mature work. Yet other key elements of his style are already in place: he disregards the order of time in the poem while highlighting the splendorous, vast poetic space, which is one of the hallmarks of his poetry—the space is imagined, often beyond the field of view. The Three Gorges, about five hundred miles away to the east, would have actually been absent from sight, but he mentions them as if they were visible. There are also the temporal and spatial leaps that his poetic mind is fond of performing, from morning to afternoon and from the cityscape to the Yangtze River flowing east.

Yet despite comparing the experience to a heavenly tour so as to show his freedom from the earthly world, Bai in fact could not escape his worries. He was anxious to hear from Su Ting, the man he saw as his best hope. It was a long wait. In the evenings Bai would strum the lute while Dansha would play the bamboo flute. They were both skilled with their instruments: the pageboy was able to mimic all kinds of bird cries with the flute, and Bai could play the lute as well as he could wield a sword. But now the two of them were playing simply to kill time as they waited. It had been a lonesome month, and good news from Su Ting seemed less and less likely.

In fact, Governor Su had decided not to recommend Li Bai, primarily because the young poet had begun to gain notoriety for his questionable practice of prescribing remedies for the sick though he lacked the proper training. Whenever Li Bai encountered someone who was ill, he would feel the person's pulse, offer some medical advice, and prescribe a remedy, usually medicinal herbs. He had learned some rudimentary medicine from Zhao Rui, and enjoyed practicing it in Chengdu. But in doing so, he couldn't help but mix with all sorts of people in streets and alleys and was very openhanded with money. Such behavior smacked of quackery and imprudence to Su Ting. That, combined with Bai's modest background, caused Su to have misgivings about Li Bai's suitability as a protégé. Su Ting's caution was justified from his point of view, because the court would hold the advocate accountable if the man he had recommended caused trouble. No official would put his own career at risk by endorsing someone he didn't fully trust.

Meanwhile, Bai continued to network with noted local figures. Most of them, however, were not welcoming toward him. When he recited his poems to them at dinner parties, they would shake their heads and sigh, saying he hadn't followed the rules of versification and would ruin his art if he persisted in such a way. He often argued with them heatedly, regardless of their titles and fame, and even said that he abhorred the stiff poetry produced by poets in the capital and wanted to write something new and unique. But his arguments only made him appear more arrogant. Occasionally he was able to impress others with his wide knowledge and quick mind, but their compliments were always measured, if not stingy. Wherever Bai turned, he encountered the same contempt in people's eyes, which seemed to say that he was nothing but a country bumpkin in an expensive robe. Soon he began to lose heart.

Finally, he decided to give up waiting and leave Chengdu.

He thought of returning home, but changed his mind and headed toward Yu Prefecture (modern Chongqing). He knew that

Li Yong (674–746) was in charge of the government there, and wanted to try his luck with him. Li Yong's father had been a well-known man of letters and had compiled an anthology, *Zhaoming Selected Masterpieces,* that was widely used by students and aspiring young scholars. It was the very anthology Bai had imitated three times during his childhood studies. Li Yong's own work also had a sterling reputation. He was a great calligrapher—an original master in the cursive script, *caoshu*—and he also specialized in composing commemorative essays for stone tablets. Most important for Li Bai, he was famous for befriending and supporting literary young men in their endeavors.

As soon as Li Bai arrived in Chongqing, he went to see the prefect. He had learned from his failed effort with Su Ting, so this time he presented his poetry instead of a rhapsody. On his way to Chongqing, he had collected folk songs from the people he encountered and even written poems in the same style because the songs were so full of life and raw experience. He had begun to think about how to give his poems the same kind of fluidity, how to render them as spontaneous as natural speech while also maintaining a high level of energy and intensity. He imagined a style that seemed regulated but not burdened by restrictive rules, free but in good order.

Among the poems he presented to Li Yong, the first was "A Local Woman's Song," which he had just finished:

巴水急如箭　　巴船去若飛
十月三千里　　郎行幾歲歸

　　《巴女詞》

The water of the Ba River is flowing like arrows,
The boats are darting away as if in flight.

Ten months gone and three thousand li *away,*
When will my man come back?

Understandably, Li Bai's new poems were inappropriate for such an occasion. The prefect was too serious and conservative a man to appreciate folk songs, especially one from a female point of view about the absence of her lover. Though Li Yong did receive Li Bai, he saw the poems as frivolous work. Bai again talked at length about his view of the world and his political ambitions, but Li Yong had already formed his opinion about this impudent visitor. He turned aside and whispered to his assistant Yuwen to show Bai the door but to give him some money, as he always treated his guests generously.

Despite the perfunctory treatment he received from Li Yong, Bai was again hopeful. Because they shared the same family name—that of the royal clan, no less—he regarded Li Yong as a relative of his, an uncle of sorts. At the interview, the prefect had even acknowledged that the two of them might be related. But a month passed, and still there was no word. Bai attempted to present another batch of poems to Li Yong through the hands of Yuwen, who had come to deliver to Bai the financial gift from his boss. As it turned out, Yuwen enjoyed Bai's poetry and treated him warmly. Yuwen must have revealed to him the truth: Li Yong had dismissed Bai's poems as common.

Yuwen was a Sien-pi name, and the man was a descendant of a northern tribe, likely Mongolian. Li Bai, because of his own mixed heritage, looked and even acted like a foreigner, with fierce and sparkling eyes. The two could commiserate with each other about their feelings of outsiderness. They shared a flask of wine, and the man had brought the poet a souvenir: a gorgeous bamboo pot for holding letters. The pot, with words carved around its side, was made of a special kind of material called peach-bamboo: its trunks are solid inside and the plants have smaller leaves than regular bamboo. The gift touched Bai so much that he wrote a poem in return. Having described the gift elaborately, the poet concludes, "I shall treasure this on my way to Emei Mountain / And always keep it around so as to think of you" ("In Return for Official Yuwen's Bamboo Pot"). Li Bai might also have shown Yuwen a poem he had written about his boss, the prefect. It is titled "To Li Yong" and opens with the declaration, "One day the great roc shall fly with the wind / Soaring higher and higher heaven- ward." Bai's pride was evidently wounded by the official's dismissal and long silence, as the poem ends on a note of complaint: "Even Confucius says that the young are to be respected. / Never should an older man look down on a young man." He did not hear from Li Yong again, though they would cross paths many years later and renew their friendship.

Twice Bai had failed in his attempts to woo a patron. It was very difficult to break into the official world. Later Li Bai would lament, "The roads to Shu are hard, as hard as ascending to heaven." It looked as though there was no way for him to join officialdom. Many like him had attempted time and again, and he couldn't see the possibility of success in the near future. Now it was time to go home.

3

BACK IN HIS HOMETOWN

All Li Bai chronologies give 720 as the year that he left Yu Prefecture. Early in the fall, he came back to his hometown of Jiangyou, exhausted and dejected. His return must have embarrassed his parents, who had expected him to obtain a position in Sichuan. According to local customs, a man his age, almost twenty, should already have started a career and a family, but Bai's life seemed to be stalled. Worse yet, he could not enter for the civil-service examination like many other young scholars whose families were affiliated with officialdom or aristocracy. Some people sympathized with Bai, saying he was too great a talent for this backwoods county, and in due time he would find his place in the world. As if in confirmation, soon word reached Jiangyou that Governor Su Ting in Chengdu had praised Li Bai's writing, calling his literary talent "unstoppable." Those officials, having heard their superior compliment Bai, had spread the word, even though they secretly had the young poet dismissed.

Around the same time, the county magistrate, apprised of the governor's praise, invited Bai to serve at the local government. This was not due to any direct effort from Su Ting. The county head, a dilettante at poetry, intended to earn credit for himself by employing the young man. Who was to say that Li Bai might not hold a high post someday? It would be better to help him start here. Bai accepted the offer, likely at his father's urging. For a long time, this episode in his life was glossed over by scholars, since it contradicted the romantic image of the poet. How could "the great roc" allow himself to be caged in the tiny office of a county administration? Li Bai himself also seemed to find this period embarrassing and made no mention of it in his writings. Yet several historical sources confirm his service with the county, such as a stone tablet at Daming Temple erected in 1068, which states: "The Royal Academician Li Bai, when he was young, served as a small official in Dang County (modern Jiangyou) and then stayed in this mountain, studying books."[1] Several other sources document this period of his life in more detail. Without question, Li Bai became a petty bureaucrat of the magistrate soon after he returned from Chongqing. This episode is crucial for us to understand the turmoil and struggle he must have experienced. He must have been tormented by his decision to accept such a humble job, the likes of which his teacher Zhao Rui had warned him to shun categorically. But he was determined to start his official career, even from the bottom of the official echelon, so that he could test the skills and knowledge that Zhao had given him.

The local records and folk memories preserved in Li Bai's home region[2] contain several notable incidents in this period of his life that illustrate his unhappiness about his job. One day, near the entrance to the *yamen,* the government office, Li Bai caught sight of a boy leading an ox. He approached the cowhand and borrowed the animal. Without announcement, Bai led it through the yard in front of the trial hall. It was a disruptive and defiant act and was noticed by the magistrate's wife immediately. She was incensed. How could a petty clerk let a beast of burden trespass on the tribunal's ground? She was about to yell at Li Bai, but then refrained and turned to her husband, her eyes ablaze. Bai saw the anger on her face, but before the magistrate could open his mouth to scold him, Bai began to chant a poem, improvised on the spot, that eloquently flattered the woman: "A lady without makeup leans against a rail, / Then a sweet voice rises from over there. / If it's not the Weaving Girl, / Who would ask about the Herd Boy?"

These verses are based on a folktale of a pair of star-crossed lovers. As the story goes, a herd boy and a weaving girl once fell in love and married. The girl had been a heavenly maiden who had stolen down to earth together with six other maidens. They bathed in a river and meant to return to heaven before daybreak. But the herd boy's old ox told him that he should pick one of the maidens as his wife by hiding her clothes. The boy loved the youngest of them, the most beautiful, and put away her clothes so that the girl could not go back to heaven once it was light. The two fell in love and married.

But soon after the births of their two children, the couple were forced apart: Goddess Wang Mu, the queen who ruled over the maidens, was angry at the girl and threw a seemingly uncrossable river between her and the herd boy. He pined away helplessly on the riverbank, gazing in her direction, holding their children in two baskets with a shoulder pole. Their love moved thousands of magpies, who formed a bridge on July 7 so that the herd boy could cross the water to meet his wife. Every year the couple could be together, but only for one day. This day—the seventh day of the seventh month by the lunar calendar—has come to be observed by lovers, especially by those kept apart, and has now evolved into "Chinese Valentine's Day."

In his improvised verses, Li Bai teased the petulant magistrate's wife, but with a compliment, alluding to the tale of the herd boy and the beautiful weaving girl. The woman was mollified, her anger dissipated. Her husband no longer had to intervene and was relieved.

Having witnessed Li Bai's poetic flair, the magistrate began to take him to banquets and parties so that Bai could compose poetry for the occasions. The official would also bring Bai along when he went on inspections. From time to time the magistrate would throw out a couple of lines of poetry himself to show off his own skill and to test Li Bai further. Once, observing a brushfire rage on the ridge of a hill, the magistrate let out these lines: "After the wild-fire passed the hill / People have returned but the fire continues."[3] At this he stopped, unable to proceed beyond such a clunky start. To save his superior's face, Bai stepped in, chanting, "The flames are receding with the scarlet sun / While the mountain is waver-ing with the evening clouds." Instead of appreciating the assist, however, his boss merely felt annoyed, outshone by Bai in front of his inferiors. Li Bai was irritated by this incident as well, because it showed that the magistrate didn't care about the farmwork—and people's livelihood—that had been disrupted by the fire.

On another day, his boss led a group of underlings to the riv-erside to check a flood condition, which could present a danger to crops and villages. A corpse appeared in the water, bobbing to the surface. It was the body of a young woman. Unmoved by the pitiful sight, the magistrate smiled and recited these lines: "Whose daughter is this sixteen-year-old? / She has been floating along the reedy bank. / Birds observe the jade above her brows / While fish touch her rouged lips." Again he stopped, unable to continue. His callousness was too much for Li Bai to stomach, so Bai retorted, "Her glossy hair is scattered among the waves / And the red of her cheeks has disappeared in the flood. / When will she find a righ-teous judge / To voice all her grievances?" Again the magistrate took offense, but Li Bai was too upset to care and strode away. Soon afterward he quit his job, which he realized had become intolerable. Later, a historian described his time at the county administration as "a stranded dragon swarmed by ants."

Throughout his life, Li Bai dedicated flattering poems to petty officials right and left. Some are laced with extravagant lines; for instance, he praised a minor official for possessing an elegant manner "like a phoenix's" and "a graceful air like a deity's" ("For Official Wang in Xiaqiu"). He didn't always feel contempt for the recipients of those poems, and even liked and respected them, partly because he hoped to become a high official himself. His response to his home county's magistrate's lines was different—Li Bai simply couldn't see his boss as his artistic equal, and despised his callous indifference to the suffering of the people in his charge. It should be mentioned that none of the three poems composed in 720 have been included in the standard collection of Li Bai's writings. They have been kept in the local annals and in the memories of the denizens, so the Li Bai Museum in Jiangyou has listed the three poems as work produced when he served in the county government. In other words, there is another Li Bai preserved in folklore, whose validity usually can be corroborated by historical writings and records.

Having left his position, Li Bai went to stay in Daming Temple on Kuang Mountain instead of rejoining Zhao Rui, whom he now regarded more as a friend than as a teacher. He wanted to go his own way and live a monastic life dedicated to the study of poetry and books. His father's influence could still be felt in Bai's choice of shelter; without Li Ke's support, the temple might not have admitted him. He would study on his own on Kuang Mountain for more than two years before he set out on the road again. His failed attempt to seek a post must have agitated him and thrown his mind into turmoil.

For centuries Sichuan (also known as the land of Shu) had been viewed as a place of marvels and deities, surrounded by high mountains and hidden in endless mist, nearly inaccessible to people from central China. The land is fertile, with an abundant water supply, and its warm climate nurtures bumper crops. Throughout history, the Sichuanese have become known for their ability to enjoy life and for their distinct culture. The region is also regarded as a place that produces poets and other artists—a habitat of crouching tigers and hidden dragons (secluded figures of great talent). Before him, a number of illustrious men from Sichuan had made their fame in the capital by serving the country's rulers. These men were not just courtiers: many were accomplished poets and essayists. Among them are the great writer of rhapsodies Sima Xiang-ru, the statesman Zhuge Liang, and the poet Chen Zi'ang.

The work of Chen Zi'ang was vital for Li Bai's progress as a poet. Chen had grown up in a nearby county, Shehong, which Li Bai often passed through on his way to see Zhao Rui. Li Bai viewed Chen as a kind of fellow townsman, even though Chen had died shortly after Bai was born. When he reentered Daming Temple, Bai had not yet studied Chen's poetry thoroughly, but now an older monk presented him with a volume of Chen's collected poems, a rare book Bai had long been seeking. Studying the book gave Bai great joy. He loved Chen's simple, straightforward verses—they had a singularly distinguished aura, expansive and timeless. Bai was moved by lines such as these: "I cannot see ancient people ahead of me, / Nor can I see people coming after me. / Observing heaven and earth, I feel sad and can't help my tears." Those verses expressed a kind of existential despair and loneliness that resonated with Li Bai. He began to imitate Chen's poetry as part of his "apprenticeship." More fundamentally, Chen's work helped Li Bai form his own poetic position. Chen believed that the poetry of the last five hundred years had grown mannered, thin, enervated, and in need of reform. He insisted that poets look to earlier times for inspiration, such as the works written in the Jian'an period (196–220), which were charged with passion, grief, and austere beauty. Chen, like Bai, emphasized the spirit of literature instead of technical rules. Bai even went further and claimed that the only worthy poetic model was the *Book of Songs*.

The volume of 305 songs is one of the five ancient Chinese classics and was compiled by Confucius, who had selected the poems—mostly folk songs—from a period between the twelfth and sixth centuries BC. Bai's claim was of course an oversimplification (in fact, later he would embrace other traditions as well), but he was utterly earnest about his proposition. He learned a great deal from the *Book of Songs,* particularly the ancient folk songs. He envisioned a kind of poetry rooted in the raw experiences and feelings of common people's lives.

Unlike other Tang poets, Li Bai wrote numerous poems from a female point of view, a tradition that can be traced back to the folk poetry in the *Book of Songs.* He also wrote songs in the voices of courtesans, foreign women (*huji*) from the western regions, barmaids, and weaving girls—people he often encountered during his wanderings. These song poems distinguished his work from that of the other poets of his time. Later he summed up his principle of poetic composition this way: "Lotus flowers come out of limpid water, / Natural without any decoration." His principles also included emphasizing poetic immediacy and the sensation of thoughts: "Bright moonlight comes in straightaway, not allowing the mind to guess." Indeed, his best poems have a kind of spontaneity and straightforwardness that seem to pour out of the speaker, with the underlying structure absent or invisible.

Li Bai also continued to study the history of political events and policies, the art of war, and government management. Now that his effort to climb up from the bottom of officialdom had failed, he was all the more eager to find another approach to transforming himself into a man of consequence. Since ancient times, there had traditionally been two ways to achieve such a goal. One way, counterintuitively, was to withdraw from society and live an eremitic life in solitude. A recluse's detachment was seen as an indication of integrity, an indifference to fame and material gain. Ancient Chinese rulers tended to be drawn to those who stayed far from the center of power and often promoted them to consequential positions, partly because they embodied the fresh energy vitally necessary for government. Li Bai had learned about this passive path from Zhao Rui. Yet this approach also had drawbacks. Prolonged seclusion could easily cause one to become lost in oblivion, and deep isolation could narrow one's vision, limit one's understanding of the world, and make one fall behind the times.

The other approach was to travel to cultural and political centers so as to spread one's name and befriend important figures. A more poetic term for this kind of travel is *yunyou*, "wandering like a cloud." Many Tang poets used this approach, mingling with the rich and powerful in the capital and other major cities, waiting for opportunities. Some were successful in the endeavor, while others failed utterly. Now Li Bai kept his eye on the central land down the Yangtze, beyond the Three Gorges. He planned to travel extensively in the coming years, but first he had to study hard and prepare for the arduous journey ahead.

4

LEAVING SICHUAN

All Li Bai chronologies and biographies place 724 as the year that he prepared to set out on the road again. This time he planned to leave Sichuan for the central land, where he would attempt to find his way into the official world. He wouldn't go directly to Luoyang, which had become the East Capital a decade before; nor to Chang'an, which remained the West Capital, seat of the central government and the court. Instead, he would travel widely through the lands of Chu and Wu (present-day Hubei and southern Jiangsu and northern Zhejiang). Such a journey was surely planned carefully before his departure. The Chu and Wu regions were prosperous, rich with farmland and brisk commerce. They were crisscrossed by water routes—rivers, lakes, and canals—that connected the major cities and functioned like today's network of railroads. Goods and foodstuffs were continually shipped to Luoyang through these waterways, which also facilitated communications between Chang'an and the lands of Chu and Wu. Li Bai's plan was to build up his reputation in that part of the country so as to attract the attention of court.[1] Indeed, it would have been rash to enter the capital directly.

For Bai, this coming journey would also turn out to be a long poetry tour of sorts—not only of performance but also of composition. As he traveled, he would leave hundreds of poems in his wake. These poems, especially those with a female persona, became songs performed in taverns, inns, and restaurants along the waterways. People loved his verses, and this helped spread his name. "The River-Merchant's Wife: A Letter," best known in the West from Ezra Pound's masterful translation, was composed on this journey. His most popular poems tend to be shorter, easier to set to music and to memorize.

In the fall of 724, Li Bai and his pageboy Dansha left Jiangyou and headed first for Chengdu. The memory of his failure in seeking office there three years earlier still stung, so he didn't stay long and continued south toward Mount Emei, one of the four sacred Buddhist mountains in China. Bai had a habit of traveling long distances to seek *xian* in famous mountains. He had visited Mount Emei before—this was where he had met Monk Jun at White Water Temple—but this time he didn't make an excursion to the monastery, having heard that Guang Jun had left for the south. Now Bai simply roamed the mountainous area. As a Daoist, he believed that *xian* resided in the caves of every mountain. A high mountain, to his mind, was an intersection between heaven and earth, a place where deities and humans could meet. That was why the country's rulers and countless pilgrims would ascend to the summits of mountains to pay homage. Although Li Bai didn't find any divine figures he had imagined in Mount Emei, he was inspired by his journey nonetheless.

On a clear fall night, as he was leaving the mountain and sailing down the Qiang River, he was touched by the tranquil beauty of the waterscape and suddenly felt homesick. Overwhelmed with emotion, he composed this poem:

峨眉山月半輪秋　影入平羌江水流
夜發清溪向三峽　思君不見下渝州

《峨眉山月歌》

The autumn moon is rising, halfway out of Emei Mountain,
Its shadows floating on the Qiang's currents.
Tonight we left Qingxi, heading for the Three Gorges,
And I miss you, but have to sail down to Yuzhou.

"SONG OF THE EMEI MOON"

The poem is a milestone in his poetic career, and its beauty can be fully appreciated only in the Chinese. The language in the poem is colloquial and transparent, the setting clear and immense, the music of the words fresh and fluid. There are five place names in the four lines, but they pose no impediment to the verbal flow, and instead generate propelling energy. The poem is a perfect and seemingly effortless piece of art. A work like this couldn't come into being by luck and talent alone—it was clearly the result of Bai's past three years of study at Daming Temple. He must have worked very hard to shed all the traces of imitation. Now he was an original poet in every sense.

Before making his way toward the Three Gorges, Li Bai lingered in Wan County in Sichuan for about half a year. We cannot know why he stopped there for so long—it is likely that he enjoyed the peace and mystery of the place, where he explored mountains, pored over books, and played chess while drinking. Literary historians have long argued about his motivations and searched for more evidence, but to date little is known about this long stopover. There should be no question, however, about his presence in Wan County. Numerous landmarks commemorate Li Bai's visit to the area: the words *Tai Bai yan* (Li Bai's Rock) were carved on the face of a cliff, still visible to this day, where it is said he used to sit and play chess. Similar words appear at other spots as well. Legend says that there is a fountain believed to have been opened by a wine cup Li Bai dropped when he was drunk. For centuries local breweries have used its water for making wine, which has evolved into the modern brand-name product Tai Bai Wine. In the Ming dynasty, a temple named after Li Bai stood in this area. It is claimed that he came to Wan County three times throughout his life, though the exact number is still a point of contention.

After passing the Three Gorges, Li Bai reached the region of Chu, sailing down the Yangtze toward Jing Prefecture. The mountains were behind him now, and the land ahead opened as the river widened. He was eager to enter a place where numerous ancient figures had once wandered, such as the statesman Wu Zixu (559–484 BC), the flood-control expert Sun Shu-ao (630–593 BC), and the poet Qu Yuan. Along the way he composed poems and shared them with those he met at the river ports. People recognized that his poetry was strikingly original: bright in imagery, fantastic in vision, spontaneous in feeling. Coming out of the town of Jingmen—an entryway to the land of Chu—Li Bai was swept up with emotion and composed this poem:

渡遠荊門外　來從楚國遊
山隨平野盡　江入大荒流
月下飛天鏡　雲生結海樓
仍憐故鄉水　萬里送行舟

《渡荊門送別》

Having left Jingmen far behind,
I am approaching the State of Chu.
Hills have receded to the end of the land
And the river flows into the vast wilderness.
Below the moon a heavenly mirror flies
While the clouds unite to raise a mirage.

How I am attached to this water from my hometown—
It's still sending my boat downstream.

"SAYING GOODBYE TO JINGMEN"

Although he is more than five hundred miles from Jiangyou, he views the water of the Yangtze as a continuous flow from the Fu River that runs through his hometown. In a way this is true, because the Fu is a tiny branch of the Yangtze. Another truth is that Li Bai would never return home again. He had no strong feelings of attachment to any place in his life, not even his hometown back in Sichuan, but as he was sailing down the Yangtze, he must have sensed that he was about to become rootless. He would have to accept his homelessness in this world. He began to feel the pain of bereavement and couldn't help lamenting it. Yet as a constant traveler, his essence would exist in his endless wanderings and in his yearning for a higher order of existence. But for now, he was to roam through the central land as a miraculous figure of sorts, as people later fondly nicknamed him the Banished Immortal. This moniker, which he embraced readily, implied that he belonged to heaven and was here only because he had misbehaved up there. It became essential to his sense of identity—it gave him a narrative for his extraordinariness and a kind of entitlement to proper treatment from the rich and powerful. He was fond of the expression "to be equal among princes and marquises."

Jiang-ling was the capital of Jing Prefecture (modern Hubei). It was a major city in central China, serving as a transportation hub with Sichuan to the west, Luoyang to the north, Jinling (Nanjing) to the east, and Hunan to the south. In Li Bai's time, it already had a history of more than a thousand years and had once been the capital of Chu State. Li Bai was familiar, through his reading, with the historical sites in the city, but he was most taken by the songs performed in its restaurants, taverns, and teahouses. They were folk songs, full of feeling, that often lamented the loss of love, the separation between women and men, and the passage of time that inevitably diminishes youth and beauty. Sometimes Li Bai was so touched by the honesty and grief in the songs that he turned tearful, wrote the lyrics down, and even memorized them. Since his father had provided him lavishly for this journey, through Dansha's hand he was able to pay the singing girls generously to show his appreciation for their art.

Soon Bai began to write his own folk songs in the local style. Some of his attempts were unsuccessful, and he threw them away. But there were also efforts that stood out as minor masterpieces. Here is his "Song of Jingzhou":

白帝城邊足風波　瞿塘五月誰敢過
荊州麥熟繭成蛾　繰絲憶君頭緒多
撥穀飛鳴奈妾何

《荊州歌》

Around Baidi Town rise too many waves.
Who dares to pass Qutang Gorge in May?
In Jingzhou silkworm cocoons have become moths.
Pulling and rolling the silk, I'm full of worries,
Oh more helpless while cuckoos fly and cry.

In late spring the cocoons grow into moths, signaling that the time for harvesting silk has begun. The woman speaking here boils the cocoons and untangles the natural silk. It is a long, laborious process. As she works, her mind is pregnant with thoughts of her man who has traveled up the Yangtze to Baidi Town, which was in Sichuan near the Hubei border. The endless strands of silk, tangled and knotted, embody the constancy and complication of the woman's feelings. She tries to forgive him, blaming the waves and the perilous gorge for his delayed return. The cuckoo indicates the passage of time—another spring is nearly gone while the woman grows older and her dejection deepens. The poem has been widely praised. Some scholars even say that in all of Tang poetry, this piece alone deserves to be ranked among the marvelous folk songs of the Han dynasty.

A fellow townsman of Li Bai's turned up in Jiang-ling. His name was Wu Zhinan, a skinny young fellow with asthma who had studied with Bai at Daming Temple. Bai was delighted to see his childhood friend, who had been roving the Chu region, and the two decided to travel together. Zhinan heard that Sima Chengzhen (647–735), a grand Daoist master, was passing through the city on a pilgrimage to Heng Mountain, where there are many temples and monuments. Li Bai remembered his teacher Zhao Rui praising Sima Chengzhen for his study of Daoist texts, so Bai was eager to meet the master and seek enlightenment. It was an opportunity to network as well, because Sima was well connected with the royal family: he was a teacher of the emperor's sister, Princess Yuzhen, and had issued Emperor Xuanzong a Daoist diploma four years before, which meant he had accepted the emperor as his disciple. Xuanzong and his father, the previous emperor, had both invited Master Sima to court to preach.

Bai and Zhinan went out in search of Sima. There were many visitors rushing to see the master, mostly local officials eager to hear his secrets of longevity and the prospects of their careers. Master Sima, already in his late sixties, lounged on a wicker chair with his eyes almost closed. Now and then he flickered his horse-tail whisk to show he hadn't dozed off. At the sight of Li Bai, the master sat up and looked spirited. He was struck by Bai's appearance, which was strapping, carefree, and confident. Bai sat down with him. The two of them discussed Daoist principles, Li Bai asking questions as the master gave succinct answers. Bai revealed his political ambition to the master. Sima emphasized that the best way to run a country was to follow the natural way without pressuring its populace or undertaking too many expensive projects. This echoes the Daoist principle of "ruling without action." He praised Bai, saying he had an otherworldly demeanor and should have high expectations for his future. But what was Bai's goal in pursuing an official career? Without hesitation Bai replied, "When I have accomplished great deeds and made a name for myself, I will retire into the wilderness." The master smiled and waved his whisk in agreement.

Li Bai's answer sounded stock on its surface, but had meaningful and even moving resonances. It implied that he accepted his limitations as a human being and was aware of the perils in a political career—if one did not withdraw from the court after achieving success, one might become enmeshed and destroyed. This is a concept found repeatedly in the *Tao Te Ching,* the fundamental scriptures of Daoism—"After success, do not stay on" (chapter 2); "To withdraw after your success, this is the way of heaven" (chapter 9). It is a Daoist principle that reflects the rise and fall of fortune that all disciples must follow.

Bai's meeting with the Daoist master moved him so deeply that he revised his rhapsody "The Great Peng." In the new version, he portrays Sima Chengzhen as the only other divine bird who can appreciate the grandeur of the roc, Bai's self-styled symbol for himself. His meeting with Sima reinforced his belief in his own extraordinariness as a supernatural being, and he was convinced that he too might become a Daoist master someday if he didn't succeed in his official career.

His friend Wu Zhinan, however, didn't seem to share his excitement about the meeting with Master Sima. Soon the two young men started out for Dongting Lake in the south. It is the largest lake in central China, more than a thousand square miles in size. The Yangtze flows into it and the water spreads to the end of the sky like an ocean. The two of them planned to acquire a boat so they could enjoy sailing on the lake. But then Zhinan fell ill and they had to stay at an inn. Li Bai cared for him and treated him with herbal medicine, but to no avail. His condition grew worse and worse, and within a few days he died.

Heartbroken, Li Bai wore a white hooded mourning gown and wept over his body. He decided to bury his friend on the lakeside, where he would rest until Bai could find a way to bring him home. According to Li Bai's own words, after the burial he lingered at his friend's grave for a long time. A large tiger appeared, scattering people in every direction, but Li Bai drew his sword and confronted the beast until it retreated. Later, in his "Letter to Deputy Prefect Pei of Anzhou," he cited the incident as evidence of his loyalty to his friends. By his account, three years later Bai returned to Zhinan's burial spot and exhumed the body. He cleaned the bones, placed them in a sack, and carried the bundle away on his back. Having no money left and unable to have his friend's remains shipped back to their home region, he chose an auspicious site east of Ezhou (near modern Wuhan) and buried him there.

Li Bai's description of this second burial for his friend is quite bizarre—it does not coincide with the traditional practices of the time. In the mid-1990s, scholars began to reinterpret this incident. They asserted that Li Bai had in fact followed a foreign burial ritual. The practice he describes, which was called "the burial of scraped bones," can be traced to southern minority tribes.[2]

Thus the controversy around this burial gives rise to a more fundamental issue—the question of Li Bai's birthplace and origins. There is further textual evidence for Li Bai's alien background. Some of his letters, as he claims in his poetry, are written in Tocharian script—a now-extinct language of the Indo-European peoples of Xinjiang—which would not be possible if he had not lived among them at some point. At the end of 761, when he believed he was dying, Li Bai recounted his life to Li Yangbing, a devoted friend who Bai claimed was his uncle; in his account, he said that his ancestors had originally been banished "for some groundless accusation" to the vast region west of China, and that later his family returned inland and settled in Sichuan when he was a young child. Some Sichuan scholars have asserted that he was in fact born in their home province, not in Suyab, Kyrgyzstan, as is the general consensus of opinion. This is a matter of pride and cultural inheritance—and business opportunities. The Kyrgyzstan government recently expressed its interest in using Li Bai as a tourist attraction. The truth is that the poet has long been uprooted from any specific place and belongs to the world. For our purposes, it is entirely reasonable to assume that he was originally from Central Asia, if not a half Chinese.

What is more significant is that Li Bai unwaveringly viewed Jiangyou as his hometown and treated people from Sichuan as his kin. In many of his poems, he speaks about his homesickness, longing for the land of Shu. He also claimed that he was "from Mount Emei" although he was not Buddhist and had no religious ties to the sacred mountain. In this sense, we can say with complete certainty that he believed his roots were in Sichuan. Nothing matters more than Li Bai's own sense of belonging.

5

DISSIPATION

Li Bai took his time as he wandered farther south. As this journey was meant to gradually build his reputation as a knight-errant and itinerant bard, he traveled at his own pace, often without an immediate destination. Whenever possible, he would make an excursion to sightsee or visit luminary figures. According to the Li Bai chronology by Zhan Ying, late in the summer of 725 he arrived in Jiangxia (modern Wuhan), where the legendary Yellow Crane Tower stood on a small hill, commanding a panoramic view of the Yangtze. This was the place where Li Bai would develop a minor poetic rivalry lasting many years. Before going to the tower, he planned to write a poem on a wall there (it was customary for poets and dignitaries to leave their words on historical sites). Such an inscription served as both a permanent advertisement and a memorial—provided that the writing and calligraphy were good enough to win the admiration of subsequent visitors. In Li Bai's time, Yellow Crane Tower was a spot frequented by literary figures and officials. It has remained so. In modern times, even Mao Zedong wrote a poem there.

The view of the waterscape moved Li Bai. But as he was about to compose his poem, he found another already up on the wall. Its author was Cui Hao (704?–754), who was three or four years younger than Bai but already an official in the palace. The poem on the wall looked to have been inscribed recently:

昔人已乘黃鶴去　此地空餘黃鶴樓
黃鶴一去不復返　白雲千載空悠悠
晴川歷歷漢陽樹　芳草萋萋鸚鵡洲
日暮鄉關何處是　煙波江上使人愁

《黃鶴樓》

Someone already rode the Yellow Crane away
And only left an empty tower here.
The crane, once gone, will not return,
White clouds floating for thousands of years.
Along the river ancient trees stand clear, one another,
While green grass covers Parrot Island.
In such twilight where can I find home?
The misty waves on the river make me grieve.

"YELLOW CRANE TOWER"

The poem is based on a local legend, which centers on an old man who used to frequent a tavern and drink there without ever paying his bill. The owner never asked him to settle it. This went on for half a year. Then one day, the old man picked up an orange peel and with it painted an enormous crane on a wall in the dining room of the tavern. The owner thought the painting was simply the old man's grateful gesture, because the crane was a symbol of longevity and immortality. But soon he discovered that whenever customers sang or music was played, the bird on the wall would flap its wings and dance. Thanks to this marvel, the tavern's business boomed and the owner grew rich. The old man wasn't seen again until ten years later, when he returned, summoned the crane off the wall, and rode it away. Cui Hao's poem begins at the end of the tale and envisions the aftermath of the bird's disappearance.[1]

Li Bai felt that his work might not surpass Cui Hao's, and so decided not to put a composition of his own on the wall. It is also said that he wrote a piece then tore it up. There have been legends about this moment when he abandoned his own poem. One even claims that he composed a doggerel, which reads, "I smash Yellow Crane Tower with my fist / And kick over Parrot Island. / Such a beautiful view I cannot describe / Because Cui Hao's poem is already there." According to the Japanese scholar Mori Daiki, these lines are a joke, and their authorship has nothing to do with Li Bai. However, Bai did write something similar. In a later poem, he tells a friend, "I will smash Yellow Crane Tower for you / And you must turn Parrot Island upside down for me" ("Composed in Jiangxia for Nanling Magistrate Wei Bing"). His jealousy is understandable—Cui Hao was a court poet and had passed the civil-service examination at age nineteen.

No doubt Bai felt challenged poetically. In Tang poetry, Cui Hao's "Yellow Crane Tower" is traditionally considered a perfect execution of its form.[2] Li Bai was not strong in this form, which was popular among capital poets. Throughout his life, Bai would return to Yellow Crane Tower both in person and in his verse to face Cui Hao's poetic challenge. More than fifty of his poems refer to this site. But at the moment, he had to concede the superiority of Cui Hao's poem.

Li Bai left Wuchang in the fall of 725 and continued east to Jiujiang, where he wished to see Mount Lu. This trip was clearly dated by his masterful poem "Watching the Lushan Waterfall." The mountain was known for its fine scenery and for its temples deep in the forests. It was also a place where many devoted Buddhists had gathered to study scriptures. From Xunyang, a river town, Li Bai and his pageboy Dansha rode south across hills and streams for more than ten miles and arrived at the East Woods Temple, built three centuries earlier in honor of Master Hui Yuan (334–416). Though not a Buddhist, Bai admired the detached spirit of the master and had heard about the tranquil beauty of his temple. The grand monk had lived there for over thirty years without ever leaving Mount Lu, dedicating himself to the study and translation of Buddhist scriptures. Li Bai and a handful of local friends were put up at the temple. They stayed there a few days, during which he paid homage to Hui Yuan's study and residence, which had been kept as a miniature shrine with a tiny altar in it, its walls decorated with paintings and calligraphy. Bai looked through the master's books and lit two sticks of incense for Hui Yuan's spirit. He also went to visit some tombs of Buddhist saints.

Accompanied by monks, Li Bai climbed to the top of Mount Lu, wearing sandals and a straw hat, a hemp rope tied around his waist. The young monks used machetes to cut a path in the bushes as they progressed. The climb was arduous, but Li Bai was captivated by the gorgeous views. On this trip he composed several poems, one of which was about the waterfall below Incense Burner Peak. It is a signature poem of his, still memorized by schoolchildren today:

日照香爐生紫煙　　遙看瀑布掛長川
飛流直下三千尺　　疑是銀河落九天

《望廬山瀑布》

The sun shines on the Burner Peak, raising purple smoke.
Look, far away a waterfall hangs on the river ahead,
Its stream flying down three thousand feet.
I wonder if it's the Milky Way descending from heaven.

"WATCHING THE LUSHAN WATERFALL"

Bai did not return to Xunyang with his local friends. Instead, he and Dansha rode back with them for a few miles, then parted company, going their own way.

. . .

About eight miles north of Mount Lu was a hamlet called Shang-jing. The poet Tao Yuanming (376–427) had once lived there. It was remarkable that Li Bai journeyed to the small village to look at Tao's homestead and pay his respects at his grave, which had fallen into disrepair, the words on the stone hardly legible. Like his deserted homestead, Tao had remained obscure for more than three centuries after his death. Only two decades prior to Li Bai's visit had Tao's poetry begun to be recognized by Tang poets, particularly for his presentation of immediate experiences in nature and the daily life of the countryside. Evidently Li Bai was one of his new admirers. Viewed from Tao's homestead, Mount Lu loomed in the distance, often half-hidden in clouds, against which birds sailed in the misty sky. The sublime scene depicted in Tao's poem "Drinking Wine" must refer to this view: "Picking chrysanthemums under my eastern hedge, / I raise my eyes and see the mountain in the south."

Li Bai's visit showed the esteem he held for Tao. There was no doubt that he liked Tao's simple natural poetry, which had founded the pastoral tradition in Chinese literature, but the two poets were very different in disposition and outlook and in their approaches to their art.

Tao Yuanming had been from a minor aristocratic family. His great-grandfather had been a high-ranking officer in charge of eight prefectures' military affairs, his grandfather the governor of Wuchang, and his father the prefect of Ancheng. In his early years, Tao Yuanming served at several official posts and then as the magistrate of Pengze County in the northeast of Jiujiang for less than three months before he decided to resign. He couldn't stand the obsequious official decorum and "wouldn't bend his back to petty lackeys for five pecks of rice" (his monthly salary). He left behind his official ribbon and seal and returned home. In his own words, "Trapped in the net of dust for so long, / At last I can return to nature." The word "nature" here also refers to his own disposition and to the state of freedom—he believed that social structures and rules were the source of evil, and he wanted to escape them. He worked as a farmer for the rest of his life. When he could find a respite from his work, he would read books and write poems, many of which were gradually discovered and embraced as masterpieces after his death. He wrote lines like these: "Life has its own way, / Where food and clothes form the root. / If you don't earn your own keep, / How can you ever feel at peace?" ("Gathering Rice in the West Field in September 410"). This stands in stark contrast to the romantic sentiments of Li Bai, who claimed, "Heaven begot a talent like me and must put me for good use / And a thousand pieces of gold, squandered, will come again" ("Please Drink"). Tao is viewed as a saint of poetry and Li Bai a god—one belonged to earth and the other to heaven. Tao's poems are calm, dignified, and painful but without malice, while Li Bai's poems are wild and passionate and often give the feeling that they tumble down from another world. More fundamentally, Tao embodied a kind of cultivation and dignity beyond Li Bai's grasp—that is, the dignity in serving neither a ruler nor a country, and in farming his own two acres to earn his living by the sweat of his brow. Like the plain surface of his poetry, there was nothing romantic or glorious in the life Tao had chosen. At times when his grain jar was empty, he even begged in nearby villages, though people respected him and treated him decently. He accepted poverty, loneliness, illness, and death with serenity, as he says at the end of the preceding poem: "I hope this kind of life will last forever / And I mustn't sigh about tilling my own fields."

Li Bai must have seen in Tao Yuanming the true state of a return to nature, which could not be separated from labor, hardship, and humility. Tao's way of life provided a point of reference for Li Bai, and served as a reminder of a stark reality. Never would Li Bai pursue Tao's kind of seclusion.

. . .

Most Li Bai chronologies agree that he arrived in Jinling (modern Nanjing) in the spring of 726. The city was a cultural and commercial center in the south. It was strategically located, and many dynasties had founded their capitals there: it faced the Yangtze to the north and Zhong Mountain to the south, believed to be easy to defend and hard to attack. It was also thought to have an imperial aura, an auspicious site for a capital. Legend holds that some ancient emperors even buried gold in this location in order to preserve its imperial spirit—this is why it is called Jinling (Gold Hill). But despite all this, throughout history the city has fallen to rebels and foreign invaders many times, so it is a heartbreaking place as well. In recent centuries, the Taiping rebels seized Nanjing in 1853 and made it their Celestial Capital, which was meant to be equal and even superior to the royal capital in Beijing; a decade later, the imperial army took the city back and slaughtered half a million people. In December 1937, the Japanese army captured the city and committed the infamous Nanjing massacre. In reality, Jinling seemed quite vulnerable to invasions. But it was a vital place geographically and economically in the Tang dynasty. It controlled the waterway transportation down to the ocean in the east and up to the interior in the west. Salt, grains, timber, iron, and other products were all shipped through the city. The surrounding regions were fertile and abundantly supplied with water. The mild climate and copious rainfall allowed double cropping of rice and even triple cropping of some produce. This made the region affluent, and the wealth helped create a colorful culture. The area was known as the Wu land, also called "the land of rice and fish." Thanks to its plentiful resources, the land of Wu was viewed as the empire's economic backbone, and a good place for training and keeping troops.

It is believed that Li Bai's family had a business in Jinling, probably a shop, and that he stayed there after arriving in the city. He was fascinated by the fleets of wooden boats loaded with goods sailing up and down the Yangtze, and by the city's marketplaces glutted with merchandise, some of which he had never seen before. As he explored the city, Bai began to make friends, wining and dining at expensive places whenever he could. He often gave away money generously to those in need. By his own account, in a single year (725–26) he spent a huge amount of cash, the equivalent of more than a dozen pounds of gold. At the same time, he began the process of *ganye,* introducing himself to officials in order to find patronage. He paid visits to many dignitaries and powerful men, but for the most part he was not well treated. Many simply declined to receive him. To make matters worse, the emperor had just announced that he and many of his courtiers were to visit Mount Tai in Shandong. The central government ordered every prefecture in the country to send its representatives to the sacred mountain to participate in the royal ceremony. Mount Tai is about four hundred miles north of Nanjing; most officials in the city were busy preparing to join the emperor there and had no time for an obscure man like Li Bai.

Meanwhile, Bai continued to give parties, where the wine flowed nonstop. As he drank, he would compose poetry, especially at the tipsy stage, inebriated but still lucid, which was believed to be the most intense and productive moment. Among Chinese artists both ancient and modern, alcohol has been regarded—even revered—as a way to stimulate creation, particularly in poetry, painting, and calligraphy. Even today, some artists still purposely become drunk so that they can achieve a kind of spontaneity in their works. Li Bai himself wrote, "Your mind will open naturally when you have imbibed enough wine." He often drank to access the emotion needed for his poems. But drinking was also a way to blunt his despair at failing to find patronage and entering the official circle, and to numb his homesickness. He wrote, "When the cup is emptied, sadness won't come."

Frustrated over his career prospects and at times lonely, he would remember his friends elsewhere and even imagine some new ones. Try as he might, he couldn't make real friends in Jinling; most of those he befriended were merely fair-weather ones who enjoyed his largesse. Instead, he began to spend time with women. He admired the fine figures, delicate skin, and soft accents of the women of Wu, and composed numerous poems about them. One was nicknamed Jinling Girl, a prostitute who appears in a few of his poems. In his verses, he idealizes her:

金陵城東誰傢子　竊聽琴聲碧窗裡
落花一片天上來　隨人直度西江水
楚歌吳語嬌不成　似能未能最有情
謝公正要東山妓　攜手林泉處處行

《示金陵子》

Whose daughter is this girl in the east of Jinling?
I listen to her music rising from a curtained window.
She's like a flowered cloud that fell from heaven
And she floats with her lover across the western river.
She sings in the Wu dialect, but her soft voice accented,
And this imperfection makes her sing with more feeling.
I think of Master Xie who took girls from Eastern Hill
Through all the woods and mountains and streams.

"FOR JINLING GIRL"

Throughout his life, Bai wrote many great poems about women, especially those spoken in female voices, which belong to the classical category of *yuefu* poetry, folk songs collected by the court. "For Jinling Girl" does not reach that level of greatness. It is too easy, rather frivolous, and is thought by some to be indicative of a larger lack of seriousness in his poems composed during this period. The poet and scholar Wang Anshi (1021–1086) of the Song dynasty even remarked that Li Bai's "vision got lower and lower—nine out of ten of his poems are about wine and women."

During his stay in Jinling, Bai did indulge in a kind of debauched poetry that tended to view women superficially. The last two lines of "For Jinling Girl," however, may reveal something deeper at work. They allude to Xie An (320–385), a statesman and calligrapher who had been the prime minister of East Jin State, and had once with his army of eighty thousand men defeated an invading force of a million troops. Before becoming a prime minister, Xie An had lived in Jinling, where Bai was now, spending his days with young courtesans on the mountains and rivers. Li Bai couldn't help comparing his situation with the ancient master's. He was twenty-five years old, confused and lost, and dreamed that his path, though seemingly frivolous now, would follow Xie An's to greatness.

Soon Bai's money ran out. It's believed that his family's business suffered a downturn at this time and was no longer able to provide for him. From this point on, he would be completely on his own. Most of his newly made friends deserted him, and as his situation in Jinling grew more unbearable, he decided to leave. The hardship, however, did not diminish his buoyant spirit, and the poetry he produced was still extravagant, full of energy and ease. At the farewell party attended by a few (so-called) friends of his, Li Bai composed a poem ending with these lines: "Please ask the river that's flowing east / Which is longer—its water or our attachment to each other?" These lines expressed his belief in friendship and his longing for loyal companions, but the others at the table were more struck by his reinvention of the flowing river image. Traditionally it has been a metaphor for sorrow, but here it refers to friendship and affection. Li Bai often expanded the space in his poetry to the maximum. In this case, friendship is stretched as vast as a river.

Before the end of the summer, Li Bai arrived in Yangzhou, a city sixty miles east of Nanjing. The weather was still summery, cicadas humming here and there in spite of the sultry heat. Bai noticed many affluent young men lounging around the downtown, and he asked after the powerful people of the city. Without delay he began to pay visits to them. But before he could fully embark on this new round of self-introduction, he fell ill. Now destitute and with no friends in the area, he was helplessly stranded. The tavern where he was lodging refused to let him stay on credit any longer—he had to pay or leave. The desperateness of his situation made him miserable and homesick. He wrote a letter in the form of poetry to Zhao Rui, saying he couldn't come home because he had not yet realized his ambitions, though he had little faith that his efforts would produce results. He mailed the letter the next day through the unreliable official post service, which mainly functioned to ensure the delivery of administrative orders and treated personal letters carelessly. Bai knew he might never hear from his teacher—he couldn't give a return address.

One night, unable to sleep, he watched the moonlit sky out the window for a long time and then composed this poem:

床前明月光　　疑是地上霜
举头望明月　　低头思故乡

　　《静夜思》

Moonlight spreads before my bed.
I wonder if it's hoarfrost on the ground.
I raise my head to watch the moon
And lowering it, I think of home.

"REFLECTION IN A QUIET NIGHT"

This would go on to became his best-known poem, which over a millennium every Chinese with a few years' schooling has learned by heart. On March 20, 2015, the United Nations Postal Administration issued a set of six stamps to commemorate World Poetry Day. Each design bore a poem in its original language. There are poems in English, Chinese, French, Russian, Spanish, and Arabic. Li Bai's "Reflection in a Quiet Night" was printed on the stamp exemplifying poetry written in Chinese.

Finally Bai realized that he couldn't buy lasting friendship with money. He was lying miserably in bed. Dansha tried desperately to nurse him back to health, but in vain. They were both starving now. Fortunately, a local official named Meng Rong, an admirer of Li Bai's poetry, came to his aid. As soon as Rong heard that Bai was in town, he hurried over to see him. He gave Bai some cash and helped him settle his arrears with the tavern. Rong was the deputy magistrate of Guangling County, which was part of Yangzhou. The owner of the tavern knew Meng Rong and from then on treated Li Bai decently. Rong also sent for a doctor, and within a month Li Bai recovered. Together Rong and Bai visited Buddhist temples and historic sites, which show up in Bai's poems. Rong advised Bai to stop wandering and seeking the appreciation of those men who were inferior to him in every aspect except for the posts they held. Rong knew office-seekers who had ruined themselves that way, becoming bankrupt and utterly lost, so he believed that Bai should first find a home or a haven that could act as a solid base. Rong had some friends in the official circle and suggested that Bai go to An Prefecture, more than three hundred miles west of Yangzhou.

Rong knew the renowned Xu family in Anlu, the capital of An Prefecture. The Xus had a daughter, who was in her mid-twenties and was still unmarried. We don't know her given name, though we do know that she later became Bai's wife. Over the previous three generations, her family had produced many preeminent statesmen. Her great-grandfather had been a classmate of Emperor

Gaozu, and her grandfather, Xu Yushi, had been a chancellor at the Tang court. Xu Yushi, however, had been demoted and banished from the capital because of his attempt to protect his son—who had killed a man in a hunting accident—from charges of manslaughter. Yushi was demoted to a far-off prefecture and eventually managed to return to his hometown of Anlu. It is recorded that while serving as a prefect, he was known for his leniency—when he found his subordinates involved in corruption, instead of punishing them he would give them a verse titled "Poem About Cleanness" so that they might repent their wrongdoings and reform themselves.

That was almost half a century back, and the Xus were no longer as prominent. Still, because they were a wealthy and renowned family, it was not easy for a man to join them by marrying their only daughter. As a result, Miss Xu had almost become an old maid by the standards of the period. Her father, Squire Xu, had asked Meng Rong to keep an eye out for a suitable match for his daughter. Rong worshiped Li Bai, who he believed was "overflowing with talent and lofty aspiration." He was convinced that Bai would become a great poet, "as famous as Chen Zi'ang," as he said to Squire Xu, so when he told Bai about Miss Xu's family in Anlu, he had him in mind as a prospective bridegroom for her.

Li Bai, however, was not inclined to marry now—he felt he had not yet accomplished anything and it was not time for him to settle down. Moreover, he felt uncomfortable "marrying into" a family and living under his in-laws' roof. Tang marriage law didn't even mention this kind of union, which meant it was abnormal and looked down upon. The accepted custom was for a successful man to bring home his bride, who ideally should be a daughter from one of the five most prestigious clans in the country: the Wangs (in Taiyuan), the Zhengs (in Henan), the Lis (in southeastern Gansu and southern Hebei), the Cuis (in Qing-he, Hebei), and the Fans (in central Hebei). The daughters of those clans were better educated and more capable of managing social life, and could bring wealth and powerful connections to their husbands.

Despite his uneasiness Li Bai agreed to go to Anlu, which was closer to Chang'an, the Tang capital. Meng Rong had friends in An Prefecture who should be able to help Bai get a post. Rong couldn't leave his work to travel with Bai, so he wrote a letter of recommendation that could secure help for him along the way.

6

MARRIAGE

Li Bai didn't go to Anlu directly. He traveled westward hesitantly, accompanied by Dansha. Anxious about the prospect of marriage, he seemed to avoid Anlu and sailed farther north along the Han River to Xiangyang. He had heard that the great poet Meng Haoran (689–740) lived in that area, and Bai wanted to visit him. At the time, Meng Haoran was equal in fame to Wang Wei (699–761), the two often being referred to as the best living nature poets. But Meng had failed repeatedly in the civil-service examination, whereas Wang Wei had passed on the first attempt and become a court official at age twenty-one, in part because he was from a well-connected aristocratic family. Despondent, Meng Haoran returned to the countryside to care for his parents. After they passed away, he became a recluse in Deer-Gate Mountain near Xiangyang Town. Li Bai had long been fascinated by this legendary town, where several master statesmen had stayed in seclusion before they came out to serve their lords.

Though Meng Haoran was a provincial, many capital poets appreciated his poetry. Their acceptance made him all the more extraordinary. He was twelve years Li Bai's senior but received the young man with open arms. He had a small farm and a house, both of which he had inherited from his parents. He cleared a room for Bai and his pageboy. Bai loved Haoran's properties, where the Mengs had over the decades planted more than a thousand fruit trees—orange, peach, date, and pear. A brook flowed by the fields—Haoran often sat fishing by the waterside after sunset. During the day he and Bai read each other's poems, and at night they talked about the ancients they admired and about the capital poets, whose works they found lacked vitality and life experience. They were both from humble origins and had come to the poetry scene from the margins, without the privileges the court poets enjoyed. Bai was delighted that he and his host had similar tastes and opinions. Haoran was especially fond of the ease and freshness of Bai's poetry. He was also fascinated by the distinct poetic personality manifested in Bai's work, which differed from anything he had read before.[1] Bai was particularly pleased to find that they shared similar political ambitions. In spite of his seclusion and self-sufficient farmer's life, Haoran insisted that the palace was "still on his mind and he would like to serve a good and wise emperor." That was exactly what Li Bai intended to do. Though by disposition they were very different—Bai would never engage in farmwork, viewing nature as mainly a religious and aesthetic space—their shared vision cemented their friendship, which was to last a lifetime.

Bai wrote several poems about Meng Haoran to express his deep feelings for him. One of them declares:

吾愛孟夫子　　風流天下聞
紅顏棄軒冕　　白首臥鬆雲
醉月頻中聖　　迷花不事君
高山安可仰　　徒此揖清芬

《贈孟浩然》

I love Master Meng,
Whose gallantry is known everywhere.
When young, he despised carriages and crowns;

White-haired, he lounges against pines and clouds.
In moonlit nights he gets drunk in an elegant manner
And possessed by flowers, he won't serve the emperor.
I can't praise enough this man who's like a high mountain,
So all I can do is clasp my hands to show my respect.

"FOR MENG HAORAN"

Bai told Haoran about his possible marriage, for which he was supposed to go to Anlu. To his surprise, his friend urged him to accept Miss Xu if he liked her, because her family was affluent and well connected. It would be foolish for Bai to continue to bumble around seeking patronage. To Haoran, the whole business of *ganye* was a joke, a way for young talents to waste their money and lives. Bai had better put down roots in Anlu and wait for a good opportunity to come to him there instead of hunting for it. What's more, it was said that the Xus had a magnificent collection of books. By all means Bai should consider the marriage seriously.

So a few days later, Li Bai left Deer-Gate Mountain for Anlu. Anlu was in the northeast of Hubei and had a slightly sloping landscape—endless farmland spread across the south, while hills and mountains rose in the north. It was connected with China's central plain through both roads and waterways. Traditionally Anlu was viewed as Hubei's gateway to the central plain. Li Bai's feelings about the town had changed some, thanks to Meng Haoran's positive words about it. When Bai reached Anlu, he ran into Yuan Danqiu, a friend he had known on his visit to Mount Emei back in Sichuan. Bai had always admired this man, calling him a "carefree fellow" who had a mild, detached manner. Yuan Danqiu was a Daoist master, and was rarely seen outside of Mount Song (the site of the modern Shaolin Temple), where he had secluded himself. We don't have the dates of Danqiu's birth and death or many facts of his life other than the few recorded by Li Bai, in whose works there are at least eleven poems about this man. In the introduction to one of his poems, Li Bai writes, "Nothing can surpass our long friendship and deep feelings for each other."

It happened that Danqiu had a friend in Anlu named Ma Zheng-hui who was an officer in charge of the military affairs of An Prefecture. Danqiu had come to visit Officer Ma. Knowing that Bai had been looking for a position, Danqiu introduced him to the officer right away. Ma liked Li Bai—although he was a military man, he was quite literary—and expressed his willingness to help the poet. According to Bai's own account, Ma commended Bai to his subordinates, saying, "Li Bai's writings are fresh, carefree and abundant, packed with marvelous words and expressions. His poems and essays glow and vibrate, every sentence shining and translucent with emotion and senses. Absolutely moving."[2] Being the top officer in the prefecture, Ma held real power and was involved in civilian affairs as well. He knew the Xu family well and told Bai that he ought to count his blessings if he could marry Squire Xu's daughter, who was pretty, intelligent, capable, and good-natured, and would make an excellent wife. Though the Xus were no longer powerful, the family was wealthy and prestigious. Li Bai was pleased to see an important man like Officer Ma support him.

Unexpectedly, Meng Rong came to Anlu from Yangzhou. His timely visit was meant to facilitate Li Bai's meeting with the Xus. It is likely that Squire Xu had urged him to come and serve as the matchmaker. Bai was delighted by his friend Rong's arrival in Anlu, where he felt he had been received warmly and could imagine himself staying. Rong took him to the Xus' residence. Bai's meeting with the family went well: although Squire Xu was unsure of his guest's family background (Li Bai claimed that his genealogical record was lost), he was struck by the young man's learning and good manners. Bai showed him his writings, mostly his recent poems. The host relished poetry and could tell that the young fellow was an extraordinary talent. Among the poems Bai presented was this one:

漢水波浪遠　巫山雲雨飛
東風吹客夢　西落此中時
覺後思白帝　佳人與我違
瞿塘饒賈客　音信莫令稀

《江上寄巴東故人》

The waves on the Han River stretch away
While the clouds over Mount Wu fly with rain.
The east wind carries the traveler's dream west
Back to that distant place.
Waking up, I again think of Baidi Town
Where you didn't come to meet me.
So many merchants return from there.
Please send me a word now and then.

"WRITING ON THE RIVER TO A FRIEND IN BADONG"

Badong was a prefecture in Hubei, near the Three Gorges. The poem is most naturally read as a love poem: the subject seems to be a woman and the speaker expresses hurt and disappointment—if not humiliation—by an unfulfilled tryst. The poem was an odd choice for the occasion (Bai was meeting his prospective father-in-law). Before the visit, the Xus had made clear that they were seeking someone who would marry into their household, and such a marriage for most men at the time had a tinge of dishonor. Bai's poem seems to deliberately subvert any expectations the Xus might have had of him as a conventional family man. The woman in the poem is speculated to be one with whom Bai had formed an intimate relationship several years earlier while visiting his younger brother up the Yangtze in Badong. The two brothers don't appear to have been close—Bai mentions him only once in his writings, and after this visit he would not cross paths with him again. Yet it was during his stay with him that Bai met this woman, and whatever intimacy they shared made him remember her fondly in his work.

Squire Xu seemed to understand the subtext of Bai's poem, but wasn't bothered by it. He saw the exuberant talent in the writing and became more convinced that Li Bai would go far in his official career and help his family regain their lost prestige. He could hardly contain his excitement. He told a maid to go and fetch his daughter. A few moments later Miss Xu appeared. She was a delicate young woman with a bony face and glossy hair. Her complexion was a bit pallid, but she had vivid, intelligent eyes. She was familiar with Li Bai's poems, which had been circulating somewhat widely, and she loved them. She was struck by the appearance of the young man seated next to her father. To her, Bai was more solid than handsome, and she was delighted by the prospective groom chosen for her.

Soon after Li Bai left, Squire Xu met Meng Rong again and expressed his wish to have Bai as his son-in-law. Meanwhile, Li Bai mulled over the meeting with the Xus. He not only liked Miss Xu's calm and graceful demeanor but also was impressed with her family's library, a massive collection with numerous rare books. There was no doubt that if he made his home here, he would have a solid foundation for his work and the full support of the Xus. He was tired of wandering around to beg officials. Although he was not yet ready to have children and raise a family, he realized that it would be better to settle down and study for a number of years, grow his reputation, and prepare himself for an opportunity.

The wedding took place within a month. It was attended by many local powers, including Li Bai's friend Yuan Danqiu and his advocate, Officer Ma. Li Bai was pleased with his gracious bride, who was well read and knowledgeable about history, literature, music, and the arts. She had a quick mind and could easily catch allusions he used in his poems and conversations, and she had her own tastes in poetry. Intellectually she was his match.

Soon after they got married, Li Bai wrote a poem, as a letter, to the woman back in Badong:

清水本不動　　桃花發岸傍
桃花弄水色　　波蕩搖春光
我悅子容豔　　子傾我文章
風吹綠琴去　　曲度紫鴛鴦
昔作一水魚　　今成兩枝鳥
哀哀長雞鳴　　夜夜達五曉
起折相思樹　　歸贈知寸心
覆水不可收　　行雲難重尋
天涯有度鳥　　莫絕瑤華音

《代別情人》

The clear water hardly moves
As peach blossoms spread on the bank.
The blossoms are playing with the water
And waves keep rocking the spring scene.
I am ecstatic about your beautiful looks
While you fall for my writings.
The breeze blows away the notes from my green lute,
Its melodies flapping with purple mandarin ducks.
That was long ago when we were fish in the same water,
But now we are two birds in separate woods,
Who warble plaintively every night until dawn.
I break a twig from the Lovesick Tree
And send it along as a sign of my heart.

The spilt water can no longer be gathered
As the clouds, once gone, can't be found again.
Yet there are birds treading the sky,
So please let them convey your word.

"FAREWELL TO A LOVER, ON BEHALF OF ANOTHER"

The title of the poem is an obvious mask—Li Bai must not have felt able to declare openly that this poem was for a secret lover of his own. At that time, it was common for poets to write love poems on others' behalf, just as writers today may compose love letters for others. This kind of ghostwriting has been an ancient practice, but this poem is much more intimate, peculiar, and complex. The speaker regrets that they cannot be together despite their love for each other. Although a union is not possible, he still longs to hear from her. And the speaker in the poem is actually a writer himself—as the line "While you fall for my writings" indicates—so why would he need a ghostwriter? The speaker must be Bai himself.

Some scholars have conjectured that the subject of this poem is a courtesan in Nanjing named Madame Duan Seven, but this argument is not convincing, because he had already written such a poem, "For Madame Duan Seven," which contains unrestrained praise of her beauty: "I'm not afraid to drown myself in this green wine / Because your fiery beauty maddens me." If this farewell poem were meant for her, Li Bai wouldn't have hesitated to put her name on it and his language would be more lavish. Furthermore, the woman in the poem was in Badong, while Madame Duan was in Nanjing. It is more reasonable to conclude that this is a poem to another former lover. In these verses, he claims that he has to end their relationship,[3] though he does not wish to lose touch with her entirely. Following this interpretation, we may even argue that Li Bai, in spite of his ungovernable heart, accepted his marriage—

and thus his separation from his former lover—as a fait accompli and tried to make the best of it.

It is generally held that Li Bai was not a good husband. Some even argue that since he had only two children with his wife, the couple's sex life must not have been active. That is a skewed view. The evidence shows that Li Bai did love his wife. Soon after their marriage, he took her to Yingcheng County, about forty miles south of Anlu, to bathe in a hot spring so that she could "float in the water and inhale the orchid fragrance / With a flushed face blooming like peach blossoms" ("Composed at the Yunü Hot Spring in Yingcheng, An Prefecture"). He wrote a number of poems for her and about her—a significant fact because poets prior to Li Bai had rarely written about their wives. His work made more room for poets to address their wives openly and honestly. In one of his poems, he addresses her and jokes about himself with a touch of self-reproach: "Three hundred sixty-five days a year / Every day I got drunk, collapsed like mud. / How awful, you became Bai's wife? / It must feel like having an idiot as a husband" ("For My Wife"). Understandably, he must have been unhappy about his dependent role in the marriage, and so attempted to drown his sadness in alcohol, but he must have also felt grateful to his wife for providing an anchor for his turbulent life.

Li Bai had another source of unhappiness. His wife had a cousin who had been living with the Xus in the role of her older brother. Her father's older brother had died many years before, and Squire Xu, without a son himself, had adopted the boy so that his household could have a male heir. The moment Li Bai married Miss Xu, his brother-in-law had regarded him as a rival, fearful that Bai might be given a good part of the inheritance when Squire Xu died. The old man doted on his daughter and had provided a generous dowry when she married. The squire placed hope of the family's recovery on Li Bai. Therefore, his adopted son grew more and more jealous—he not only begrudged Bai his role in the family but also seized every opportunity to vilify him in town. By and by rumors cropped up, and some in power began to view Bai as untrustworthy. As a result, no matter how hard Li Bai tried to join the local official circle, his effort always came to nothing. He sensed that his brother-in-law might be behind the hostility against him, but he couldn't prove his suspicion.

The Xus kept a country house in North Shou Mountain, which was twenty miles northwest of Anlu and could be reached in half a day by horse. The mountain was small but exquisite, heavily wooded with wall-like cliffs and domed peaks. Squire Xu's father, the disgraced chancellor, used to stay in the cottage from time to time, reading books. It had fallen into some disrepair but was essentially intact. With some work, it could be restored and fully habitable again. To avoid his brother-in-law and to help maintain his peace of mind, Li Bai persuaded his wife to let him move there so that he could devote his time to reading and writing. The squire granted permission—he agreed that Bai needed to concentrate on his work. So he set out for North Shou Mountain with Dansha, who was a young man now. They brought along a cartload of books from the Xus' library. After they arrived at the mountain, the two of them restored the bamboo fence to keep away monkeys and cleaned and repaired the cottage, rendering it livable again in just one day.

MARRIED LIFE

Li Bai, by his nature, couldn't be a good family man. He seemed to need to conserve time and energy for himself and for his work. His father-in-law often insinuated that he should try harder to enter civil service and even helped him get in touch with local officials, but the efforts still produced no result. Officer Ma, who had once admired Li Bai's talent, fell under the sway of Bai's brother-in-law and changed his mind about him. Even though Bai was now living away on the mountain, his brother-in-law continued to create obstacles for him, whispering that Bai was a devious, vainglorious man with a dubious family background.

All Li Bai chronologies indicate that late in 727 he heard from his friend Meng Rong. Bai was surprised by the formality of the letter: it came in the form of an official missive, delivered to him through the local government, as if his friend meant to emphasize the seriousness of its contents. In the letter Rong criticized him, saying Bai shouldn't have stranded himself in North Shou Mountain, which was far too small a place for a man of his ability, and that he should instead redouble his efforts to promote himself in official circles. Rong spoke figuratively, writing that if the tiny mountain retained Bai for itself, it would fail in its duty to nourish, sustain, and eventually release his great talent to the world. It is likely that Bai's father-in-law had complained to Meng Rong about his son-in-law's stagnant career, prompting Rong to rebuke the poet.

Li Bai was perturbed and even a bit incensed. In reply, he picked up Rong's figurative language and wrote a full essay in the voice of North Shou Mountain, describing himself as an accomplished Daoist: "He lounges around against clouds and with the mandolin in his arms; he drinks nectars and swallows elixirs of life."[1] The letter goes on to say that although North Shou Mountain was an obscure place, not much bigger than a hill, it could still "gather clouds and rain and provide shelter for deities." The mountain ventures to claim, "Heaven does not secrete treasures, nor does earth conceal gems. If good talents do not excel, that is because the emperor's supreme order has not prevailed yet." The letter, in the mountain's voice, assures the recipient that Li Bai is not lost. He is resolved to study books by the glorious ancients and will eventually emerge to restore the order and peace of the land. Once he has achieved that, he will leave his post for the wilderness, where he will enjoy himself in tranquility. As we have seen, this became Bai's refrain throughout his life: a plan to succeed in the world and then withdraw to nature. It went beyond a conventional Daoist creed Li Bai had adopted; it evolved into a personal belief. "I have observed the sages of ancient times— / Whoever did not resign after success would suffer destruction" ("It Is Hard to Travel"); "Since ancient times, not retreating after success / Would bring about more suffering" ("Ancient Songs 16").

Meng Rong seemed to understand the message contained in Bai's reply; he became more sympathetic and—though he still worried that his friend was indulging his reveries—didn't pressure Bai again.

Although he had sequestered himself on North Shou Mountain, by nature Li Bai was actually quite gregarious—he forced himself to stay on the mountain so that he could concentrate on his studies. Yet it was impossible for him to remain in total isolation and obscurity, especially as his poetry continued to gain popularity in the country. Whenever friends passed through Anlu, he would come out to meet with them and would also visit with his wife. In the spring of 728, his friend Meng Haoran informed him by letter that he was to make a trip to the region south of the Yangtze. Eager to see the older poet, Li Bai wrote back and asked to join Haoran in Jiangxia (modern Wuhan). They agreed to meet in the river town, more than sixty miles south of Anlu.

Li Bai was the first to arrive in Jiangxia. A young local scholar named Liao, a fan of Li Bai's, turned up at the inn where Bai was staying. Liao treated Bai to dinner and volunteered to be his sightseeing guide. Bai accepted the offer and inscribed for him a short poem, a piece of calligraphy, as a keepsake. Liao knew many of Bai's poems by heart—he was especially fond of those that had been set to music and were performed by singing girls along the river, such as "Spring Thoughts," "Song of Ba Girl," and "The River-Merchant's Wife." He asked Bai to share the secret of his poetic composition. Bai confessed to his new friend that his lines had come to him naturally and that he had simply recorded them—there was no secret at all. To show Liao how he had written the poems, Bai suggested going to the port in the north together, saying they might discover poetry there. Liao agreed and they started out the next afternoon. When they arrived, they took in the sights of the port, watching the boats as they sailed up and down the river. Then they entered a tavern.

As they were conversing over rice wine, a young woman walked in and asked a barmaid if a boat was coming in from Yangzhou. The girl told her there were boats from that city every other day. This meant that one would arrive tomorrow. At that, the young woman's face clenched and she began to complain, saying that her man had promised to come back within a year, but now three years had elapsed and there had been no word from him. The bargirl sighed and said there were many women in her situation. She added that if their men hadn't returned within a year, they might never come back. Li Bai listened attentively to their conversation. Another bowl of wine later, he and Liao left the tavern.

The next morning Liao asked him why they had not encountered any poetry at the port. Bai showed him a piece of paper that bore this poem:

憶昔嬌小姿　春心亦自持
爲言嫁夫婿　得免長相思
誰知嫁商賈　令人卻愁苦
自從爲夫妻　何曾在鄉土
去年下颺州　相送黃鶴樓
眼看帆去遠　心逐江水流
隻言期一載　誰謂曆三秋
使妾腸欲斷，恨君情悠悠。。。

《江夏行》

I recall my small waist and delicate limbs
And my young heart full of pride.
I wanted to marry you so that
We wouldn't miss each other miserably.
Who could tell I chose a merchant
Only to sink myself in sadness and pain?
Ever since we became a couple
You've rarely been home.
Last year you left for Yangzhou
And I saw you off at Yellow Crane Tower,
Watching your boat sailing far away
While my heart was following the current.
You said you would be back within a year,
But three autumns have gone by.

You've filled me with worry and sorrow
And my hatred of you flows long like this water. . . .

"JIANGXIA SONG"

This poem was somewhat derivative of Bai's other works, similar in sentiment to his masterwork "The River-Merchant's Wife." It feels facile and slightly forced—Li Bai must have grown a little glib, given that there were so many of his songs loved by the folks along the Yangtze. Moreover, there is a temporal discrepancy in this poem: the woman says her husband left a year ago, but in the same breath she claims that "three autumns have gone by." Li Bai seems to have composed the poem in haste, perhaps too eager to impress his new friend. Nonetheless, Liao couldn't help but marvel at the poem and shower the poet with praises. He nodded as Bai explained that a poet must have a sensitive mind and a sharp ear to catch things others might miss.

A few days later, Meng Haoran arrived in Jiangxia. Bai and Haoran were overjoyed to see each other, and together they visited places and friends in town. Bai showed his new poems to Haoran, who liked them but didn't comment in detail. Haoran was the more famous of the two, and so in spite of Bai's brilliance Haoran treated him like a younger brother, a growing poet. He observed, "I can see that you are good at composing folk songs. Ancient poetry tends to be low in style and sentiment, while contemporary poetry is restricted by forms and metric patterns. Only folk songs can be flexible without a fixed form and have longer or shorter lines. My brother, you are a natural talent and this kind of poetry suits you best. . . . I think that those who have written folk songs—both ancient and contemporary poets—tend to go so astray from the real art that they only end with the name of folk songs, as they just call their poems folk songs. Or they could be so dutiful in their composing that the songs are like mere imitations of ancient works. I believe that even though you want to learn from the old masters, it's still better to start with the poetry within yourself. . . . Brother, if you work hard on folk songs, in a matter of a few years you will be able to blaze your own path."

Meng Haoran's advice—"to blaze your own path"—stuck in Li Bai's mind from then on.[2]

As planned, Haoran was to sail down the Yangtze River to Yangzhou. Bai went to the waterside to see him off. He stood below Yellow Crane Tower after his friend departed, watching Haoran's boat bobbing away until it vanished beyond the horizon. This was the very spot where Bai had once attempted to write a poem but had stopped once he'd seen Cui Hao's superlative work on the tower wall. But now, even though Cui's masterpiece still stood there, Bai composed a more personal poem, one that didn't emphasize historical awareness or the beauty and grandeur of the land. He simply chanted:

故人西辭黃鶴樓　煙花三月下揚州
孤帆遠影碧山盡　惟見長江天際流

《送孟浩然之廣陵》

My friend is sailing west, away from Yellow Crane Tower.
Through the March blossoms he is going down to Yangzhou.
His sail casts a single shadow in the distance, then disappears,
Nothing but the Yangtze flowing on the edge of the sky.

"AT YELLOW CRANE TOWER,
SEEING MENG HAORAN LEAVING FOR GUANGLING"[3]

The poem became one of Li Bai's best works. He could not have been unaware of the significance of those lines, knowing that he was still in some sense competing with Cui Hao. As the centuries have gone by, this four-line farewell poem has in a way outshone Cui's, becoming part of the Chinese language. It is still quoted when people celebrate friendship and when they see their friends off, especially the last two lines.

On his way home, Li Bai stopped at Anlu to see his wife, and then took more books back to his cottage in North Shou Mountain. He continued with his studies, but often felt frustrated, at times even hopeless. Like most of the poets of his age, he was unable to escape the pressure of social hierarchy. There were very few ways for talented people to rise socially: peasants were bound to their land and had to pay heavy taxes, artisans were treated as mere handymen, and merchants were spurned by aristocrats and unprotected by the state. Like most men of his time, Bai had a strong sense of class—the stratification had already become a long-standing formation in Chinese society. This explains why Li Bai felt so proud of belonging to the royal clan despite the fact that, obscure and disadvantaged, he had to continue to hunt for office. There was simply no other outlet for his energy and gift. Even exiled, poets in ancient China couldn't wander beyond the geographic borders of their country, which confined their ambition and vision. Li Bai was no exception, and like other underprivileged talents, he had to go out in search of opportunities. Even when he stayed home, he had to study books to equip himself with more learning to prepare himself for an official career.

Although Li Bai stayed in North Shou Mountain most of the time, his brother-in-law continued to scheme against him. By the end of 728, Officer Ma had left Anlu for a new appointment elsewhere. A local official, Deputy Prefect Li Jingzhi, took charge of the Anlu government. Li Bai's father-in-law urged him to try his luck with the deputy prefect and even managed to have Bai introduced to him. Li Bai attended parties held in honor of Li Jingzhi and official visitors. At these gatherings, he often composed poems, which were praised by the attendees. Sometimes he also performed a sword dance, which was also well received. Everyone was convinced that he was a remarkable talent, and the deputy prefect told him that he would do his best to recommend him to a suitable post. In return for the official's heartening words, Li Bai eulogized him excessively in front of others. He didn't know that his brother-in-law had already gone ahead of him by cultivating a personal relationship with Li Jingzhi, in whose eyes Bai gradually became an inveterate troublemaker with a reckless temper, an impertinent attitude, and an unclear background.

One night Li Bai went to a party, a gathering attended by a few friends. They drank heavily and did not break up until after midnight. Bai was tipsy, and as he was walking back to the Xus', he saw a carriage with lanterns dangling on both sides coming toward him on the road. Rather than step aside to let it pass, he went up to the vehicle—he had caught sight of the deputy prefect Li Jingzhi and meant to greet him. His approach startled one of the horses, and the carriage plunged aside and nearly veered off the road. Two bodyguards dismounted and seized Li Bai: by law, any pedestrian had to keep a distance of a hundred feet from a high official's vehicle (such a practice is still common in China, where the police keep pedestrians aside to open the way for senior officials' cars), so Bai's act was criminal. Worse still, he was also in violation of curfew, which throughout the country forbade anyone to roam the streets after midnight. A commoner who committed such crimes would be flogged in public, but Li Bai was a scholar, a member of the local gentry, so they would not manhandle him. He apologized to Li Jingzhi, who flew into a fury, saying Bai had no respect for officials and had intentionally startled his horse. The deputy prefect left without accepting Bai's apologies.

Li Bai feared this wasn't over yet and talked to his wife. She was alarmed and so was her father. At their urging, Bai went to the prefecture's administration the next day and wrote out profuse apologies, using language like "I was frightened spiritless," "I should have knelt in front of your Excellency to receive a thorough flogging," and "now I am willing to accept any punishment." It was humiliating, but he had to bow to the powerful man. In appearance the deputy prefect seemed appeased, but Bai knew that his chance for an official recommendation was dashed.

Fortunately, it happened that Li Jingzhi transferred to another post soon afterward. Li Bai was relieved and even elated when he heard that the new appointee to the office was Pei Kuan, who was well known for promoting young men and often threw parties at which everyone was welcome. On September 8, 729, the date of the emperor's forty-fifth birthday, celebrations were held throughout the country, so Pei hosted a sumptuous party as well. Li Bai attended the event and performed a sword dance, which was applauded. He met Pei at the festivities and had a good feeling about him.

At his father-in-law's suggestion, Li Bai wrote Pei to introduce himself. He was still mortified by his brother-in-law's backstabbing and by the treatment he'd received at the hands of Pei's predecessor. Afraid that there might still be negative words about him in the government files, he could hardly maintain his composure in the letter. He asserted that he had aristocratic ancestors and was from the royal clan, that he had been generous to others—especially young scholars in need—and loyal to his friends. He wrote that he had studied devotedly for many years, learned from his teacher Zhao Rui how to remain detached from earthly affairs, and traveled thousands of miles to see the country, often wearing his long sword on the road. He listed the praises others had sung of his writings. He went on to flatter the official, saying Pei Kuan was "keen like an eagle and dignified like a tiger," his "teeth white like two neat rows of shells" and his "gait sturdy and striking." He continued to mention many great virtues and honors that people believed Pei possessed.

As he continued his letter, Bai could no longer hold back his anger at the rumors against him. One by one he tried to refute them. His writing grew at once more extravagant, more servile, and more arrogant. He ended the letter with, "I hope you will grant me a great opportunity. If you are delighted by me, please continue to bestow favors on me and increase my gratitude. Bai shall certainly do everything in return for your kindness and shall spare no cost or effort. If you are displeased, even angry, and will not allow me to follow you, I still will kneel in front of you to thank you. Then I will depart like the yellow crane that vanished in the sky. At which lord's gate can't one dance with a long sword?" ("Letter to Deputy Prefect Pei of Anzhou"). To "dance with a long sword" is a figure of speech referring to putting one's ability and ambition into practice.

Unsurprisingly, Deputy Prefect Pei was disturbed by the letter and felt that Bai was unstable—perhaps unreliable as well. In spite of his talent, the young man seemed full of himself, as if this prefecture were too small a pond for a big fish like him. So Pei Kuan didn't bother to respond. Although the court often urged local officials to recommend talents, whoever endorsed a problematic man could stain his own career and might even be held responsible if the recruit misbehaved in his office. Pei simply wouldn't have wanted to run such a risk.

Pei's silence discouraged Bai. It became clear that he was still a problematic man to the local government. Soon Bai concluded that it simply wouldn't be possible to find an official post in a small, claustrophobic place like Anlu and that he had better go elsewhere.

8

IN THE CAPITAL

Li Bai became restless again. He had been talking to his wife about leaving Anlu for some time so that he might have a better chance at entering civil service. At first she was reluctant to let him go, but she soon yielded, realizing that as a poet he needed to see the larger world and meet other literary men. She also understood that it was emasculating for Bai to stay under her family's roof for too long and that he was eager to found their own home and to secure their livelihood with a regular income. Her father had also been urging Bai to try his fortune elsewhere.

In the early summer of 730, Li Bai set out again. He traveled alone, heading for the capital, Chang'an, which was almost four hundred miles away in the west. By then, Dansha, his pageboy, was married, so he stayed behind. Together Dansha and his wife, a servant maid, were to attend to the household work and the mistress. Bai proceeded at his leisure and stopped here and there along the way. He detoured to Fang Town (present-day Fang County in Henan), where his friend Yuan Danqiu was staying at a temple. Danqiu was not expecting Bai but was thrilled to see him. He loved Bai and always gave his friend a hand whenever he needed it. In his eyes, Bai was an extraordinary genius whose poetry would undoubtedly endure. He often told others that whatever Bai put down on paper sparkled with brilliance and that no one could match his talent. Together the two men traveled to Dengfeng,

Henan, and spent more than ten days visiting historic sites. They also went to Longmen (Dragon Gate), said to be the very place where, twenty-seven centuries before, the ancient hero Yu the Great had opened a channel in the mountain to relieve the flood of the Yellow River. Along the way, Li Bai wrote several poems praising the beauty of the landscape and the deeds of the ancient heroes who had passed through before him. About thirty miles north of Longmen lay the city of Luoyang, the second-biggest metropolis in China at that time. Bai and Danqiu went to visit the city but didn't stay long, because Bai wanted to reach Chang'an before the end of the summer.

The entire trip to the capital took him nearly two months. When he reached Chang'an, it was midsummer.

With a population of more than half a million, the city was the largest in the world at the time. It was also a commercial center, a hub on the Silk Road. Bai was amazed by the high city wall that surrounded the capital. It was more than fifty feet thick, thirty feet high, and about ten miles in length. Armored soldiers on horses moved along the top of the wall. Bai stopped his horse and gazed up at the gate in front of him, above which were the words "Bright Virtue Gate." He had been told that there were twelve gates to the city and that five of them were similar to this one, composed of three entryways. He saw that pedestrians went in through the left and came out through the right. Both of the side entryways were narrower than the middle one, which was for vehicles. Having entered Bright Virtue Gate, he was struck by the wide street stretching north. This was the famous Red Bird Avenue leading to the center of the city. He had read that Chang'an had eleven north–south streets and fourteen east–west streets, which together formed more than one hundred blocks. Passing through a marketplace, he saw foreign merchants among the Chinese, hawking their wares and haggling with customers. The street was lined with stalls and shops, some of which specialized in jewelries, musical instruments, wines, fabrics, candies and pastries, tools, and sport-ing goods—even polo equipment and big kites were on display. Some owners of the shops were Persians and Kucheans wearing turbans of various colors. Their headwear reminded Bai of the men he had met in his childhood, back in Central Asia. Then he caught sight of an inn and went toward it. He had to find a place to stay, lest he break curfew when it got dark.

The next morning he went to find the home of his relative Xu Fuqian, who was a distant cousin of his wife's and a minor offi-cial in the palace, in charge of a catering section. Before Bai had left Anlu, his father-in-law had written to Fuqian, asking him to introduce Bai to consequential men at court. Fuqian received Bai cordially. He told him that he supervised only the supply of some foodstuffs in the palace and had no direct contact with high-ranking officials, but he would see what he could do. At the moment, most of the courtiers had left for their summer retreats in the countryside or in the mountains, but the catering department was still busy, preparing to celebrate a prince's birthday, so Fuqian suggested that Bai stay with him for the time being. Bai eagerly accepted the arrangement.

When Fuqian began to explore the possibilities, he found out that Chancellor Zhang Yue was regarded as the man most active in recommending talents to court and that many young men had started their official careers under his aegis. The old chancellor was not only an expert in solving thorny legal cases but was also, like many of the courtiers, fond of classics and the arts. Moreover, he was deeply trusted by the emperor because he had, seventeen years earlier, presented His Majesty with a dagger, signaling that the emperor ought to take action without delay to wipe out an enemy faction headed by Princess Taiping (665–713), the emperor's aunt. The emperor acted on his advice, put the court in order, and seized the throne. However, lately Chancellor Zhang had become ill and was seldom seen at the palace. The heartening news was that he had three sons, all well versed in classics, poetry, arts, and music—particularly the middle son, Zhang Ji, who was already a powerful figure at court, married to a daughter of the emperor's and holding the third rank, a full minister. The emperor was very fond of this young son-in-law and often granted him favors.

Undaunted by Fuqian's report on Chancellor Zhang, Li Bai decided to call on the old man himself at his home. Legend had it that for this visit, he designed a card the size of a book, on which he inscribed these words: "Li Bai, Turtle Angler on the Ocean." When the old chancellor saw Bai's card, he was baffled by the fanciful courtesy name, Turtle Angler, a nom de plume coined just for this occasion, and his curiosity was piqued. Having seated Bai in the front hall, the host asked him, "The ocean is so vast, with what can you catch turtles?" Bai answered, "I use a rainbow as the fishing rod and the crescent moon as the hook." This befuddled the old man even more, but he persisted: "What bait will you use?" Bai replied, "Wicked and corrupt men." Astonished, the chancellor felt uneasy about his guest's answer. Yet after reading the writings that Bai had brought along as samples of his poetry, the older man couldn't help but become more polite, because he saw that the young man, though brash and unpolished, was truly gifted. So he told Bai that owing to his frail health, he had stopped handling official affairs, but he would like to have his son Ji talk with him.

In no time Zhang Ji stepped into the hall. He was a dashing, urbane man, even something of a dandy. In his eyes, Li Bai must have looked hopelessly provincial, with his heavy Sichuan accent. But as he read Bai's poetry, he was surprised by its abundant energy and fresh voice and flowing ease. It was completely different from the mannered and subdued works written by capital poets. Moreover, Bai's calligraphy was strikingly beautiful, absolutely unique. Beyond any doubt, this visitor was an original. As Zhang Ji grew more courteous and conversed with Li Bai more cautiously, a rush of envy rose in him. By any means he must keep this young provincial away from court or he might become a serious rival. Outwardly he promised to help Bai but left the timeline vague, saying that at the moment the palace was nearly empty and they had to wait for an optimal time. Unfamiliar with the intrigues of the official circle, Bai believed that he had finally found someone who appreciated him. He left the Zhangs' elated, full of hope.

Two days later, Zhang Ji paid a return visit to Li Bai. He told Bai that he had an idea: Emperor Xuanzong had a beloved sister named Princess Yuzhen, who was a pious Daoist and had become a nun a decade before. She had a villa on Zhongnan Mountain, built for her by His Majesty, and she would go there regularly, staying a month or two each time. She loved poetry and enjoyed discussions about the *Tao Te Ching* and *Chuang Tzu,* and so if Li Bai went to the mountain and got to know Princess Yuzhen personally, he would beyond all doubt open an avenue for himself.

Bai in fact knew of the princess—his friend Yuan Danqiu belonged to the same Daoist sect as she. Yet Bai had misgivings about Zhang Ji's suggestion—since Princess Yuzhen was not a court official, he asked, how could she recommend someone for a position? Ji smiled and explained that if she took a liking to him, she could speak to the emperor directly on his behalf. That would surely expedite the promotion process, because she could circumvent all the overelaborate procedures and formalities. So Li Bai was convinced. He had of course heard of the legendary Zhongnan Mountain, which was the birthplace of Daoism. Lao Tzu (fifth–fourth century BC) had lived there and written the *Tao Te Ching* there. Happily, Bai agreed to go and stay at the princess's villa as a close friend of her nephew Zhang Ji. He thanked Ji profusely.

Zhang Ji assigned a servant to accompany Li Bai to Zhongnan Mountain. Bai and Ji's man started out early the next morning, riding east unhurriedly, and arrived at Zhongnan Town in the afternoon. After a late lunch, they continued south up the mountain, on which stood many shrines, monuments, archways, and villas. Some of the constructions had been there for centuries—evidently this tranquil place had long been a favorite retreat for Daoists and officials. No wonder the area was also known as the Land of Bliss. Princess Yuzhen's villa was on a slope on the west side of the mountain. The sun was sinking behind a rocky ridge as they approached, so Bai couldn't see the house clearly from a distance, but he felt that the whole place was supernaturally quiet. From the town to the villa, they had not encountered a single soul.

But the sight of the princess's villa disheartened Bai. It was vacant as if deserted, its front yard overgrown with grass, among which was a vegetable patch, its green a shade darker in the dusk. Inside the house, furniture was broken and dust blanketed everything. Clearly Princess Yuzhen had not been here for a long time. There was only an old guard at the property, who unlocked a wing of the house for them. Hurriedly Zhang Ji's servant helped Bai tidy up a room, in which the two of them spent the night. The next morning the man told the old guard to help Bai settle in and to let his wife cook for him from now on. Without further ado, the servant headed back to Chang'an.

For several days Li Bai was restless, wondering if he might have been taken in. The place was dull and he felt lonely, unsure of why Zhang Ji had sent him here. He spoke with the old guard about Princess Yuzhen, who, Bai learned, hadn't come to this place for more than a year. In fact, she had numerous residences of this kind in and around the capital and this one was not among her favorites. Fortunately, the princess had left here a shelf of books, mostly religious texts, which helped Bai pass the time. As the days went by, he grew less worried. He spent the daytime reading books and copying out ancient folk songs. He also practiced calligraphy and swordsmanship. The old couple were impressed but they were illiterate, and Bai could hardly converse with them at length. Literate people were few at that time, especially in the countryside; it was not uncommon that a whole village didn't have a single person who could read and write. Meanwhile, Bai's money was running low, and he began to pawn away his belongings in the town below the mountain. He let the old man take away his clothes and even his books in exchange for wine, which they would drink together. When Bai was drunk, he bragged that he would be summoned to court for a high post at any moment and someday he might become a chancellor in the palace.

In truth, he believed that Zhang Ji would send someone to fetch him soon, since Princess Yuzhen hadn't arrived. Day after day he waited, and then the rainy season set in. Gradually he lost his patience and felt dejected. Every meal was the same fare, boiled millet or corn with salty vegetables. The old couple could not afford cooking oil, so the food was watery. Bai hadn't tasted meat for more than a month and had no idea how long this situation would continue. He had no winter clothes with him, and the thought of weathering the cold and snow unsettled him. He wrote two poems addressed to Zhang Ji expressing his unhappiness. The second of the poems shows him no longer holding back his anger, as it ends with these lines:

何時黃金盤　一斛薦檳榔
功成拂衣去　搖曳滄洲傍

Someday I will use a huge gold plate
And offer you a whole hu *of betel nuts.*
After my success, I'll leave everything behind,
Floating around in the wildness.

"FOR SUPERVISOR ZHANG,
FROM PRINCESS YUZHEN'S VILLA ON A RAINY DAY"

The *hu* is a container with a narrow mouth and a wide bottom, able to hold a hundred liters. The gold plate and the betel nuts refer to an anecdote from the Nan dynasty (429–589). A poor but capable man named Liu Muzhi married a woman of an affluent family, but the couple's home had little food, so Muzhi often went to his in-laws' to cadge meals. For that, his wife's brothers looked down on him. Once they held a dinner party, to which Muzhi went (though uninvited), and after the courses of food, he began to chew betel nuts. His brothers-in-law ridiculed him, saying that it was common knowledge that betel nuts accelerated digestion, and he should have known to let his meal settle in his stomach first. Muzhi was humiliated and could never get over the insult. Years later when he became a top local official, he gave a sumptuous dinner to his in-laws. After the main courses, he told them that he would like to share something. He motioned for his servants to come into the dining room, and they carried in an enormous gold plate that contained a whole *hu* of betel nuts. Clearly, incensed though Li Bai was, he could voice his anger at Zhang Ji only indirectly, through an allusion.

Meanwhile, he was still hoping that Princess Yuzhen would come to the villa. He tried to imagine what she was like and even wrote about her. In the poem titled "Lines for Yuzhen, the Celestial Being," he envisions her as follows:

玉真之仙人　　時往太華峰
清晨鳴天鼓　　飆欻騰雙龍
弄電不輟手　　行雲本無蹤
幾時入少室　　王母應相逢

　　《玉真仙人詞》

Yuzhen is truly immortal,
Frequenting the peaks of Taihua Mountain.
Early in the morning she beats the drum
As she exercises like riding a pair of dragons.

With both hands she gathers all her force
As if floating on white clouds.
When will you fly to Mount Shaoshi
Where you can meet Heaven's Queen?

All through September Bai indulged in such reveries. When he was drunk, he even bragged to the old couple that he and the princess knew each other, so she would be coming to see him at any moment.

As fall deepened and crops were gathered in, Bai grew more anxious. He feared that he might not be able to survive the winter if he was stranded here for too long, so he returned to Chang'an. He went to Xu Fuqian's home, but to his dismay, his wife's cousin no longer welcomed him. A footman told him that the master was not in and handed him a small sum of cash. Displeased though Bai was, he accepted the money and turned away to look for cheap lodgings.

He did not expect to be received by Zhang Ji either, because the old chancellor, Ji's father, had just died, so instead of calling on the young dandy, Li Bai mailed him the two poems he had composed. He thought he might hear from Zhang Ji nonetheless, but no word ever came. Soon Bai realized that Ji had wanted nothing more than to wash his hands of him and would never contact him again. It would make no sense for him to wait in Chang'an any longer, so before the first snow, he left the capital.

Bai went to Binzhou (modern Shan County, Shaanxi), about a hundred miles northwest of Chang'an. It was something of a frontier town, where Bai faced a vast desolate landscape; he likely was drawn there by a subconscious longing for the far-flung land of his childhood. He wrote poems that attempted to evoke the sentiment of the borderland, where the sun looked more distant, the mountains more solemn and immense, even the geese crying more gutturally and sending down a heavy note of sadness to travelers' hearts. The open expanses made him miss a sense of home, and he yearned to return to his wife.

The prefect of Binzhou, Li Can, was a hospitable man who kept an open house for a wide range of visitors. He received an annual salary of two thousand *dan* (one *dan* is approximately one hecto-liter) of grain, which was unusual and similar to the yearly earn-ings of a circuit governor or a full minister, and he could afford to throw dinner parties for his guests every two or three days. Musi-cians, dancing girls, singers, and acrobats often performed in his hall until midnight. When he met Li Bai and heard his predica-ment, he was sympathetic. Considering that they shared the same surname, it was possible that they were blood relatives—a connec-tion Bai openly claimed, calling the prefect a cousin of his. Li Can saw Bai's talent and, though it was impossible to recommend him for any post at the moment, wanted to keep tabs on him. He didn't mind feeding an extra mouth, so he invited Bai to stay in his resi-dence. Bai, eager to find a place near the capital, accepted the offer.

For two months Li Can held frequent parties and banquets, at which Li Bai accompanied the guests. They watched dances, lis-tened to songs, and composed poems as they feasted. Bai enjoyed the food and wine and the merriment in the beginning, but soon began to feel he was merely wasting his time. If he continued to live like this, he might ruin himself with nothing accomplished. So he began to write poems addressed to the host or honored guests to convey his longing (while at the same time heaping praises on them). Nonetheless, he couldn't help drawing a contrast between his own plight and Li Can's privileged life. One of his poems reads:

忆昨去家此为客　　荷花初红柳条碧
中宵出饮三百杯　　明朝归揖二千石

宁知流寓变光辉　胡霜萧飒绕客衣
寒灰寂寞凭谁暖　落叶飘扬何处归。。。

《豳歌行，上新平长史兄粲》

When lotus flowers were pink and willows green
I left home and have become a guest.
At night I go out downing three hundred cups,
Dreaming I will be paid two thousand dan *of grain.*
By now I am familiar with the light in guestrooms
And also the frost and chilly winds of the frontier.
Who can warm the cold ashes and melt my loneliness?
Or tell me where the leaves are heading in the wind? . . .

"SONG OF BIN, FOR BROTHER LI CAN PREFECT"

Bai's claim of "downing three hundred cups" a day is not a groundless boast. In addition to high-alcohol wines, low-quality wines, which contained little alcohol and were mostly home-brewed, were also available, and so it was not entirely implausible for one to consume such a large quantity.[1] In addition, the cups were small and usually each held only two or three ounces.

The poem, mild as it was, provoked mixed feelings in Li Can when he read it. What Bai said made good sense, but he seemed also to complain that Li Can had not helped him enough, and as a consequence, he was stranded in Binzhou.

This made Li Can reassess Bai's case. He began to suspect that the poet might be essentially ungrateful, with deeply entrenched character flaws; otherwise, how else could Bai have encountered one setback after another for so many years? Now Bai even coveted his benefactor's kind of salary, two thousand *dan* of grain annually. Li Can saw Bai's extraordinary ambition, which to some extent unnerved him, so he decided to let Bai go. The sooner he got rid of this recalcitrant fellow, the better. He sent for Bai and told him that Wang Song, a councilor at the government of Fang-zhou (modern Huangling County, Shaanxi), needed an aide and that Bai should go there to seize the opportunity.

Li Bai had no choice but to leave for Fangzhou, which was about seventy miles north of Chang'an. Like Li Can, Wang Song was fond of company and of songs and dances performed in his residence. He treated Bai decently, inviting him to dinner parties now and then. He introduced him to his other guests, some of whom later became Bai's friends. As before, Li Bai composed poems to please his new host and to impress the guests, but from time to time he could not help alluding to his own predicament in the hope that Wang might recommend him for a suitable position at the local government. Wang Song, like his friend Li Can, didn't make an effort to help Li Bai's career, unsure of the poet's character and afraid of becoming implicated if Li Bai caused trouble. More-over, as a mere councilor at the prefecture's administration, he had little power—people respected him mainly as a figurehead.

When Bai saw the true situation he was in, he decided to leave. Out of courtesy Wang gave him a handsome amount of cash for his travel expenses, which Li Bai badly needed. He calculated that with this money he would be able to stay in the capital for quite a while, so he decided to head back to Chang'an.

Wang Song's parting generosity touched Bai. Before leaving, he wrote a poem to express his gratitude and reiterate his aspiration: "I hope to help a righteous lord. / After I succeed, I will return to my old woods. / Why did I come west all the way? / To make true friends while bearing a long sword. / Birds love green mountains far away / And fish dive into ocean vast and deep." The poem ends with the hope that Wang Song and Bai will one day visit each other so that they can stay on a mountain and enjoy the music of the lute ("Farewell to Councilor Wang Song").

During this time Bai missed his wife back in Anlu, but he could not return to join her without any achievement to show in his quest for office. Instead, he kept working on a group of eleven love poems addressed to his wife, collectively titled "To the One Far Away." It is believed that Li Bai mailed some of these poems to her in his letters home, which she perhaps never received since mail was unreliable. These poems are uneven and a few seem unfinished, but some of them express the love and attachment between him and her:

六
陽臺隔楚水　　春草生黃河
相思無日夜　　浩蕩若流波
流波向海去　　欲見終無因
遙將一點淚　　遠寄如花人

《寄遠》

6
Your terrace is beyond the Chu water
While spring grass spreads along the Yellow River.
My thoughts of you torment me day and night
Like the river's tumbling waves
That are flowing toward the ocean
And fading from view in an instant.
All I can do is gather some tears
For the one like a flower blooming far away.

We can see that Li Bai could hardly say anything original about his feelings for his wife. He even romanticizes the recipient of the letters as an ideal, unavailable lover, as Poem 10 states that he writes in a foreign script for the lover who lives far away at the western frontier. By nature he was not a family man, and though he undoubtedly missed his wife, his poems for her seem generic, spoken in conventional tropes. He labored to complete those poems and make them original, and yet they don't stand out among his larger body of love poems.

In the spring of 731, Li Bai started out for the capital. He no longer had a foothold there: his wife's cousin, Fuqian, would surely shun him, and inns in the city were expensive. By now he had spent a good part of the cash Wang Song had given him, so he passed Chang'an without entering it. He went farther south to Zhongnan Mountain, where he had once stayed in Princess Yuzhen's abandoned villa. This time, however, he lodged at a local temple, where he could always find a bed. He called the place Secret Lair of Pines and Dragons. He also went to visit a local friend, a farmer named Husi. Li Bai was very fond of this man and his farmstead. Bai's lodging place, the temple, was on the southern side of Zhongnan Mountain, but Husi's home was on the northern side. We know nothing about the circumstances in which Li Bai had befriended Husi, whom he affectionately called "Mountain Man," but evidently he cherished their friendship and loved the farmer's home. In a poem, Bai describes the idyllic beauty and the tranquility of the place:

暮從碧山下　山月隨人歸
卻顧所來徑　蒼蒼橫翠微
相攜及田家　童稚開荊扉
綠竹入幽徑　青蘿拂行衣
歡言得所憩　美酒聊共揮
長歌吟松風　曲盡河星稀
我醉君復樂　陶然共忘機

《下終南山過斛斯山人宿置酒》

At dusk I descend the green mountain,
The moon following me all the way.
As I turn to see the road I walked

The endless woods stretch like emerald swells.
My friend takes me toward his farmhouse
Where his kids open the bramble gate.
Along the bamboo we stroll on a quiet path
As turnip leaves flap against our clothes.
Happily we chat, completely relaxed
And raise our cups now and again.
We sing loudly with the wind in the pines.
When we're done, stars turn sparse.
The host grows more delighted, seeing me drunk—
Together we have forgotten this world.

"DESCENDING ZHONGNAN MOUNTAIN AND STAYING AT
MOUNTAIN MAN HUSI'S HOME, WHERE WINE FLOWS"

Such a bucolic poem is rare by Li Bai, since he was not fond of the rustic life. We can see that the poem echoes the spirit of Tao Yuanming's poetry about nature and farmwork. It celebrates a harmony, albeit momentary, between humans and their surroundings. To some extent, it also speaks of the ideal space to which Li Bai imagined retiring if he ever succeeded in his political ambitions.

Li Bai was good at relating to common people, capable of understanding their lives, joy, pain, and suffering. During this time, when he traveled to and around Chang'an and when he actually stayed in the capital itself, he wrote other poems about common people; some of them are in the form of folk songs and are among his best. Here are two poems from his "Midnight Songs" composed during this period:

三
長安一片月　萬戶搗衣聲
秋風吹不盡　總是玉關情
何日平胡虜　良人罷遠征

四
明朝驛使發　一夜絮征袍
素手抽針冷　那堪把剪刀
裁縫寄遠道　幾日到臨洮

SONG 3

The moon shines on the City of Chang'an,
Where ten thousand households are beating laundry.
The autumn wind blows endlessly,
Always sending over feelings from Jade Pass.
When shall we subdue the barbarians
So our men can stop battling far away?

SONG 4

The emissary will start out tomorrow morning,
So we are busy tonight sewing robes for our men.
Bony hands are pulling cold needles
And it's hard to handle scissors for a whole night.
What we've made will travel a long way
Though we have no idea when they will reach Lintao.

Jade Pass and Lintao, far west of Chang'an, were the frontier areas where the Tang army often fought the tribal forces that troubled the borderland. The persona here is a collective female voice, speaking from the perspective that of the women left behind by the soldiers on the expedition. These poems have completely shed the decadent sentiment of singing girls and courtesans present in so many of Li Bai's early poems about women. The dignified folk songs embody the new depth and maturity of his art, conveying a historical drama that is often absent in his earlier poems with female personae. His frustrations and suffering in the Chang'an area must have made him a more compassionate man, and his poetry benefited from that.

At the end of the winter, he returned to the capital, planning to enjoy springtime in the city, which was said to be gorgeous, but Chang'an disappointed him yet again. He spent plenty of time at restaurants and taverns, believing that he might encounter powerful men there and even accomplished poets. But now he kept running into hoodlums, who were mostly from rich and influential families, good for nothing and only abusing the poor and the weak. Several times he even fought with them, since he was skilled with the sword and always ready to meet challenges. Once he was nearly beaten up by a band of gangsters, but a new friend of his summoned the police and rescued him just in time. Yet during this stay, Li Bai also made several genuine friends who were in a similar situation and had come to the capital to seek office. Together they reveled and vented their discontent and anger. At parties and restaurants he saw that some insolent young officials were actually ne'er-do-wells, incapable of office work and unable to use arms. They held positions largely because they were knowledgeable in irrelevant subjects such as ball games, cockfights, dogfights, cricket fights, even running kites—"expertise" that was apparently appreciated by some top officials and lords. These upstarts had mansions, land, businesses, packs of bodyguards. They would bully people at random and have pedestrians driven aside when they passed through the downtown. Their horses and carriages threw up dust and upended vendors' stands while their lackeys beat gongs and barked at people.

The more Bai encountered such parvenus, the more outraged he became. He composed a set of poems titled "Hard to Travel," which allegorically expressed the impossibility of men of humble origins to advance through society with honesty. He chanted one of these poems at a party: "It's hard to travel, hard to travel! /

There've been so many forks and wrong turns / That I no longer know where I am. . . . / The road is broad like heaven / But I alone have no way out." At another party, he wrote a poem that ends with these lines: "What I enjoy is a jar of wine when I'm alive. / Why should I need a name of ten thousand years after I'm gone?" His friends all shared his misery and could not see a ray of hope. The capital was full of young office-seeking scholars like them, all desperately trapped in such an impasse. Bai realized that he must not mingle with those derelict souls for too long, because that would only lead to despair.

In the spring of 732, he decided to leave Chang'an and head home.

9

AWAY FROM THE CAPITAL

Bai didn't go back to Anlu directly—he chose to travel by boat down the Yellow River to Bianzhou (modern Kaifeng). From there he could continue home by land—such a trip would be faster than the usual route via Luoyang City. He also wanted to see Liang Park on the Bian River near Bianzhou. The park was a historic site, originally used as a retreat by the royalty of the Han dynasty. It was immense, one hundred miles in circumference. In Li Bai's mind, the grounds were splendid, with buildings, pavilions, charming lakes, and blossoming bushes, but when he arrived at the park, he was quite disappointed. In front of him spread endless ruins— half-dead trees, dried-up streams, broken walls, and shards of tiles among weeds. There was no trace of the splendor described by so many ancient writers. Such a desolate scene cast a dark shadow on Bai's mind.

From the park he went to a nearby town and sat in a tavern on a hill slope, from which he could catch the view of the Yellow River in the distance, its ocherous waters nearly motionless. He ordered strawberries, and as he ate them with fine salt, his mood began to lift. He was amazed to see a burly servant with a shaved head waving a large fan in the dining hall, because it was only May, the weather quite mild. This gave Bai the illusion that it was already midsummer. He reminded himself to enjoy everything while he could. Life was too short to be wasted lamenting ruins and losses.

These details are recorded in his poem "Song of Liang Park," composed at the tavern. Toward the end of the poem, he turns meditative and shows misgivings about his fruitless quest:

昔人豪貴信陵君　今人耕種信陵墳
荒城虛照碧山月　古木盡入蒼梧雲
樑王宮闕今安在　枚馬先歸不相待
舞影歌聲散綠池　空餘汴水東流海
沉吟此事淚滿衣　黃金買醉未能歸。。。

《梁園吟》

Lord Xinling was once rich and powerful,
But today crops grow on his grave.
Moonlight bathes the ruined town and park,
Where old trees stretch toward boundless clouds.
Where is Emperor Liang's palace?
Where are talents like Sima Xiang-ru and Mu Cheng?
The shadows of dances and the tunes of songs were scattered
On the green ponds, though the Bian still flows toward the sea.
To lament these things makes me tearful
And I squander gold for wine, reluctant to go home. . . .

As Bai wrote, tears trickled down his cheeks and wet the front of his robe. Yet the grief didn't crush him, and he still dreamed of rising above his circumstances to realize his ambition, which he also believed was his way to help the common people who would always benefit from peace and responsible governance. This emotional push and pull reflected the torment of his soul and became a dramatic pattern and source of tension in his poetry.

Again he avoided returning to Anlu directly. Instead, he wandered westward to visit historical sites that interested him. Mount Song, in the west of Henan, was the birthplace of the Quanzhen Dao, the main branch of Daoism. The site was known as a retreat for many accomplished Daoists. Throughout history, masters had made their homes there, and some had even started their own sects and created their own versions of Daoism on the mountain. Today, the Shaolin Monastery sits on Shaoshi Hill, which is part of Mount Song.

Li Bai went to the mountain because he had heard of a female Daoist known as Master Jiao, who was said to be over two hundred years old but looked in her fifties. She was an expert in making pills of immortality. She was said to be in robust health despite her extraordinary age and her weak vegetarian diet, and was also said to be able to travel on foot more than two hundred miles a day. In every way she was imagined as a *xian*. For weeks Li Bai climbed the thirty-six hills of Mount Song in search of Master Jiao, but she was nowhere to be found. So he composed a poem both to express his admiration for this traceless master and to record his pilgrimage to her place. Although he had not found her, he firmly believed in her existence, because other poets of his day, such as Li Qi and Wang Changling, had written verses to her and about her, celebrating her accomplishments and even describing their meetings with her. Li Bai's poem concludes with these lines: "If you can teach me your sacred knowledge / I will be your most devoted student" ("For Master Jiao of Mount Song"). Likely his recent frustrations had intensified his desire for the otherworldly existence that she exemplified.

There were a number of legendary sites on Mount Song, and Li Bai wandered around to visit them. By sheer luck, he came upon his friend Yuan Danqiu's cottage at the foot of a hill. The encounter delighted both of them, and they stayed late into the night chatting and playing the lute. Before Li Bai had gone to the capital, the two of them had met and traveled together for more than ten days, but Bai hadn't known that Danqiu moved here to pursue his religious cultivation. Bai admired his friend's peaceful place and composed a new poem for him:

故人棲東山　　自愛丘壑美
青春臥空林　　白日猶不起
松風清襟袖　　石潭洗心耳
羨君無紛喧　　高枕碧霞裏

《題元丹丘山居》

My dear friend lives on a mountain in the east.
He loves the beauty of valleys and hills.
In the springtime he sleeps in empty woods
And won't get up even though it's already light.
The fresh pine breeze cleans his robe
While stone pools cleanse his mind and ears.
My friend, I admire your life without noise or strife,
Your head is pillowed on colored clouds.

"COMPOSED FOR YUAN DANQIU'S MOUNTAIN RESIDENCE"

As for Master Jiao, Danqiu assured him that he had only heard
of such a woman and had never met her in person. She couldn't
possibly live on Mount Song. Ever warm and loyal to Bai, Danqiu
mentioned that he had a cousin, named Yuan Yan, who was now
in the nearby city of Luoyang. If Bai went there, he could stay with
him. Two years before, on his way to Chang'an, Bai and Danqiu
had spent a few days in Luoyang but hadn't had time to explore,
and Yuan Yan had not yet moved there. Now Bai indeed wanted
to return to the city. He seemed intent on delaying his return to
Anlu. Not having achieved anything since he'd left home, he surely
felt ashamed to face his wife and in-laws.

Five days later, Bai bade Danqiu goodbye and departed for
Luoyang, where he planned to stay a month or two if he liked it
there. Although it was not a political center, the city, as the East
Capital of the country, was as prosperous as Chang'an. The mar-

ketplace stretched for miles along the Luo River, which divided the city into its north and south halves. Some of the bridges on the river featured lively entertainments—music and songs, short plays, kung fu, acrobatics, stilt dances, dancers with painted faces and dressed in colorful satin and silk. Without difficulty, Li Bai found Yuan Yan's home. The man was happy to play host: he took Bai around the city and also showed him the palace, which was somewhat deserted since most courtiers and the royal family lived in Chang'an.

Li Bai showed his host the poem he had composed for Danqiu. Yan admired it so much that—having heard from his cousin about Bai's wonderful calligraphy—he asked the poet to write it out as a piece of artwork. Bai obliged him by inscribing the verse on a large piece of Xuan paper, used specially for painting. Bai's calligraphy greatly impressed Yan, who said he would have it mounted right away and hang it in his main hall. The two of them had become close friends; they planned to meet again in the future so that they could travel together to eastern prefectures and to the south of the Yangtze. Unlike Bai, Yuan Yan was not eager to acquire office or pursue the Daoist religion. He simply admired Bai and wanted to spend more time with him.

Except for his new friendship with Yan, however, Li Bai felt somewhat let down by Luoyang. It was not the place of political opportunities that he had hoped for. Yet there was unexpected beauty: whenever Bai went out, he heard folk songs performed by girls and women in taverns, open-air theaters, and marketplaces. One day, listening to a tune played on the flute, he became reflective and composed this poem:

誰家玉笛暗飛聲　散入春風滿洛城
此夜曲中聞折柳　何人不起故園情

《春夜洛城聞笛》

From whose house are the flute notes floating?
They blend into the spring breeze all over Luoyang.
In the tune I heard expectant hands break willow twigs.
Who wouldn't think of home at such a moment?

"LISTENING TO THE FLUTE IN LUOYANG CITY
ON A SPRING NIGHT"

Conventionally, the breaking of willow twigs was a gesture of longing and nostalgia, and the music reminded Bai of his wife. He missed her all the more, so without lingering any longer, he headed south for Anlu.

He had been away for almost three years and was finally home. During his absence, his wife had sent him letters, but they had never reached him because he had no permanent address. She had also asked others who were going to the capital to find out how he was faring. Rarely had she heard from Bai—he had written her only once or twice a year. His return surprised and delighted her. But to Bai's dismay, his father-in-law had died the summer before, and now his brother-in-law was fully in charge of the household. The man had inherited nearly everything Squire Xu had owned, leaving his sister and Bai only a few acres of poor farmland. The meager inheritance didn't bother Bai much—he had told his brother-in-law long ago that he wished for nothing but the library of books, which his wife had kept for him.

Fortunately, Dansha and his wife remained at the household—they were loyal to the mistress and helped her manage the domestic work. In recent years, Miss Xu's health had deteriorated and she had become frail. Li Bai took his wife to the calm, restful slopes of North Shou Mountain, the site of his former study. Against the cottage he and Dansha now added a lean-to, and in the front yard they set up a stone table with four stools around it. The small homestead was cozy and peaceful. It was already mid-fall, with tree leaves floating in the air and the weather turning chilly at night; Bai and his wife were happy there together and the days passed uneventfully.

But soon Li Bai became restless again. Now that his father-in-law was no longer around to help, it was imperative that he find a way of supporting himself and his wife. He went to visit his friend Meng Haoran in Xiangyang to seek advice. After the two of them had parted company at Yellow Crane Tower in Jiangxia four years before, Haoran had traveled to the south and eventually wandered to Chang'an. But when Bai had arrived in the capital the next summer, Haoran had left—the two men had just missed each other. Now they were happy to be together again. Having heard Bai's account of his recent struggles, Haoran told him not to lose heart—a new opportunity might be on the horizon. An acquaintance of his, Han Chaozong, had just gone to Jing Prefecture, a neighboring region, to assume the role of its military commander—Bai should try his luck there. Li Bai had heard of Han, who was highly regarded for his straightforward honesty and for his generosity in helping young people. According to a popular saying, "You don't need to seek to be a duke, so long as you get to know Han Jingzhou." (Han Chaozong was nicknamed Han Jingzhou—"Jing Prefecture"—implying that he embodied the entire region in his control and commanded a good deal of resources.)

Following Haoran's advice, Bai set out for Jing Prefecture, about a hundred miles to the south. Unbeknownst to Bai and Meng, however, Han Chaozong was harboring an old grudge toward Meng Haoran. A few years back, Han and Haoran had agreed to meet in Chang'an so that Han could introduce him to a top courtier as a reputable poet, but when Han went to Haoran's inn outside the palace to fetch him, he found his friend dead drunk, unable to speak coherently or recall their arrangement. Han had no choice but to give up the plan, and left in a rage. He felt slighted and could not forgive Haoran for such negligence. Worse yet, Haoran, absentminded by nature and unfamiliar with the decorum of official life, never sent him a word of apology or showed any signs of regret for his gaffe. None of this boded well for Bai's visit. Now, like his friend, Bai had no awareness of the old grudge.

Following convention, Bai composed a long essay in anticipation of his meeting with Han. He piled praises on him, calling him a savior of countless young scholars and aspiring statesmen. Han's writings, Bai wrote, were like the work of a deity, and his virtues were powerful enough to move heaven and earth. Bai heaped praises on himself as well: he had become an expert swordsman at fifteen and had begun to converse with local officials in his late teens; at thirty, he had met many great men in the country. He was loyal, grateful, and righteous. If Han gave him an opportunity, he would surely go a long way in his career. When Bai found his own success, "soaring into the splendid clouds," he would bring honor to Han too. Bai went on to celebrate Han as a demigod who could shower favors and kindness on people with abandon. He implored his potential benefactor to try him, offering to compose an essay or a lengthy poem right in front of him—he could produce ten thousand words of fine prose in a single day. And also, he wrote, please treat him to dinner so that he could speak in person about his vision and aspirations.[1] He even challenged Han indirectly, asking, "Why should dukes and marquises cherish the tiny squares of ground in front of their doorsteps so much as to prevent Bai from standing in one of them, giving utterance to my heart and letting my spirit soar toward the clouds?"

The passionate essay indeed impressed Han, who could see that Bai was an extraordinary talent, full of energy and imagination, but he was also unsettled by Bai's grandiloquence. He worried that Bai might be impulsive, impertinent, self-centered. He had heard that, unlike other members of the local gentry, Bai did not follow the prevalent custom to bow or kowtow to high officials. What if he made trouble with his insubordination after he took a post? Then Han would be held responsible. Han tossed the essay aside and refused to receive Bai. The refusal, an affront to Bai's pride, was a crushing blow that for many years put an end to his quest for office.

Li Bai's talent was so prodigious that whenever an opportunity presented itself, he couldn't help but demonstrate a level of brilliance that unnerved others. He was too great an artist to be useful in a worldly way. Crestfallen by Han's rejection, he returned to his wife in North Shou Mountain and fell back into drinking. He abandoned his hopes for a career and sighed, "A hundred years have thirty-six thousand days / And every day I must drink three hundred cups."

In spite of these lines, that winter Bai didn't drink as heavily as he once had—he didn't have the money or the company of friends. His family's income mainly came from the rent collected from the poor farmland, and the Lis could barely make ends meet. Bai had to live modestly so that the others in the household would not starve. By springtime, his wife's health had improved, and their life became more stable and domestic. The truth was that even if Li Bai had wanted to embark on a new trip, there were no longer funds available to finance his travel. Later, reflecting on this period of his life, he would say that he "wasted ten years, drowned in alcohol," meaning he had stopped making efforts to seek office. Ironically, however, this uneventful time, more than any other period of his life, most closely resembled the reclusive retirement he had always dreamed of. His wife's love and generosity provided a haven for him in the midst of adversity.

IN THE NORTH

One day in the late spring of 735, Li Bai received a letter from Yuan Yan, the friend he had made in Luoyang eighteen months before. Yan wrote that he now held the position of inspector in Haozhou, Henan. It was an inconsequential job, but it enabled him to travel. At the moment, he was planning to go to Taiyuan, a northern frontier city, where his father was serving as a military commander, guarding the border against Mongolians and other tribesmen. Yuan Yan invited Li Bai to join him on this trip, generously offering to cover all expenses. If Bai was interested, they should meet in Luoyang City and from there they would travel north. Bai, who had always longed to see the northern frontier, jumped at the invitation. Two months later, he went to join Yuan Yan in Luoyang, and without delay they set off for Taiyuan.

Taiyuan was a large city, nicknamed the North Capital, though it was not as prosperous and grand as Chang'an or Luoyang. Li Bai found the landscape around the city quite unusual. The land was flat and vast, with grassy plains stretching to the edge of the horizon. Bands of camels were passing south and north. The southbound caravans were loaded with furs, nuts, and medicinal herbs, while the northbound ones carried grains, fabrics, salt, bricks of tea, and utensils. It was already summer but hot only around midday—a cool breeze always flowed from the Mongolian steppe, and the air turned cool after sunset. At night Bai had to cover himself with a thick blanket. He was told that fall came early in this area, in late August. Autumn was the best season for hunting, which was a major sport among the locals. He noticed that the people of Taiyuan were more straightforward and quick-tempered, likely because of the influence of the tribal folks in the north. The region was especially significant to the Tang rulers because it was their ancestral land—before the Lis seized the throne, they had lived here. So in a way, Li Bai, as a "relative" of the royal clan, might have felt that this was a kind of homecoming. He would carry deep memories of this trip and write about them in his poetry.

General Yuan, Yan's father, was in his late forties with a weather-beaten face, but he was still sturdy and spirited, physically nimble and acute in his perception. He was delighted by the arrival of his son and Bai. By then Li Bai, despite his isolation and financial struggles, was well known, his poetry cherished by many fans as the work of a genius (although few thought of him seriously as a soldier or a statesman, as Bai viewed himself). General Yuan presented him with a marten robe, worth hundreds of pieces of gold, and a dappled steed. With the horse, Bai could go to the prairie and the border with Yan, and wearing the fur robe, he could attend parties and banquets as a respectable guest. His presence in the city brought honor to the general, who presented him to the local dignitaries. Bai was invited to many gatherings, at which he composed poems and short essays in honor of the hosts. Soon he became popular among some of the officers. He admired their dedication and bravery and often went to watch them drill their troops. He even practiced archery, of which he was already a master of sorts. In one poem, he even claims that he once killed two tigers with a single arrow—most likely a boast, though it shows his pride in his archery.

One day he found a few gray hairs on his head and realized that he was thirty-four—already more than halfway through his lifetime by the standards of the era. This realization saddened him and made him pensive. He wondered if it might be better for him simply to stay in the Taiyuan area, serving in the army. He was good with a sword and knowledgeable about military strategies and tactics, and believed he could be a capable officer, useful to General Yuan.

But when Bai broached the topic with Yan, his friend was opposed to it, saying Bai was unaware of the hardships that his father's soldiers had been suffering. Yan went on to explain that the central government had no consistent policies for border defense, and as a result, battles and expeditions were often started at the frontier at random, regardless of long-term consequences. Worse still, the court had not been fair in issuing rewards and meting out punishments. His father's troops had been garrisoned in this area for more than a decade, but there was still no word about transferring back inland. Some men had grown too feeble to fight any longer. In fact, those who had stayed behind, safe and comfortable in the central land, might never come to the front. Yan feared that his father might die in the Taiyuan region without ever seeing their hometown again. That was why the general had insisted that Yan, his only son, hold a civilian job elsewhere, as a way to preserve their family's bloodline. It was not too much to say that the men stationed here were in a hopeless situation—Bai must not be misled by the officers' brave faces.

Yan's words were a revelation to Li Bai, who gave up the thought of staying in the frontier permanently. He began to observe the soldiers more carefully and saw their predicament and hardships with new eyes. He wrote poems that empathize with their misery. Here is one, written in the style of ancient songs, fresh and realistic and straightforward:

代馬不思越　越禽不戀燕
情性有所習　土風固其然
昔別雁門關　今戍龍庭前

驚沙亂海日　飛雪迷胡天
蟣虱生虎鶡　心魂逐旌旃
苦戰功不賞　忠誠難可宣
誰憐李飛將　白首沒三邊

《古風其六》

The northern horses don't think of the south
Where animals cannot long for the north.
Their indigenous habitats have shaped
Their habits and lives.
Long ago we came out of Goose Pass
And ever since have stayed in the barbarous land.
Sandstorms distort the view of the sun and the steppes
And flying snow blocks the foreign sky.
Lice infest our clothes and leather mail,
Yet we resolve to keep our banners aloft.
So many bitter battles won but without rewards,
Our devotion never recognized.
Who has ever taken pity on General Li the Swift,
Who lost his white head in the desert?

"ANCIENT SONGS 6"

General Li was the legendary commander of the Chinese army in the remote western reaches of the Han dynasty, the very man Li Bai's father had claimed as their ancestor. The soldiers' plight in Taiyuan must have reminded Bai of the unjust fate of the great general, who was never granted an official post despite his many victories on the battlefield, who had never been able to return home, and who out of despair had committed suicide in the frontier. So many heroic men had gone unrecognized and mistreated. The more Bai brooded about the injustice of their fates, the more despondent he became.

In recent decades, the border area had been frequented by poets who had served in the military. Li Bai greatly admired those men not only for their robust verses but also for the bravery and flair displayed by their poetic personas. He and Yan made trips to ancient battlefields, where they recited poems by the poets who, as officers, might have served and even fought in this region. They also chanted poems that had become popular songs, mostly the kind of frontier ballads called "Liangzhou Song-lyrics" (so named because they are all set in the border region). One poem goes:

葡萄美酒夜光杯　欲飲琵琶馬上催
醉臥沙場君莫笑　古來征戰幾人

Grape wine is poured in gleaming cups
And guitars urge us to drink before we ride away.
If I get drunk, I'll doze on a battleground.
Don't laugh at me. Since ancient times
How many men have returned from war?

—WANG HAN (687–726)

Another:

黃河遠上白云間　一片孤城萬仞山
羌笛何須怨楊柳　春風不度玉門關

The Yellow River rises into white clouds.
Beyond a lone fortress sits a mountain
That is tens of thousands of feet high.
The barbarian flute shouldn't blame the trees
That haven't turned green—
The spring breeze doesn't reach Jade Pass.

—WANG ZHI-HUAN (688–742)

Although these two poems were written by contemporaries of Li Bai, he admired the music and the space of these verses so deeply that he regarded them as classics and their creators as already immortalized. He too tried to create vast spaces in his own works to give them more magnitude and grandeur.

After the last snow, the weather grew windier and the willows began to sprout buds on their drooping branches. Li Bai decided to return home. In addition to a farewell dinner, General Yuan gave him a large sum of funds for the road. Bai went back alone—Yan would stay on a little longer to help his father with some administrative work.

On his way back, Bai again ran into his devoted friend Yuan Danqiu. They both fell into raptures about the encounter in Luoyang City. Danqiu had gone on to Mount Emei in Sichuan and was on his way back to his retreat in Mount Song, which Bai had visited two and a half years before. Danqiu invited him to stay a few days at his hermitage on Yingyang Hill in Mount Song, but Bai was eager to go home, and so they parted ways. However, Bai had hardly gotten out of the city the next morning when a messenger from Danqiu caught up with him and handed him a letter, which said that a friend of Danqiu's named Cen Xun was a longtime admirer of Bai's poetry and would love to have him over for a few days. At the moment, Cen Xun was living near Danqiu in Mount Song, so Bai should come to Yingyang Hill again so that the three of them could meet.

Bai had heard about Cen Xun from Danqiu and knew that he was from a renowned family, but had chosen not to enter for the civil-service examination in spite of his comprehensive education in classics. We don't know the dates of Cen Xun's birth and death, but it is believed that he was younger than Li Bai, and was such a fan of his poetry that he had traveled hundreds of miles to Mount Song in the hope of encountering him there. Danqui had enclosed a poem written by Cen Xun, and Bai could tell that the man was a genuine poet—someone he would like to meet. He recalled that a scholar in Chang'an had also mentioned this remarkable young talent. Bai was touched to learn that Cen Xun was such an admirer of his own work.

Both Danqiu and Cen Xun were famous recluses and heavy drinkers, so Bai's arrival made the wine flow. As the host, Danqiu gave a party, attended by just the three of them, which started in the afternoon. They drank in the yard in front of Danqiu's cottage, cracking jokes and composing verses. Cen Xun was eager to witness Bai's legendary poetic abilities, so he tossed out a line, and Bai spun a poem around it. Both Danqiu and Cen Xun were amazed by the swiftness of Bai's composition. Together the three men continued to sing songs and chant poems and play the lute, the bamboo fife, and the zither, which Cen Xun could strum with skill. When the moon was high above the clouds, Cen Xun suggested calling it a night, but Bai wanted to continue. To entertain his two friends, he even performed a dance he had just learned in Taiyuan, kicking his heels and brandishing his arms. That made them laugh.

The three men decided to move the party to Cen Xun's place on the other side of the hill; from there they could see the moon more clearly, and could catch the view of the Yiluo flowing east into the Yellow River. Although the water was hardly visible in the dark, the lanterns on the fishing boats glowed as they sailed back and forth. The men went up the slope to Cen Xun's shack and resumed their merriment. As the night wore on and Li Bai got more drunk, he asked Danqiu to get out ink and a brush for a new poem that was brewing within him. Under coppery brown light thrown by a pair of oil lamps, he chanted it slowly while Danqiu transcribed:

君不見　黃河之水天上來　奔流到海不復還
君不見　高堂明鏡悲白髮　朝如青絲暮成雪

人生得意須盡歡　莫使金樽空對月
天生我材必有用　千金散盡還復來
烹羊宰牛且爲樂　會須一飲三百杯
岑夫子　丹丘生　將進酒　杯莫停
與君歌一曲　　　請君爲我傾耳聽
鐘鼓饌玉不足貴　但願長醉不復醒
古來聖賢皆寂寞　惟有飲者留其名
陳王昔時宴平樂　斗酒十千恣讙謔
主人何爲言少錢　徑須沽取對君酌
五花馬　千金裘
呼兒將出換美酒　與爾同銷萬古愁

《將進酒》

Have you not seen the Yellow River flow down from heaven,
Rushing toward the ocean but never coming back?
Have you not seen the mirror in the lofty hall grieve the white hair
That is black in the morning but snowy in the evening?
When happy, we must enjoy ourselves to the full,
Not let our gold goblets empty to the moon.
Heaven begot a talent like me and must put me to good use
And a thousand cash in gold, squandered, will come again.
Boil a sheep and butcher an ox for our feast,
And let us drink three hundred cups at one go.
Mr. Cen and Sir Danqiu, drink without stop.
Let me sing a song, please give me your ears.
Drums and bells and sumptuous food shouldn't be cherished.
What I want is to be drunk forever without sobering up.
Since ancient times saints and sages have been obscure,
But only drinkers have left behind their names.
Prince Chen, throwing a banquet in the old days,
Got wine at ten thousand cash a gallon.
My dear host, why say you are short on cash?

Let us buy wine and enjoy it at any cost.
My dappled horse and gorgeous fur robe,
Let your boy take both to the shop
And exchange them for good wine
So we can drown our sorrow of ten thousand years.

"PLEASE DRINK"

Yuan Danqiu and Cen Xun were astounded by the energy and the madness of the poem. Looking over the transcription, they were overwhelmed by the poem's emotional intensity that verged on mania. At one moment the lines seem laden with grief, but then the mood turns to ecstasy. It is sad yet vibrant with rapture. Awestruck, they remained wordless for a good while. Later, they told others how Li Bai had composed this poem, how they had seen him pouring out lines without premeditation. Every word, every line, and every rhyme were in place—the poem was perfectly wrought at the very first attempt. This was something only a deity could do, they said, and the verses must have come from heaven. Thereafter, whenever they talked about Bai, they felt pity for him: his genius seemed too great for any office in this world.

The next morning, Danqiu asked Bai to title the poem. Bai said it should be something related to drinking. Danqiu gave it some thought and then came up with "Please Drink." The three of them liked the suggestion—it echoed a type of ancient song performed as an elaborate toast to urge people to drain their cups. Since then, the poem has become one of Li Bai's most quoted works, and its lines are often tossed out at tables where people gather to drink.

Bai stayed at Mount Song for several days, visiting nearby Buddhist temples with his two friends. Before his departure home, he composed a few more poems for Yuan Danqiu and Cen Xun.

IN THE SOUTH

Most Li Bai chronologies indicate that he returned to Anlu in the spring of 737. His wife was pleased to see him back, though she scolded him for not sending her word ahead of his return. Bai was happy too, in part because he had brought back cash and other valuable items—damask, jade, medicinal herbs. Thanks to his increasing fame, as he had traveled home he had been generously treated by the governments of counties and prefectures, whose officials presented him with small gifts. With this experience, he realized that he could make money by traveling, enjoying the admiration of others and the hospitable events held in his honor. He told his wife about this, joking that they might even become rich someday. She did not believe him but was glad to learn that his popularity had increased.

Soon Bai became restless again, tormented by a poignant wanderlust. He was prone to depression and attempted to mitigate his despair with drinking. At heart he could not accept his failure in seeking office. He was only thirty-six, his mind keener than ever and his body still strong. He believed he had to trust his talent and knowledge and mustn't give up. He wanted to try his fortune elsewhere again, convinced that eventually he would succeed. For months he had been thinking about the land south of the Yangtze, which, though he had been there before, was still slightly exotic to him. But for a trip to Yangtze, he would need to secure sufficient funds.

Since his household still depended on the rent collected from the few acres of farmland, it would be impossible for him to get the money needed for travel. He turned to his friends for help, but none was rich enough to assist him. Some offered to take him along to places where they were planning to go. Ever impulsive, Bai simply set out for Yangtze on his own, believing that his fame and ability would carry him there. He first went to Mount Song to see his friend Yuan Danqiu, who kept him there for several days. At the moment, Danqiu was short on cash as well and could only help Bai with a small sum. Bai took the money and continued south without delay.

By now, the Tang dynasty was at the peak of its prosperity—most counties and prefectures had full granaries and were flush with cash. The farmland south of the Yangtze was fertile; the local governments had grown rich collecting taxes and didn't hesitate to spend money entertaining visitors, especially officials from the north and the central land. Known for his splendid poetry, Li Bai was treated decently in most of these places, where he would attend dinner parties given by officials. Without fail he would compose verses in honor of his hosts and recite his other poems. Most officials, vain but generous with public funds, valued Bai's presence at their gatherings as someone extraordinarily artistic, someone who could offer them entertainment of a different order from the common dances and songs performed by girls and courtesans. Some officials, usually friends of Bai's, would put him up for ten days or even a month. By now he seemed to have friends everywhere thanks to his poetic reputation. Most officials were highly literate and often knowledgeable about literature and the arts, so they sought the company of a literary luminary like Li Bai. Before he left, they would present him with a small amount of cash for the road. He now considered such money as earnings that he should be securing regularly, and always saved a portion for his family. Indeed, he was more careful about his expenditures than before.

But gradually he discovered that he was still just a poet, with talent and showmanship but no power or influence, and so even as his popularity grew, officials would rarely receive him as a truly important guest. Above him, there were always personages that they would lavish with flattery and gifts. At times these honored guests were merely sons of powerful officials in the central government, incapable and ignorant with no achievements of their own. Bai couldn't help but feel resentful whenever he came upon such young dandies.

After revisiting Nanjing, where contrary to his expectation he didn't find any friends, Li Bai arrived at Yangzhou in July. There he wanted to see Meng Rong, his old friend who had introduced him to his wife, but he soon learned that Rong was no longer in the city. He had been transferred west, Bai was told, but no one was sure of his exact whereabouts. Bai was disappointed, unable to find out anything more about his friend. Then a number of admirers and well-wishers, having gotten word of Bai's arrival, came to his inn, eager to see him. His literary reputation had spread widely now, even preceding him on the road, and some of his short poems were known all over the country. A few of these visitors were especially friendly and invited Bai to restaurants and taverns. There was a sense of warmth and familiarity: Bai knew a number of the men already, from his previous visit more than a decade back, and even those who hadn't met him before felt connected to him because one of his most famous poems, "Reflection in a Quiet Night," had been composed in this very city twelve years before. Li Bai remembered the difficult time he had been going through then, ill and penniless in a downtown tavern. It had been his dear friend Meng Rong who had cared for him and helped him recover. Where was that sweet man now? How Bai wished to see him again!

As they reveled about town, the local literary figures, who were meeting Bai for the first time, asked him about his friends, particularly those to whom he had dedicated his poetry. They loved the farewell poem he had composed on seeing Meng Haoran off at Yellow Crane Tower and the short verses titled "Midnight Songs." Bai was flattered, not having expected to meet so many fans in the city. When the wine had loosened his tongue, he told his new friends about his humiliating experience in the capital, how Zhang Ji had taken him in and dispatched him to Zhongnan Mountain. They were offended on his behalf, cursing the vainglorious and duplicitous men in the palace.

After a heartening stay in Yangzhou, Bai sailed down the Yangtze, continuing toward the coast. He wanted to reach the end of the land, to see the ocean for the first time. His destination was Wenzhou, the east end of this land, though he might wander elsewhere. He wanted, indeed, to see the entire country, believing that his mind would be expanded and that, in turn, his poetry would gain greater spirit and depth. For him, travel was not simply entertainment; it was how he learned and grew. He was determined to make himself more capable, to become a better poet and a wiser statesman. He still clung to his political ambitions, though his quest for an official post had, after years of rejection, become half-hearted and he was somewhat detached.

After a few days on the water, he arrived at Jingkou (in modern Zhenjiang). From there he took a skiff west to Jin Hill and Jiao Hill, which lay in the middle of the river. The pair of hills, thickly wooded, were a kind of resort frequented by visitors. The land and feel of Jiao Hill resonated deeply with Bai; there he composed this poem while gazing at another island far away that had a hill on it too.

石壁望松寥　宛然在碧霄
安得五彩虹　駕天作長橋
仙人如愛我　舉手來相招

《焦山望寥山》

From the cliff I'm watching Songliao Hill
Feeling like I am standing in clouds.
I'd like to grab hold of a colored rainbow
And raise it as a celestial bridge.
If a goddess is fond of me
She will surely wave me over.

"GAZING AT SONGLIAO HILL FROM JIAO HILL"

He continued to sail down from Jingkou, and soon the estuary came into view. He could see the two waters of the river and the sea, pushing at each other and tossing wavelets and eddies. In the distance rose a few dark reefs that resembled tiny knolls. Seabirds—petrels and gulls—glided in the air and let out their cries. Far away, the horizon shifted with the tumbling water. Bai was enchanted by the endless waves and couldn't help imaging the world beyond the ocean in the east. He had heard of Japan, which to him seemed a wonderland inhabited by gods and spirits. Someday he thought he might take a boat sailing that way, or ride a crane there as a *xian*. In his mind, the celestial sphere would always be accessible to him once he was done with his life on earth. He would be able to accompany the divine bird through the universe without any attachment to this earthly existence.

On the canal he traveled south down to Wuxi, Suzhou, then Hangzhou. The West Lake in Hangzhou, the waterscape of breathtaking beauty that the city has boasted for more than a millennium, hadn't been fully constructed yet, but he liked the coastal climate and visited Tianzhu Temple, accompanied by the prefect Li Liang, whom Li Bai thought might be a distant relative of his. He wrote about this visit in a poem, addressing Li Liang as his nephew. It is believed that this gesture, far from ingratiating himself to Liang, only irritated and alienated the prefect. In his eyes, Bai was just another office-seeker vying for his favor, and he couldn't wait to get rid of him. Bai likely composed numerous other poems on this leg of the journey around the coastal area, but most of them have not survived. From Hangzhou he took a boat up the Fuchun River to Wenzhou, which he had planned as the destination of this trip on the seacoast. Then he turned back inland, passing Lu and Wu prefectures along the way (present-day Tong-lu and Jinhua). In Jinhua, he stopped at Yiwu Town to pay homage to Luo Binwang (619–687), one of the four great early Tang poets (the others were Wang Bo, Yang Jiong, and Lu Zhaolin).

Luo was one of Li Bai's heroes. At age seven, Luo had composed the most popular nursery rhyme in Chinese—it is the first poem that tens of millions of people hear in their childhood: "Goose, goose, goose / Stretches its neck and sings to the sky, / Its white feathers floating on green water / And its red webs paddling blue waves." Li Bai commented about Luo's work, "Luo Binwang's poetry is high in style and lofty in spirit. His poems read like something made in heaven, where deities gather, riding clouds like cranes and floating about with ease."[1] Yet despite Luo's fame as a prodigy and his career as a leading voice in Chinese poetry in his time, his official career was fraught with frustrations and setbacks. Time and again he was demoted, banished to the borderland in penal servitude, and once even imprisoned, because he wouldn't stop criticizing the extravagance and corruption of the court and speaking on behalf of common people at the bottom of society. His parents had been poor, and so he empathized with their plight.

At age fifty-six, when Luo was a county magistrate, he wrote a "Proclamation Against Empress Wu" and then joined the rebels, led by the banished duke Li Jingye (636–684), in fighting the imperial army and attempting to topple the court. In belligerent language Luo called Empress Wu, the only empress in Chinese history, "a fake ruler" and claimed that "her promiscuity had ruined her court." But when Her Majesty listened to the condemnation, she couldn't stop smiling; in spite of the criticism, she couldn't help but appreciate the beauty and vigor of Luo's writing. Toward the end of the reading, at the sentence "The earth of the late emperor's grave is still wet while the royal heir has no idea whom he can trust," she turned to a chancellor and asked sternly, "Why have we neglected such a gifted man?"

When the rebels were finally suppressed, Luo vanished. There was some talk that he had been killed by imperial troops, but other rumors claimed that he had become a monk in a secluded temple and still roved the wilderness.

Undoubtedly Li Bai was a greater poet than Luo, but his official career, if there was one, had been even more difficult. Still, he viewed Luo as a kindred spirit. He made a special trip to Luo's adobe house in Loujia Village, paid his respects at the cenotaph built for him, and fed the waterbirds in the pond next to his house. From Yiwu Town, Bai headed back to Anlu. Along the way he visited numerous legendary mountains and resorts, especially those associated with ancient figures. He traveled homeward unhurriedly and often stayed in a city or town for ten days or more at a stretch.

In late fall Li Bai arrived at Xiangyang, about 140 miles south of Anlu. Bai hoped to see his old friend Meng Haoran, but when he arrived at his friend's farm in Deer-Gate Mountain, Bai was stunned to find that Haoran had just died. He had succumbed to running sores on his back after indulging in a binge of drinking with his visiting friend, the poet Wang Changling (698–756). Haoran had suffered from this ailment for a long time, but before his friend's arrival, the sores were in remission and his doctor had urged him to avoid seafood lest they break out. But on the dining table was a braised bream from the Han River, and the fish was so fat and tempting that Haoran couldn't help applying his chopsticks to it. He and Changling regaled themselves with both savory dishes and alcohol. As a consequence, the sores burst on his back and he died two days later. Li Bai was devastated to hear of his friend's passing—he threw away the wine he had brought for Meng and couldn't help but lament how precarious life was.

After having wept and grieved at Haoran's funeral, Bai left two days later, heading south to the Dongting Lake region. In Baling Town, he encountered Wang Changling and told him the news of Meng Haoran's death. Changling was only two years older than Bai but had been an official for more than a decade. He was known as a master of short poems, especially the type called *jueju,* which is a quatrain, strictly rhymed and with elaborate metric patterns. He was a leading capital poet, and many of his poems had become popular songs. Bai had heard Wang Changling's poems performed in taverns and teahouses and greatly admired them.

Like Bai, Changling wrote many poems about women, which was uncommon among poets then, though their approaches were different. Changling was a master of mood, his language evocative, full of drama. His "Boudoir Grief" was sung everywhere and was particularly loved by married women. It goes, "The young bride doesn't know sorrow yet. / She makes up and climbs a high tower. / Catching sight of greening poplars and willows along the road, / She regrets letting her groom seek to be a duke far away." What differentiates this poem from Li Bai's works about women is the absence of persona, or characterized voice, which Changling rarely used. Changling was also known for his borderland poetry. His best-known frontier poem is "Charging out of the Border," which praised the man Bai believed to be his own ancestor, General Li Guang:

秦時明月漢時關　　萬裡長征人未還
但使龍城飛將在　　不教胡馬渡陰山

出塞》

The bright moon of the Qin dynasty
Has seen the mountain pass of Han times.
Thousands of miles away from home,
The soldiers haven't yet returned.
So long as the Swift General stays at Dragon Fort
No barbarians' horses dare to pass Mount Yin.

Because of Bai's personal attachment to this poem, he had become fond of its author before they had even met. By this time, Li Bai's reputation as a poet was almost equal to Wang Changling's, but to date they had admired each other only from a distance. Now their meeting delighted both of them. They chatted about people they both knew and about the news in the capital. Changling felt awful about Meng Haoran's death—he had known Haoran was absentminded but hadn't thought he would be so careless about his health. If only he, Changling, had stopped him from eating the fish and drinking so much that night!

Upon hearing that Bai was on the last leg of his long trip and that he was still bent on finding a position, Changling sighed and told him about the other side of an official's life. After passing the civil-service examination, he had started his career as a county magistrate in Henan at the lowest rank, the ninth. He quickly became tired of the official decorum and drudgery; he applied for a position at the Secretariat in the palace, which seemed impossible but which miraculously he was granted. The new post sounded prestigious, but he soon discovered that the Secretariat was somewhat like an old-age home: it was filled with many senile scholars who simply did clerical work, copying and transcribing and proofreading documents. It badly needed young hands. Worst of all,

Changling said, an honest man in the palace could not survive the political maneuvers and intrigues against him. He had witnessed high-ranking officials beaten half dead, flogged with sticks in front of the emperor and dozens of courtiers for having done nothing more than to speak a few candid words. Changling always feared that he might end up in such a plight. Just now he had lost his job at the central government and had to take a post elsewhere, all because he had gotten drunk one night in downtown Chang'an and overslept and missed his shift at the office. It was only minor negligence, he argued, but the men above him had seized the opportunity to drive him out of the capital. That was why he had been demoted and sent down to a small county. In brief, it was dangerous and unpredictable to serve at court.

Seeing Bai look unconvinced, Changling pressed on. Look at their late friend Meng Haoran, who had remained a farmer recluse all his life but was still known and revered everywhere. Because he had depended on nothing but his own talent and effort, his poetry had breathed new life into the world of letters. His might be a better way to follow.

Although dismayed at the story of his friend's demotion and grateful for his honest words, Bai couldn't give up his endeavor so easily and found Changling too pessimistic. But hearing of scholars who had gotten into trouble for presenting petitions to the emperor curbed Bai's desire to write to His Majesty directly—he would go on to abandon his half-finished letter addressed to the court. In appearance the emperor always welcomed petitions, but it was hard to predict what contents might offend him. Li Bai had dreamed that his writing might impress His Majesty and earn him a favor directly from the emperor. Now it was clear that even if he had dispatched a letter to the court, it might never have reached the Son of Heaven. Changling also mentioned that the central government was shifting its focus to promoting warriors rather than scholars. This planted a new idea in Bai's mind, as he also thought of himself as a soldier. If the country needed more military talents, he was skilled with the sword and knew the art of war well—he was good officer material. But he told Changling that he would think about his advice.

It was getting cold, and Bai realized he must not linger on the road any longer and must get home before winter began. So he headed back to Anlu without further delay.

By Zhan Ying's chronology, early in 739, Li Bai's wife gave birth to their first child, a daughter. We don't know how Bai felt about the arrival of his first child, who wasn't born until the twelfth year of his marriage, but we are certain that when she was growing up she was very attached to her father. Bai named her Pingyang. The name, which had associations with historical royalty, indicated that he had high hopes for her. It was the namesake of Emperor Han Wu's sister, a woman who lived a troubled but extraordinary life (having survived three husbands), and it was also the name of the first Tang emperor's third daughter. This daughter had been a commander of troops, fighting for her father in order to found the dynasty. Prior to her time, few women had ever played such a role. When she fell on the battlefield, her body was retrieved and she was memorialized as a valiant officer, her funeral accompanied with a military salute. Li Bai must have hoped that his child would grow up to be noble, beautiful, and courageous like those extraordinary women.

We know little else about Bai's daughter. His biographers have inclined to touch on her very briefly, partly because of the paucity of information we have on her and partly because traditionally, scholars tended not to focus on an ancient literary figure's domestic life. But it is necessary to know as much as we can about Bai's family life and his relationships with his children if we want to understand him intimately.

There are three crucial pieces of information that can help us approximate a rough sketch of Pingyang's life. One is from Wei Hao, Bai's devoted disciple in the poet's later years. In his introduction to Li Bai's collected writings, Wei Hao states that Pingyang "died soon after she married." The other two pieces of information are from Li Bai's poetry. He wrote a handful of poems about his children (he might have composed many more, but only a few are known to us), and one, the famous "To My Two Young Children in East Lu," contains these deeply felt lines:

南風吹歸心　飛墮酒樓前
樓東一株桃　枝葉拂青煙
此樹我所種　別來向三年
桃今與樓齊　我行尚未旋
嬌女字平陽　折花倚桃邊
折花不見我　淚下如流泉
小兒名伯禽　與姊亦齊肩
雙行桃樹下　撫背復誰憐。。。

《寄東魯二稚子》

The south wind blows my heart back home
And it lands before my lovely wine drinking house.
In front of it stands a peach tree,
Whose branches and leaves are haloed.
I myself planted that tree before I left—
It's been almost three years now.
Now the tree must be as tall as the house,
But I'm still on the road, unable to return.
My daughter, named Pingyang,
Picks flowers next to the peach tree.
As she goes, she cannot find her dad
And her tears flow like a spring.

My young son, named Boqin, is already
Tall enough to reach his sister's shoulder.
They are both under the peach tree,
But who would pat their shoulders
And take pity on them now? . . .

The poem is universally believed to have been written in 749 when Li Bai was staying in Nanjing, separated from his family in Shandong. We know he had again left home for the south in late 746, and as he writes in the poem, he hasn't seen his children in three years. At the time, Pingyang must have been around ten years old, as suggested by the "young children" in the title and her tearful response to her father's absence, more characteristic of a small girl than a teenager.

In the preface to another poem written in 755, six years later, Li Bai says, "My disciple Wu E is a righteous man with a steady disposition. He admires the knight-errant Yao Li, hunting and fishing on rivers and lakes without caring about worldly affairs. But upon hearing of the outbreak of rebellion in the central land, he hurried west to see me. My beloved son is still in Lu, and I implored Wu E to go and fetch him before the arrival of the barbarous forces. Tipsy and grateful, I am writing this poem for him" ("For Wu Seventeen E").[2] The rebels, led by An Lushan, the emperor's adopted son, had just occupied Luoyang and were going to Chang'an to overthrow the dynasty, so Li Bai was asking his disciple to go to Shandong and rescue his family. But what is notable is that Wu E was supposed to bring back only Li Bai's son. The absence of Pingyang here gives us our third piece of information, signifying that she must have died by then ("soon after she married," as Wei Hao wrote). If she were alive, she would have been sixteen.

In the Tang dynasty, girls could legally marry at age thirteen; the most common age was fifteen, but a great many brides were still in their early teens. So we can be fairly certain that by the time Wu E went to Shandong (Lu) to rescue Li Bai's family in 755, his daughter was already dead. This is consistent with the preceding poem that portrays her as a young child in 749, and further points to 739 as the year of her birth.[3] Most Li Bai scholars have placed Pingyang's birth many years earlier, as far back as 728, probably because his children were not that important in the conventional Li Bai scholarship and because information on his daughter's birth was insufficient. This has created a good deal of confusion and inconsistency in the resulting biographies of Li Bai. We must clarify this issue because Pingyang's birth seems to be a pivotal moment in Bai's life. Once he became a father, he seemed more attached to his home and viewed himself as a family man. Although he would not spend much time with his children throughout their lives, it is evident that he loved them and would always have them taken care of.

12

MOVING TO THE LU REGION

After giving birth to their daughter, Li Bai's wife grew feeble. She became pale and listless and often took to her bed. She had little appetite and was malnourished and could hardly breast-feed their child. Bai sent for doctors and bought fish and wild game meat for his wife. In spite of the costly herbal medicine and the rich food, her condition did not improve. In late fall a doctor revealed to Bai the prognosis, which was dire. Her pulse was weak and irregular, thin like a thread, and she might not have many days left. Bai was devastated and stayed home with her during the winter.

But miraculously, when spring arrived, some of the color returned to her face and her health improved a little. She could move about and even embroider with their maid. As his wife's condition stabilized, Bai's old restless self began to return. He had been here in North Shou Mountain too long, and no longer felt any attachment to the region. And so, despite his wife's health, he decided to relocate the family from Anlu permanently. He wanted to move to the Lu region about two hundred miles away in the northeast, and again his wife yielded to him. They sold their cottage at the mountain and their farmland, and together with the servants—Dansha and his wife—the young family set off on the road.

They headed north for Lu Prefecture, roughly where the southern part of today's Shandong Province lies. Lu was a large prefecture, comprised of eleven counties, and was rich in farmland. Confucius had once roamed there to disseminate his teachings, and his influence in the region remained strong: people respected education and followed traditional rites and values. They worshiped heaven and their ancestors, attended to filial duties for their parents, adhered to social order, conscientiously performed their domestic roles, and embraced loyalty, kindness, honesty, charity, and other virtues upheld by Confucianism. Lu had produced a number of great thinkers, such as Mencius and Mozi. Bai had relatives in Lu, and hoped he might get help from them—a distant uncle was the magistrate of Ren County, and a few cousins were minor officials in some of the other counties.

There was also the draw of the Qi region. Throughout history, Lu and Qi have traditionally been mentioned together: they were adjacent to each other, and both regions once had many Confucianists. The learned men in Qi remarkably differed from those in Lu, however. The famous men of Qi were not only notable thinkers, but also men of action, such as Sun Tzu—the general who wrote *The Art of War*—and the great strategist Lu Zhonglian.

Lu Zhonglian (305–245 BC) was Li Bai's ultimate hero because he had overcome his humble and even destitute origins to become a legendary strategist and an eloquent negotiator on behalf of the State of Qi. But despite his immense services, Lu Zhonglian never accepted a reward from his rulers, who offered him titles, money, riches, even towns and cities. As soon as his greatest feat was accomplished—writing a letter to the commander of the invading Yan army so persuasive that the enemy troops withdrew from the occupied capital of Qi State (the Yan commander committed suicide out of shame)—Lu Zhonglian fled to the East China Sea, simply vanishing without a trace. He had always said that he preferred the freedom of a commoner to the restrictions of aristocratic life—that was how he managed to survive, and that was why, a thousand years later, he became Li Bai's idol and model. He exemplified Bai's belief that after success, one must retreat or one might suffer destruction.

Bai praised Lu Zhonglian in more than a dozen poems. In one of them, he even pictures himself achieving a similar feat: "I too can shoot a letter into Liao Town / And break the siege and throw the enemy back" ("Moving to East Lu in May and Answering the Man on the Wen River"). Lu Zhonglian's association with the lands of Lu and Qi made Bai feel he was following in his hero's footsteps, as he wrote in a poem addressed directly to the great statesman: "I am also a detached man, / Ready to float away like you" ("Ancient Songs 10").

Another reason for moving to Lu was a new approach in his pursuit of officialdom. Ever since his conversation with Wang Changling the previous fall, Li Bai had been thinking about how to serve in the military—he believed he could make an excellent officer. General Pei Hao, regarded as the era's greatest master of the sword, was currently stationed in Lu Prefecture. The Tang empire was said to have three treasures: Wu Daozi's paintings, Zhang Xu's calligraphy, and Pei Hao's swordsmanship. Pei had fought many victorious battles on the northern and western frontiers and was considered one of the emperor's favorite officers. Bai was eager to learn the art of the sword from Pei, under whose tutelage he dreamed of becoming a master himself. Before he'd left Anlu, he had written to the general to express his wish to become his disciple, but despite Bai's poetic reputation, somehow Pei had made no reply.

After arriving in Lu, Bai didn't bother to look for a house and simply put up his family at his uncle's residence in Ren County. Without delay he went to call on General Pei. Pei happened to be observing mourning for his mother, who had recently passed away. The grieving period would last three years, during which he was required to shun all work and entertainment. Nevertheless, he received Bai briefly, probably because of the young man's literary fame. Also at the meeting was the general's nephew Pei Zhongkan, who knew Li Bai's poetry and was excited to meet him. Yet General Pei, though he treated his guest cordially, seemed to avoid the topic of Bai's request to study with him. After the initial visit, Bai would continue to see Zhongkan, who became his close friend. The young man was known for his gallantry and for keeping his word. He was a local power of sorts, and thanks to his excellent reputation, he often mediated for others.

Li Bai's uncle, with whom his family had been staying, was leaving Ren County, where his appointment was about to end. After this term of office, the older man would return to the capital for a new assignment. Bai had no choice but to turn to his two cousins for help. Li Yi and Li Lie served in Shanfu and Xiaqiu counties as accountants in the local governments. They were both proud of Bai's accomplishment as a poet and helped him acquire a house surrounded by a small yard on the west bank of the Si River.

Bai liked the location of his new home, which was on a sandy hill near the eastern gate of Xiaqiu Town (modern Yanzhou). Yi and Lie also helped him buy several acres of farmland on the east side of the river. Bai let his two servants, Dansha and his wife, take care of the fields, sowing, weeding, and harvesting the crops. From his house he could see the Si River flowing between his farmland and his homestead. The water was shallow but quite wide, and a stone path stretched across its surface. A short waterfall, about five feet high, dropped from the path like a white curtain, and its sound accentuated the quiet of the surroundings. Li Bai was content with the arrangements and began to live a stable, self-sufficient life. By now his wife was pregnant with their second child and, despite her unwieldy body, often went to spend time with the two servants across the river.

One day Pei Zhongkan, the general's nephew, came to invite Bai to dinner at his uncle's residence. Bai was surprised because during his mourning period, the general was not supposed to host parties. Zhongkan said this was an exception and Bai must come and see why.

Bai went to the general's and found a shining table set in the courtyard. Beside it a large bowl of ink was sitting on a stone drumstool. As he wondered what this could be for, the host stepped out together with a scrawny old man wearing a long white beard and a black hat. General Pei introduced him to Li Bai as Wu Daozi. At the mention of the master painter's name, Bai was overwhelmed. He hadn't known that the two masters, of the sword and of the brush, were close friends. The general explained that he had invited Mr. Wu to paint a mural in his courtyard in memory of his mother. The painter, more than twenty years Bai's senior, had heard of Bai but was unfamiliar with his poetry. He was pleased to see Bai and liked the poet's sparkling eyes, strong-boned face, and natural demeanor.

As the dinner continued, Master Wu asked the general to give a sword performance, saying he needed to see the spirit of Pei's swordsmanship to get the right rhythm for his own brushstrokes. Pei said he hadn't touched a sword for a long time because he was in mourning, but to make the party lively he would do what he could. He put on his leather mail and took his sword and began to perform in the middle of the courtyard.

Bai could hardly follow the swift movement of the sword, which whirled and glittered as Pei wielded it. The weapon seemed to be another limb of his, thrusting and chopping and slinging as his body danced about. As the spectators, including some servants, applauded, Bai realized how shabby and crude his own swordsmanship was. This only made him more eager to learn and master the art.

The moment Pei put the sword back into its sheath, Master Wu rose and went up to the blank wall prepared for him. Two servants placed the ink bowl and a set of brushes near the foot of the wall.

Wu dipped a brush into the ink and began to paint. His strokes seemed to be as vigorous as Pei's sword and to move just as rapidly. Soon hills, august trees, and human figures began forming on the wall. People watched with bated breath. A few moments later, the mural was done, although the master said he would add some final touches and also some colors early the next morning.

General Pei was delighted with the painting, saying his mother's soul would surely love the piece, especially the pair of cranes in flight. He nodded to thank the painter.

Li Bai was also moved: after an evening of anticipation, he had at last witnessed the two great masters at work. He stood up and again begged General Pei to teach him the art of the sword. Pei smiled and said Bai shouldn't treat the banquet room as a drill ground. His remark set the whole table laughing.

Afterward, Bai asked Zhongkan why General Pei wouldn't take him as his disciple. Was he not good enough to learn from the master? Zhongkan shook his head and told Bai that he misunderstood his uncle, who wasn't only a sword master but also a military strategist. He had once guarded the frontiers and accomplished great deeds, but now he was a general in name only, without any real authority to command. His superiors had always been jealous of him and kept him under their thumbs. Eventually he was forced to retire before he had even turned fifty. A few years earlier, the emperor had summoned him to Luoyang to give a sword performance. Although His Majesty greatly admired General Pei's swordsmanship and granted him gifts to show his appreciation, Pei became downcast after he returned to Lu, because he had become a mere performer when what he wanted was to serve as a commanding general.

Zhongkan also revealed to Bai that his uncle had in fact taught him how to use a sword. Zhongkan had mastered every skill and routine that his uncle had taught him, but he still felt hopeless in his career, which remained stagnant in spite of his young age. It would have been better if he had learned how to compose poetry instead. So, he said, Bai should be patient, because with his poetic talent, someday he would gain the recognition he deserved. Bai smiled bitterly and realized that every man had his own peculiar quandary. Indeed, wherever he turned, he saw failure and disappointment.

Soon after settling down in Xiaqiu County, Bai had begun to associate with local scholars. Most of them were Confucianists, bookish and starchy even on casual occasions. Some of them were also very careful about how they dressed, down to the last detail. Bai, carefree and a little arrogant, often found himself at odds with these men. Once after a gathering, he composed a poem to mock the Confucianists, portraying them like this:

魯叟談五經　白髮死章句
問以經濟策　茫如墜煙霧
足著遠遊履　首戴方山巾
緩步從直道　未行先起塵。。。

《嘲魯儒》

The old men in Lu love the five classics,
Sticklers for words and all white haired.
If you ask them how to run a government
They'll go blank like in a fog.
They always wear shoes designed for long trips
And headscarves made in Fangshan.
Slowly they walk on straight roads,
But before they lift their feet, dust goes up.

"MOCKING CONFUCIANISTS IN LU"

The poem outraged many local Confucianists, who regarded themselves as capable men, truly learned and virtuous. Their outcries were so persistent and overbearing that Li Bai was forced to withdraw for a time. He retreated to an area near Julai Mountain and mingled with a circle of local literary figures there. These men were all noted for being reclusive, refusing to serve in office and secluding themselves in the wilderness. Soon Bai and five other men gained the name "Six Hermits of the Bamboo Creek." Together they drank, played chess and musical instruments, and chanted poems on the mountain. Bai enjoyed their company and admired their life, detached from worldly strife.

Occasionally he still went to the local government to see if he might procure a post. Most officials either ignored him or paid lip service to his request. Only a petty official in Zhongdu, a small county, treated him with respect. They met for the first time one afternoon when the young man saw Li Bai sitting outside an eatery. He approached the poet, greeting Bai with a deep bow. Bai didn't know the man, who bowed again, saying he had been waiting to meet him for a long while. He placed a pair of live fish, apparently just bought from a vendor nearby, and a jar of wine on the corner of the table and introduced himself as Feng Seven, a devoted fan of Bai's poetry. He wanted to treat the poet to a meal because he had known Li Bai for many years, he claimed. Surprised, Bai could not recall where they had met. Feng Seven explained that he had cherished Bai's poems for so long and knew them so well that it was as if he had been with the poet himself all these years. Delightedly Bai accepted his gift of fish and wine; they had the fish cooked at the eatery and together they regaled themselves.

Feng Seven asked Li Bai a favor—to write a poem for him. Already tipsy, Bai wielded a brush and dashed off these lines:

魯酒若琥珀　　汶魚紫錦鱗
山東豪吏有俊氣　　手攜此物贈遠人
意氣相傾兩相顧　　斗酒雙魚表情素
雙鰓呀呷鰭鬣張　　蹳剌銀盤欲飛去

呼兒拂幾霜刃揮　　紅肌花落白雪霏
為君下箸一餐飽　　醉著金鞍上馬歸

《酬中都小吏攜斗酒雙魚于逆旅見贈》

The wine in Lu has the color of amber
And the fish from the Wen have purple scales.
The official of Shandong is truly gallant,
Carrying these gifts over to entertain me.
The friendship is mutual and
We open the jar of wine and clean the fish
Whose gills still open and close noisily,
Making the plate jump about.
We call the waiter to come with a knife—
One stroke reveals the red fat and white flesh.
Let us eat and drink to our fill
Then leap into the saddles and head home.

"IN RETURN FOR A SMALL OFFICIAL IN ZHONGDU,
WHO BROUGHT ALONG A JAR OF WINE AND A PAIR OF FISH
TO WINE AND DINE ME ON THE ROADSIDE"

Although Feng Seven was thrilled to see the poem unfolding right in front of him, Li Bai felt he hadn't yet done enough to repay his new friend's kindness. So he picked up the brush again and wrote on another piece of paper:

蘭陵美酒鬱金香　　玉碗盛來琥珀光
但使主人能醉客　　不知何處是他鄉

《客中作》

The fine wine of Lanling gives off a fragrance—
Held in a jade bowl, it shines with amber light.

So long as the host can make me drunk
I'll have no idea where my hometown is.

"SONG OF BEING A GUEST"

This second poem might have actually been composed on a previous occasion—Li Bai may have written it out as if it were new in order to please Feng Seven. Despite our uncertainty about its origin, it has become one of his most enduring masterpieces. Even today it is often quoted by people gathering to drink.

13

WOMEN

According to the chonology compiled by Zhan Ying, in 741 Li Bai's wife gave birth to their second child, a son. Bai was delighted by the new arrival and named him Boqin. He also gave him a pet name, Ming-yue Nu, which means "Little Bright Moon." As with his daughter, the choice of name reflected Bai's high expectations for his new child: Ming-yue Nu was the courtesy name of the great archer Hu Luguang (515–572), a local hero in Shandong whose valor and prowess Li Bai admired.[1] A courtesy name is an additional moniker one adopts, which conventionally expresses one's aspiration and disposition and even profession—to highlight a unique desired identity. Bai must have hoped that his son would become a great warrior, although the boy would not be able to live up to his expectations, as few sons with extraordinary fathers can.

After the second childbirth, his wife's health deteriorated rapidly, and soon she died. Li Bai was thrown into deep grief. We don't have any poems from him that express his mourning, but this doesn't mean he didn't write any. A great portion of his poetry is lost, and there is no way we can accurately gauge the depth of his grief. But we can say for certain that he knew he had let his wife down. She surely died with a broken heart, having seen her husband's career fraught with setbacks and failures and having led a troubled and lonely married life.

Although he was the quintessential romantic poet, Bai didn't seem to love any real woman with the level of passion that appeared in his verses. He loved his wife in his own way, which was willful and somewhat selfish. He had spent so many of his prime years pursuing his aspirations in politics and Daoism (though his religious zeal fluctuated according to his situation) that he had often neglected his familial responsibilities. Moreover, women didn't seem to form an essential part of his life. In the few poems addressed to his wife when she was alive, we can find no sense of passionate love or heartfelt pain caused by their separation. At most, Bai admits he drank too much to be able to fulfill a husband's duties. Beyond question, when he traveled in search of an official post he encountered other women, often singing girls and courtesans, especially those in Nanjing. (He was also fond of foreign women, *hunü* and *huji,* which is made clear in his poems.) He spent money on them regardless of his means and wrote hundreds of poems about them, showing sympathy and understanding of their hardships and heartbreaks; yet he didn't give enough love and attention to the woman closest to him. He wandered through the world as though he did not belong to it and was merely passing through. He had little sustained attachment to anyone except his children, whom he missed and even wept for when they were separated from him. Perhaps a genius of his caliber, full of demonic power and extravagant visions, needed to conserve the bulk of his energy and time for his art. Still, could his profound detachment be justified by his talent and artistic achievement? From the viewpoint of his family, probably not.

With his wife gone, his home felt desolate. Wherever Bai turned, he was reminded of her absence. Because his children were now without a mother, Li Bai would no longer travel as extensively as he had before. He still often wandered the lands of Lu and Qi, but within a short time he would return to his daughter and son. He loved his children, and in a number of poems he expresses his attachment to them. Yet he was not a man who stayed home for long—the freedom he yearned for was found only on the road. For now, more than anything, he needed a woman who could take care of his children, particularly his baby son. Soon he began to look around for a suitable match.

A young woman living next door caught Bai's eye. She was pretty and from a distance she often listened to him chanting his poems. Sometimes she would smile at him as if to indicate that she fully understood his poetry in spite of his heavy Sichuan accent. In her yard grew a bush of pomegranate flowers that had just begun to bloom, and when a breeze blew, the scent of the flowers would waft over to Li Bai's study. As a result, he was often reminded of her even though she was absent from view. His awareness of her was reinforced by the greetings they would exchange every morning.

One day Bai wrote a poem for her. Not knowing her name, he called her Miss Lu. It reads:

魯女東窗下　海榴世所稀
珊瑚映綠水　未足比光輝
清香隨風發　落日好鳥歸
願爲東南枝　低舉拂羅衣
無由一攀折　引領望金扉

《詠鄰女東窗海石榴》

Under Miss Lu's window
Grows a bush of rare pomegranate flowers.
Coral in green water
Cannot match them in glory and brilliance.
Fresh fragrance comes with the breeze
And birds return to them after sunset.
I would like to become the branches

That bend to caress your silk dress.
Having no chance to pick a flower,
I can only gaze at your golden door.

"PRAISING THE POMEGRANATE FLOWERS
UNDER THE WINDOW OF MY FEMALE NEIGHBOR"

The tone here is deliberately ambiguous; he might be flirting with her or genuinely eager to know her. The poem was completed, but he couldn't hand it to her directly, so it is said he attached it to an arrow and shot it toward her house. But the arrow flew across into her neighbor's yard, which belonged to an old Confucianist. The man had been hostile to Li Bai ever since Bai had written the poem ridiculing the local pedants. Now, after reading Bai's poem, he was outraged anew and shared the verse with other Confucianists. Soon Li Bai became a target of condemnation once again. In those scholars' eyes, he was a libertine, seducing women of good family without hesitation. To make matters worse, the young woman turned out to be already engaged, though her fiancé was essentially absent—he had been away on business for years and she had heard no word from him. Nonetheless, the Confucianists were ready to drive Bai out of town.

Bai's cousin Li Yi could not intervene on his behalf, despite his official position in Shanfu County's administration. Yi was merely a secretary and an accountant in the magistrate's office, of modest rank and unable to protect Bai in such a scandal. Bai turned to his friend Pei Zhongkan for help. The young man knew how influential those local scholars could be, so he urged Bai to join his hermitic friends at Julai Mountain for a time to give the Confucianists the impression that he had become intimidated and left town. Bai followed Zhongkan's advice and spent his days with the other members of the Bamboo Creek Hermits. Meanwhile, his young friend managed to dissuade the Confucianists from going after him any further. But soon Bai grew restless again and sneaked back home. To his disappointment, his neighbor Miss Lu had moved.

Throughout his life, Bai formed domestic relationships with four women: his first wife, two other women in Lu who lived with him and helped him raise his children, and his second wife. We have little information on the two Lu women, and the basic details about them are derived from Wei Hao's introduction to Li Bai's collected writings: "In the beginning he married Xu, who gave birth to a girl and a boy, who was named Ming-yue Nu, and the girl died soon after she was married. Then Bai joined Liu, who left him. Then he joined a woman of Lu, who gave birth to a son named Poli. Finally he married Zong." What is interesting in this passage is the distinction between the words "married" and "joined." By "joined" Wei means cohabitation without marriage. People tended to call such a woman a "concubine," but in Li Bai's case such a union was made mainly for the practical reason that his household was in need of a woman's care. The unmarried woman who joined him was more like a partner than a lover.

In fact, bringing a woman into his family without marrying her might have been the most reasonable solution for him. By Tang law, any man older than twenty and any woman over fifteen who had lost their spouses and passed the mourning period were required to apply for another union with a person of the opposite sex so that the new couple could live together legally. In other words, widowers and widows were urged to get married or united with others to form new households. When a local official was evaluated for his achievements, an increased number of such unions in the area under his charge would be a significant factor, because more intact households meant more stability and eventually an increase of population. Furthermore, the government did not recognize the ownership of land by women, who would therefore not pay taxes on any property under their auspices. If a man brought a woman into his household, he would benefit from her property without incurring extra taxes, and if a woman joined a man, her life would become more secure. People were motivated, therefore, to live together after they had lost their spouses. All this meant that it would be almost impossible for Bai to stay single for long.[2]

Because of this, after the loss of his wife, Bai's friends and neighbors urged him to find a woman who could help him maintain the home and raise his children. He agreed, and soon they found a suitable young woman, a commoner named Liu. Although we don't know much about her, quite a bit has been imagined and speculated. From Bai's poetry, there are a few things we do know for certain. She seems to have been worldly and practical: she most likely agreed to live with Bai because he was a minor celebrity and a man of learning. Lu Prefecture was an area where people respected books—knowledge was associated with potential power and wealth. Li Bai also had his acres of farmland, and from those was able to provide a decent home. Then, too, he was a physically attractive prospect, strong and handsome.

Although Li Bai and Liu were a good match for domestic partnership, the relationship never progressed to marriage, because her station was not appropriately high enough for Bai. We should keep in mind that his first wife had been a granddaughter of a chancellor; his second wife, whom he married years later, would be a daughter of another chancellor. It is clear that Bai, with his distinct sense of class, preferred a wife from a wealthy and renowned family.

But Liu seemed to have expected more than Bai could give— she was soon disappointed by his drinking and by the debts he accumulated at taverns and wineshops. To make matters worse, with her maintaining the household he could afford to travel more, and became absent from the home for extended periods. She often blamed him for his idleness and for his failure to earn money for the family. Ignoring her, he continued to go out with his friends for long stretches of time. Unlike his late first wife, Liu did not appreciate Bai's poetry—given her modest background, she may even have been illiterate.

Understandably, the two of them didn't get along. Bai soon couldn't stand her anymore. Later in a poem he expressed his anger: "That woman is loud as a shrieking magpie. / That woman is vulgar and stupid like a desperate wren. / I am honest and feel at ease / And wouldn't say more about this." This was very strong language—no other poet would say something so unflattering about their spouse or partner. As its title suggests—"Poem for My Friend to Counter Slander"—Li Bai was enraged because the young woman might have bad-mouthed him behind his back. Yet, for the sake of his children, he most likely tried his best to live with her, and there are moments in his poems when he seemed earnestly to attempt to understand her. In some verses he even spoke from her point of view. She must have felt lonely, insecure, deserted, like "flowers soundlessly dropped in moss." In "A Lament of the Leaving Woman," he speaks in her voice: "In the ancient days there were deserted women, / Who all had somewhere to go. / Today I am leaving you, / But where can I head from here? / My age has been growing with the years. / A cheap concubine, how long can I last? . . . / Where can I stay for long? / Who would build a life together with me?" He seemed to understand that she was entitled to leave him if the situation did not improve.

In spite of her unhappiness with Bai, Liu did accompany him on his travels south to the land of Wu (modern southern Jiangsu, northern Zhejiang, and southern Anhui). Soon after they arrived, it is said that the woman abandoned him and eloped with a merchant to the seacoast. This might also explain Bai's outrage in his poem to "counter slander."

After Liu left, Li Bai took in another woman, known as "the

woman of Lu," so that she could take care of his children and maintain the household.

All Li Bai biographers agree that in the late summer of 742, as he was traveling alone in the area around Mount Tai, Bai received an official letter in a large red envelope, which summoned him to the capital to serve at court. He was stunned but then realized how this had taken place. His friend Yuan Danqiu had once promised him to look for an opportunity for him in the palace, but Bai had never dreamed that the emperor would invite him to the palace personally. Now he had to return to Xiaqiu where his home was, about fifty miles away in the southwest, to say goodbye to his children and make arrangements for their care while he served in Chang'an. After arriving home, still full of ebullience, he wrote a poem that recorded his exultation and his reunion with his daughter and son:

白酒新熟山中歸　黃雞啄黍秋正肥
呼童烹雞酌白酒　兒女嬉笑牽人衣
高歌取醉欲自慰　起舞落日爭光輝
遊說萬乘苦不早　著鞭跨馬涉遠道
會稽愚婦輕買臣　餘亦辭家西入秦
仰天大笑出門去　我輩豈是蓬蒿人

《南陵別兒童入京》

When I return from the mountain
White liquor is just ripe in the brewery
And yellow chickens, all fat,
Are picking up grains in the autumn light.
I call the servant boy to cook a chicken
And take a jar of the white liquor
As my children are frolicking around me,
Pulling the hems of my robe.

I sing and drink to comfort myself,
Then dance to outshine the sunset.
Having traveled far and met powerful lords,
Now is the time to spur my horse for a long road.
The stupid woman used to mock her man,
But now I am going to Chang'an in the west.
Laughing loud with my head thrown back,
I walk out the front gate. How can a man
Like myself stay in the weeds for too long?

"SAYING FAREWELL TO MY CHILDREN IN NANLING
BEFORE I SET OUT FOR THE CAPITAL"

"The stupid woman" here could only refer to Liu, who had been unable to imagine that Li Bai would ascend to "heaven" in one great leap, clearing all the obstacles of the bureaucracy to serve the emperor himself.

Now his arrangement with the woman of Lu would become permanent. For his children, Bai would need her to stay in his household while he was away in the capital. Wei Hao calls the woman of Lu *fu*, a word that implies she had married before and was likely a widow. For a woman in such circumstances, joining Li Bai's family presented a good opportunity, particularly now that his fortunes had turned and he was heading to Chang'an. We have no record stating exactly when their cohabitation began, but given the need for a caretaker, we can surmise that he must have taken in the woman of Lu after Liu had jilted him. This woman differed greatly from the previous one; she faithfully took care of the children and his estates during his absences. Above all, Bai seemed to trust her.[3]

By the fall of 742, Li Bai was already the talk of the country—his official summons to court had been sent from the emperor personally, an exceedingly rare honor. Several explanations have been proposed as to why His Majesty granted Bai such a favor.

Li Bai's fame as a poet had evidently spread far enough to reach the palace, and the admirers and friends he had made through his endless travels were eager to help him. Among his advocates was a court poet, He Zhizhang (659–744), who was the first to praise Bai as a "Banished Immortal." The old court poet had come upon Bai's "Tune of Ravens' Perch," and after reading it, sighed that the poem would make ghosts and gods weep. Despite several allusions in the lines that reduce the transparency of the poetry somewhat, it is a deeply unsettling poem, even in translation:

姑蘇臺上烏棲時　　吳王宮裏醉西施
吳歌楚舞歡未畢　　青山欲銜半邊日
銀箭金壺漏水多　　起看秋月墜江波
東方漸高奈樂何

《烏棲曲》

When ravens perch on Gusu Terrace,
The beauty, Xishi, gets drunk in Wu Palace.
Wu songs and Chu dances are not over yet,
Though the sun is down, half behind the green mountain.
The brass water clock still drips to measure time
While the autumn moon falls into the waves of the river.
What can you do as the east is turning white?

It is generally held that Xishi was one of the most beautiful women in ancient China. In the poem, she indulges in revelry with her lord, but of course the party cannot go on forever and has to end at daybreak. In essence, the poem is about the sinister nature of time and the ephemerality of beauty and pleasure sustained by passion and power. In a way this is also an allegorical poem, one that resonated with the current situation at court, where the emperor was somewhat bewitched by his favorite consort, Lady Yang. But unlike Bai's other poems, the speaker here doesn't mention politics directly and simply focuses on the progression of time. As a song poem (*yuefu*), this verse should have had eight lines, but the closing couplet is cut in half to reflect the truncation of pleasure and beauty by time: the impaired form of the verse signifies the futility of human effort to make merry. In this sense, beauty and power are both doomed since no one, despite the desperate passion that may drive them, can sustain pleasure for long.

He Zhizhang must have caught the political implications of the poem and been struck by its fluidity, verbal music, and poetic virtuosity—he hand-copied it and couldn't stop sharing it with others. Compared to Bai, Zhizhang was not a prolific poet but was famous for a handful of short poems, particularly this one: "I left home a boy and returned an old man. / My accent has not changed but my hair is thin and white. / Children greet me as a stranger, / And smiling, they ask me where I'm from" ("Writing by Chance on My Return Home [6]"). Zhizhang was forty years older than Bai, and in spite of his seniority as the director of the Imperial Library, he became an unlikely supporter of the young poet.

In addition to Zhizhang's advocacy, we also know that the emperor and Lady Yang had read and loved Bai's poetry themselves, and wanted to recruit him for service in the palace. This, of course, would have been by far the strongest factor in Bai's favor.

There is another explanation for the royal summons that involves Princess Yuzhen, the emperor's younger sister. It was at her villa outside Chang'an where Li Bai had stayed for months during his first visit to the capital twelve years before. The princess never met Bai during his stay there, despite the poems he wrote singing her praises. Later, Bai's friend Yuan Danqiu, the hermit in Mount Song, became Princess Yuzhen's dependable associate. Both were devoted Daoists, though Danqiu was more senior in the religious society than she and had actually been her endorser for her induction. Yuzhen trusted Danqiu and assigned projects to him: he supervised temple renovations and managed a large shrine in Chang'an City. In recent years, Danqiu had often accompanied the princess on her pilgrimages, and on these journeys he had introduced Bai's poetry to her. In this way the princess became an admirer of Bai's and eventually recommended him, a fellow Daoist, to her brother the emperor. In every sense, Danqiu was Bai's devoted friend and helped him whenever he could. Their friendship lasted decades, a lifetime.

Legend has it that Li Bai was enamored of Princess Yuzhen, and it is even said there was an affair between them. This claim cannot be substantiated, but undoubtedly Bai longed for her attention and patronage, if not her affection or love. His wild nature, however, made him an unlikely protégé for the princess, given that she was quiet and peaceful, detached from worldly affairs. She preferred the other great poet of their time, Wang Wei, a reserved, mild man with a delicate disposition and a sensitive intelligence. He had been under her guidance since the beginning of his career. With her support, he had passed the civil-service examination and become a court official in his early twenties, in charge of musicians and other entertainers.

Here is a riddle in the history of Chinese poetry: these two great poets were the same age—the dates of their births and deaths are nearly the same—but there is no record of their paths ever having crossed. Wang Wei was an official in the palace (though he was twice banished from the capital) where Bai must have gone frequently, and there must have been occasions where he and Li Bai encountered each other. The two poets even had friends in common—both of them were close with Meng Haoran and Du Fu. Yet there are no references to each other in their writings—it is as though they lived in different times and were unaware of each other. In addition to poetic rivalry and aesthetic difference—Wang Wei's poetry is serene, rational, and restrained, rarely touching on realities of his day, whereas Li Bai's is passionate and spontaneous, often lamenting the hardships of soldiers and common people—there may have also been competition for the affection and patronage of Princess Yuzhen. This competition must have alienated them from each other to such an extent that they appeared to be strangers throughout their lives.

IN THE CAPITAL AGAIN

The journey from Lu Prefecture to Chang'an was more than six hundred miles, but Li Bai reached the capital in just fifteen days. Such a trip usually took more than a month. When he arrived, rather than going to an inn, he checked into Talent Haven, which was owned by the municipality and provided free lodging for men of special ability who came to serve the central government. While waiting for the emperor's interview, Bai worked hard on a long essay titled "A Grand Plan for Our Dynasty," which expressed his political vision. As always, he was grandiloquent in his diction and extravagant in his analogies.

Within a few days, the emperor summoned him to court. His Majesty was to give Li Bai an extraordinary reception. A eunuch led him to Gold Bell Hall in Grand Bright Palace. From its front steps Bai could see the cityscape in the distance: soaring eaves of the other palaces, ponds and lakes covered with lotus pads, weeping willows along the banks of the canal and rivers, white towers above the trees. When Bai entered the hall, he saw a man seated in the throne, dressed in a red brocade robe with an embroidered golden dragon on its front and a black hat adorned with a cut of white jade. The man had a soft face, with gray bags under his dull eyes. So this must be the emperor. At the sight of Bai, His Majesty stood and descended from his throne. He was struck by Bai's physique and demeanor—his guest seemed perfectly at ease, as if he were already familiar with this hall. He motioned for Bai to sit on a couch next to him so they could converse and share a meal. Tea was served. As the servants turned away, Bai realized this was a private interview. Emperor Xuanzong evidently already knew Li Bai's poetry and must also know they were relatives, members of the same clan. The sovereign was an accomplished composer, musician, calligrapher, and choreographer, so he treated Bai as a great poet whose lyrics would be helpful for his composition. He said to Bai, "You are without an official title, but your reputation has reached me nonetheless. If you did not possess great virtues, how could this happen?" His Majesty's compliment delighted Bai. When a porcelain terrine was placed on the table, Xuanzong picked up a bowl and ladled soup into it. He stirred it with a spoon, then let Bai taste it. A small number of courtiers were present in the hall, though they kept at a distance from the table where the emperor and Bai sat. They were all surprised—His Majesty had never done this before, personally filling a bowl of soup for a guest. The emperor seemed to be so excited that he was acting out of character. Later they spread the word about the favor that the emperor had bestowed on Li Bai. It soon became a topic of the palace, then of the capital, and then of the country.

Bai was assigned to the Imperial Academy in the palace. In spite of its lofty title, the institution was in fact composed of a miscellany of unusual men, some of whom made Bai uncomfortable and even embarrassed. In addition to the expected scholars, painters, calligraphers, and sculptors, there were also master monks, geomancers, experts on astrology and fortune-telling, and even a man who claimed that he was more than three thousand years old. All of them had no official rank and were kept by court like entertainers; though they were called "academicians," they were in reality not much different from servants. Li Bai felt out of place and despised most of these "special talents." In a poem about the academy, entitled "At the Imperial Academy, After Reading Books, I

Voice My Feelings to My Fellow Academicians," he writes, "It's so easy to be tainted by flies / But so hard to find someone attuned to your thoughts." He resolved to stay above them. It is difficult to imagine that a new arrival with this kind of contempt for his colleagues could remain unscathed for long. If only he could have worked under He Zhizhang in the Royal Library, but that was out of the question for now. In fact, the above poem was secretly held as a piece of evidence against Bai. Scholars believe that it was Zhang Ji, the man who had once fooled Bai by sending him to Princess Yuzhen's villa in Zhongnan Mountain, who passed the poem on to the emperor.[1]

However, on the surface Zhang Ji gave the appearance of warming up to Bai. As soon as Bai had arrived at the academy and settled in, Ji came to greet him, offering advice and instructions. Though he was in charge of the Imperial Academy and therefore quite senior, Zhang Ji treated Li Bai with courtesy because he had heard that the emperor admired Bai's poetry and had even stirred soup for him personally. Ji told Bai that as an academician, he was expected to remain on duty at all times in case the court needed him, but that he was entitled to a day off every ten days so he could take a bath in a public bathhouse downtown. Bai liked the warm pools in those establishments, where he could steep and scrub himself alongside other men.

The academy was in a large courtyard, planted with flowers and various types of bamboo. In the beginning Bai was quite conscientious about his job, which consisted simply of sitting in his office and waiting for summonses. Every day he would review the classics that he had already read many times, and once in a while he would stumble upon a sentence or passage that made him smile or laugh. But rarely was anyone here summoned to court, so when Bai grew bored with reading, he would revise and polish his essay "A Grand Plan for Our Dynasty." He also wrote poems that showed how he missed his untrammeled life outside the court. Many people would call on him, currying favor and asking for a poem inscribed in his calligraphy; he was also habitually invited to dinner parties. At the outset, he was excited and enjoyed the gatherings and the wine and food, which were also his meal tickets now that he wasn't paid enough to buy two full meals a day. Most of the academicians were quite poorly paid; it was assumed that they would receive bribes, fees, and favors, but Bai, a poet and a new arrival, lacked the power and influence to attract such income. Yet soon he tired of constantly eating at banquets with strangers. He was reluctant to mingle with the snobs and sycophants of the court and preferred to be alone. Unlike the other academicians, he didn't know how to fraternize with government officials, unable to walk the line between congeniality and obeisance. In short, he was completely out of place.

Meanwhile, he continued to expect the emperor to summon him to court again so he could present to His Majesty his essay on national policies. But instead of an audience, he was ordered to leave with the royal retinue for Mount Li, about twenty miles northwest of Chang'an. The area was warm in winter and cool in summer, ideal for a seasonal resort. A large palace sat at the foot of a hill there, and pools were fed by hot springs. The royal family would stay at the mountain palace during the hottest and coldest months. Now that winter was approaching, the emperor and Lady Yang were on their way there.

At first, Li Bai was happy at the prospect of getting away from the academy. He believed that by staying close to the emperor, he would have an opportunity to directly express his political ambition and views to His Majesty. He hated to think of himself as a mere poet and longed to become a consequential statesman. But the trip turned out to be only a great fanfare. Along the way to Mount Li, colored banners and pennants celebrating the emperor flew so thickly that they seemed to block out the sky. A large army of royal guards rode before and after the royal entourage, and trumpets and drums played frequently. Li Bai was told to write a poem about this procession to record the splendor.

As soon as Bai was settled near the palace at Mount Li, he went about composing this poem, which he completed on his first night there. Instead of the daytime pageant, he chose to set the poem in a nocturnal scene:

羽林十二將　　羅列應星文
霜仗懸秋月　　霓旌卷夜雲
嚴更千戶肅　　清樂九天聞
日出瞻佳氣　　蔥蔥繞聖君

《侍從遊宿溫泉宮作》

Twelve generals of the Royal Guards
Ride in order like stars arranged in the sky.
Frosty halberds raise the autumn moon
While banners wave with floating clouds.
A curfew keeps thousands of houses quiet
As music rises heavenward from the palace.
At sunrise the fine air gets more pure,
Encircling our Sagacious Lord.

"COMPOSED AT THE HOT SPRING PALACE
WHILE ACCOMPANYING THE EMPEROR"

The poem is noticeably subdued and falls below Li Bai's best efforts, lacking the exuberance and energy that mark his strongest work. Despite the somewhat forced last couplet, the emperor liked the poem and rewarded Bai with a fur robe. Bai was elated by the poem's reception and hoped there would be more such opportunities to bring him closer to His Majesty.

The palace in Mount Li was gorgeous—everywhere Bai turned, he saw luxury. Even the food was better than back in the academy, and wine flowed at every meal. A few days after their arrival, the emperor granted all the officials in his entourage three favors: they were summoned to partake in a sumptuous banquet, to climb the hills surrounding the palace with His Majesty on the following day, and then to bathe in the pools fed by the hot springs. Most of the officials felt fortunate and enjoyed the royal treatment, but Li Bai only grew more restless. He asked the servants when the emperor would grant an audience.

They looked bewildered by his question. The emperor and Lady Yang had come here to rest, they replied, so there would be no interview or audience. Bai should simply enjoy himself like everybody else. As for political and military affairs, Chancellor Li Linfu and Master Gao Lishi, the head eunuch, could handle them back in Chang'an. Bai mustn't meddle with the routines here or he might get in trouble.

Gradually, Bai realized that there would be no opportunity for him to express his political vision, regardless of how close to the emperor he might seem to be. More disheartening, His Majesty might be uninterested in listening to other voices, especially those that jar his ears. He relished praises and reveled in pleasures. Bai had no choice but to remain quiet like the others.

Most Li Bai chronologies suggest that he was back in the capital in the spring of 743. Bai made bold to present to Chancellor Li Linfu, via an intramural messenger, his "Grand Plan for Our Dynasty." Li Linfu (683–753) was from the royal clan and therefore considered a distant relative of Bai's, but he was not inclined to give the poet an audience. He was crafty and manipulative and kept a good part of the court in his clutches. He always blocked others, especially those who were capable but did not belong to his clique, from approaching the emperor. Yet Bai still hoped against hope that his essay would be passed along to His Majesty.

Li Linfu was knowledgeable about music and could appreciate Li Bai's poetic genius, but when he read "A Grand Plan for Our Dynasty," he flew into a rage, believing it was just bravura without real substance. He told his underlings that Bai was nothing but an entertainer and must not style himself as a great statesman. Bai's universe was his study—the moment he stepped out of the academy, he would make a fool of himself. Li Linfu's assessment of Bai's essay undoubtedly had some truth to it: although the text has been lost, the essay was said to be a barrel of clichés and hot air. Bai didn't know how to compromise or navigate official circles; his political vision, such as it was, came mainly from antiquated books. The chancellor's underlings suggested disciplining Bai immediately as a warning to others, but Li Linfu restrained them. In his eyes, Bai was merely a bookworm, incapable of any political action. As long as they kept him quiet and under control, there was no chance he could make waves, so Li Linfu put the long essay aside without passing it along.

Bai didn't know that the emperor would not personally read any writing that reached him. A petition or essay would be read out to him by a courtier at his side. If it was long, it would be condensed to give the royal ears a summary of the contents. It is unlikely that the emperor ever heard about "A Grand Plan for Our Dynasty."

Li Linfu was one of the most hated courtiers at the time. He and Gao Lishi (684–762), Yang Guozhong (?–756), and others have been condemned throughout history for their deceit and treachery. Gao was a eunuch with great physical strength—he was over six feet tall, and skilled in managing military affairs. He had helped the emperor suppress several rebellions and was eventually promoted to grand general. The emperor allowed him to handle most military matters independently, and he would only report to His Majesty when necessary. In spite of his notoriety, Gao Lishi was a devoted, loyal servant to the emperor, and the absolute trust His Majesty placed in him was earned. All the princes called him "older brother," royal family members of the younger generation called him "Uncle Gao," and the emperor's sons-in-law simply called him "Lord Gao."

Yang Guozhong was also trusted by the emperor, though he was much less capable than Gao. He was a distant cousin of Lady Yang's, and the emperor used him to counterbalance Li Linfu's power at court. As a result, Yang Guozhong headed fifteen key offices and eventually held more than forty positions. This seemed incredible, considering that most officials had just one. But multiple-office holders have been common throughout Chinese history; even today President Xi Jinping heads fourteen offices. Yang Guozhong had expensive taste and always spent lavishly to please the emperor.

As for his cousin Lady Yang (719–756), she was plump but beautiful, and over the centuries she has become a symbol of beguiling beauty in China. Originally she had been the concubine of one of the emperor's sons. The emperor was thirty-four years older than her; she first caught his eye when she was twenty-four. Five years later, he persuaded his son to give her up so that he could take her as his own. This was a turning point in the emperor's life: prior to her, he had been a diligent and conscientious monarch, but after she became his, he began to ignore his duties and indulge in sensual pleasures, spending most of his time with her. It is said she had bewitched him completely.

Naturally Li Bai disliked these powerful people, but they were all well above him and he had no direct contact with them. He grew less attentive about his duty at the Imperial Academy and began to spend time with a group of drinking friends. Among them were his advocate, the old poet He Zhizhang (who had a sparse goatee), the master calligrapher Zhang Xu (with a balding crown), and five others. They often gathered downtown and indulged in benders. Zhizhang adored Bai—although he was forty years older, he treated Bai as his peer and even acknowledged his poetic superiority. When the two men had met for the first time in a restaurant the previous fall, at the end of the meal it turned out that neither Zhizhang nor Bai had enough cash on them for the bill. The older poet took his amulet, a little gold turtle, off his neck and left it at the establishment as their payment. Now they met more often, together with other poets and artists. This coterie soon became a legend in the capital, not only for their drinking but also for the art they produced under the influence of alcohol. One of them was a prince, Li Jin (?–750), who admired Bai's work and personality. Du Fu, though much younger and not present at any of the drinking binges, wrote a poem to celebrate these "eight divine drinkers." He describes some of them as follows:

李白斗酒詩百篇
天子呼來不上船
長安市上酒家眠
自稱臣是酒中仙

知章騎馬似乘船
眼花落井水底眠

張旭三杯草聖傳
脫帽露頂王公前
揮毫落紙如雲煙

宗之瀟灑美少年
舉觴白眼望青天
皎如玉樹臨風前

LI BAI

After a gallon of wine
Li Bai can spin a hundred poems,

Then sleeps in a downtown tavern.
Even summoned by the Son of Heaven,
He won't get on the boat,
Saying "I'm a drinking xian.*"*

HE ZHIZHANG
When drunk, Zhizhang rides a horse
Wavering like on a boat.
Eyes bleary, he falls in a shallow well
But keeps slumbering in the water.

ZHANG XU
After three cups, Zhang Xu displays
His feat of calligraphy.
He takes off his hat,
His bald crown shiny in front of everyone,
Then he wields his brush, stirring up
Smoke and clouds on paper.

CUI ZONGZHI (POET)
Zongzhi is a handsome young man.
He raises his whitish eyes
To gaze at the blue sky.
He is so elegant
Like a jade tree in the breeze.[2]

I quote here only half of the long poem. The last portrait, above, describes a young man who has a fine figure. From this verse, the image of a jade tree in the breeze, *yu shu lin feng,* has become an idiom in the Chinese language, one that has endured for more than a millennium. Today people still use it to refer to a handsome, refined man.

Li Bai composed many poems at the drinking parties. His creative power seemed to become amplified by drink, and the poems he produced often amazed and even startled his friends. In fact, some of the poems were old work, but he would toss them out among the new verses to enliven the atmosphere. On one occasion, to urge others to drink more without qualms, he chanted, "If Heaven didn't like wine / There would be no Wine Star up there. / If Earth didn't like wine / There would be no such a place called Wine Spring. / . . . Three cups will lead you to the great Dao / And a jar will merge you into nature. / Let us enjoy the fun in the cups. / There's no need to share it with sober souls" ("Drinking Alone in the Moonlight [2]").

For all of spring and the early summer the court had been rehearsing "The Rainbow and Feather-Garment Dance." The dance was designed by the emperor, who had once dreamed of wandering in a palace on the moon and decided to re-create the celestial beauty and splendor he had encountered there. The performance involved more than two hundred people—choreographers, composers, dancers, musicians, singers, costume designers, and of course poets. The project was also meant to delight Lady Yang. Li Bai didn't take part until the rehearsal period was nearly over. One day, as he slept, dead drunk, on a couch at Prince Li Jin's residence, a group of men arrived, saying they had been searching for him everywhere. Among the group was Li Guinian, the composer in chief at court. Guinian told the others that the emperor had stopped the boys' choir from singing that morning because he wanted new songs for them, so he sent for Li Bai, who must come immediately to write the lyrics.

They tried to wake Bai up, but to no avail, so they sprinkled cold water on his face. The instant Bai sat up, Li Guinian told him that the emperor had summoned him to compose poems in celebration of "The Rainbow and Feather-Garment Dance" and that he must leave with them without further delay. They put the inebriated Bai into a sedan chair and carried him to Fragrant Pavilion, where the dance was to be performed. The swaying sedan made him sicker, and he vomited and soiled his robe.

When they arrived at the pavilion, which was a large yard paved with granite slabs, Li Bai was asleep again, his breath whistling through his nose. At this sorry sight the emperor said nothing, though the grand eunuch Gao Lishi ordered a servant to fetch a bowl of hangover soup. Bai vomited again. They put a new robe on Bai, who woke up a little but still couldn't stand steadily, so Gao told the servants to carry him to a large rattan chair under a yellow parasol. The emperor followed them to see if Bai was capable of composing a poem. To everyone's amazement, Bai raised his foot and demanded that Gao Lishi take off his boot for him. Onlookers gasped in astonishment. Gao was stunned as well, but, accustomed to serving the royal family, he went ahead and pulled off Bai's boot. Then Bai lifted his other foot, and Gao did the same.[3]

After he drank the hangover soup, made of orange peel, mint, fruit, green tea, and honey, Bai sobered up a bit. He saw His Majesty go back to join Lady Yang, who stood in the pavilion against a rail and watched the dance. Beyond them, swaths of peonies were in full bloom, swaying in the breeze. Lounging in the chair, Bai watched the dance as music rose from the band beyond the pavilion. A few moments later, he rose and moved to a table nearby, on which were prepared ink, spread paper, and a pair of brushes. He picked one up and began to write, not about the performance, but about Lady Yang's beauty:

一

雲想衣裳花想容　春風拂檻露華濃
若非群玉山頭見　會向瑤臺月下逢

二

一枝紅豔露凝香　　雲雨巫山枉斷腸
借問漢宮誰得似　　可憐飛燕倚新妝

三

名花傾國兩相歡　　常得君王帶笑看
解釋春風無限恨　　沈香亭北倚欄杆

《清平調》

1

Her gown brings to mind clouds and her looks, flowers.
The breeze caresses the rails glazed with thick dew.
If she is not at the peak of Jade Hills where gods reside,
You can find her at the Jasper Terrace bathed in moonlight.

2

The red, red peonies glisten with dewdrops.
She stops others from pining for goddesses.
Tell me, who was like her in the Han palace?
The pitiful Flying Swallow would resort to a new dress.

3

The flowers and the rapturous beauty shine on each other.
They make His Majesty smile when he looks at them.
The breeze blows away all his worries
As he and she lean over a rail at the Fragrant Pavilion.

"QING PING MELODIES"

Flying Swallow was a well-known beauty of the Han dynasty, but she had been very thin and delicate, the opposite of Lady Yang's plump beauty.

Both the emperor and Lady Yang loved these three poems, though they are in fact not extraordinary compared to Bai's true masterpieces. They are light and commonplace, particularly the analogy between female beauty and flowers.[4] Yet the royal couple were amazed that Li Bai could still produce charming lines even in such an impaired state. Lady Yang enjoyed the poems so much that she presented Bai with a parakeet—the bird was to be kept in the Imperial Academy, where a servant would teach it to utter some lines by Bai. Without delay Li Guinian began to set the poems to music. From then on, Lady Yang often sang these songs; occasionally the emperor would accompany her on the vertical bamboo flute.

Though the emperor was happy about the poems, he also felt uneasy about Li Bai's treatment of Gao Lishi. In private, His Majesty told the head eunuch that Bai looked "destined to be a pauper." The emperor was known to be well versed in physiognomy, and his opinion on Li Bai seemed to be accurate; indeed, Bai was never really wealthy during his lifetime. (He became well-off briefly over the next few years, but then grew poor again.) On the surface, the emperor's remark was meant to console the grand eunuch, but it also manifested the general attitude of a ruler toward an artist: however prodigious Li Bai's talent was, in the sovereign's eyes he was no more than a commoner. Talent alone was worthless, and at heart His Majesty may never have truly accepted Li Bai as a member of the royal clan. The boot-pulling incident also marked the point where Bai's career began to suffer, regardless of his later glorious moments at court. Although his defiant act produced a potent legend that would fire the imagination of the generations to come, by humiliating Gao Lishi he had acted out his haughtiness and his contempt for the man in a dangerous way. He'd have to pay for this.

Rumors began to crop up in the palace, calling Li Bai irreverent, if not malicious. Without question Gao Lishi was behind the gossip. Some said Li Bai mocked Lady Yang in his poems, and some insisted that he was flirting with her. The ancient beauty Flying

Swallow had once been a dancing girl and had led a promiscuous life before becoming a queen, and she was also an archetype of the ruinous seductress—it was outrageous to compare Lady Yang to her. When the calumny against Bai reached Lady Yang's ears, she was swayed by it and began to hate him. Legend has it that three times the emperor intended to promote Bai to a post, but she dissuaded him every time.

Bai disliked Lady Yang and didn't seem troubled by her hostility. It was widely believed that she had cast a spell on the emperor and was ruining the dynasty. She was wasteful, self-indulgent, unscrupulous. For instance, she loved fresh litchi, so the court set up a relay system to transport the fruit expressly from Lingnan (modern Guangxi and Guangdong provinces), horses galloping nonstop all the way from the deep south to Chang'an. It was reported that the litchi, having traveled more than a thousand miles, were still damp with dew when they arrived at the palace. But many horses died of exhaustion en route, and some pedestrians were trampled to death. Even crops were often destroyed, because the transporters, fearful of punishment for delay, would cut across the fields in order to arrive at the palace more quickly. In Chinese there is an idiom for such a terrifyingly beautiful woman—a beauty that can topple a city or a country *(qing guo qing cheng)*. Of course, it is not the beauty but the power under her spell that does the ruination.

POLITICAL INVOLVEMENT

In the fall, an emissary came from a distant land and presented a letter to the Tang court. It was clear to the top officials that the diplomat was from somewhere near Central Asia, but no one could tell from which country nor comprehend the letter. The emissary couldn't speak Chinese, so for half a month the central government was unable to ascertain his identity or mission. The emperor flew into a fury and threatened to disband the cabinet if they didn't decipher the contents of the letter within three days, so the high officials began desperately searching for someone who knew the foreign language. Chancellor Li Linfu, who was in charge of diplomatic affairs and would be held responsible if China lost face, was more shaken than the others. The emperor's son-in-law Zhang Ji was nervous as well: he headed the Imperial Academy, which ought to have been able to produce a translator for the letter.

In a way, however, this lack of preparedness was unsurprising. For many centuries China had treated the countries beyond the western frontier with little distinction. The peoples of Central Asia were all called *fan,* a term that was also used to refer to Tibetans and Mongols. There were many *fan* peoples and languages, and China had diplomatic relationships with some of those states. But no Chinese, at least no one in Chang'an, could understand the *fan* script in the letter delivered by the new emissary. And so He

Zhizhang again recommended Li Bai to the emperor, suggesting that Bai, who had once lived on the western frontier, might be familiar with the script. Bai was summoned to court. Glancing over the letter, he told the emperor that it was a script (scholars surmise that it was probably Tocharian) used in Yuezhi Country, which consisted of many tribes. Bai had often seen this script as a young boy and even had learned quite a bit of it. In a poem, he describes writing a letter in this foreign tongue: "Lu silk spreads glossy like frost, / On which I inscribe the Yuezhi script" ("Letters for the One Far Away: 10"). We should keep in mind that his mother had been from a western tribe, and that Bai had grown up in a bilingual or multilingual family. Now, in front of the entire court, he read out the contents of the letter, which contained a threat. The Yuezhi Country demanded that China cede some land to it or it would dispatch a powerful expeditionary army to Chang'an, destroy the city, and sack the palace.

The threat flustered the emperor and his courtiers—it was a message that demanded an immediate response. Li Bai assured His Majesty that he could write a reply, but he wanted Li Linfu to prepare the ink for him so that he could inscribe the script here and now. He hated Li Linfu, knowing the man had withheld his "Grand Plan for Our Dynasty" from the emperor, and he intended to humiliate the chancellor openly. Without delay Li Linfu began to grind an ink tablet on a stone, urging Bai to write the letter. Bai wrote the reply rapidly and then translated it into Chinese for the emperor. The contents of the letter wouldn't have been difficult for him to compose: the civil-service examination had always contained a section for such a diplomatic essay, and although Bai had never entered for the exam, he was familiar with the preparatory materials.

The emissary was called in to listen to Li Bai announce the reply. In a loud voice, which had a slightly metallic twang, he summarized it thus: China would not yield to their demand and was unafraid of their military. If the Yuezhi Country instigated a war, China, which was many times bigger and mightier, would retaliate, destroying all of Yuezhi's tribes. China was willing to exist peacefully with their country if they were not bellicose. Awestruck, the emissary hurried back with the official reply. Thereafter no word came from Yuezhi Country again.[1]

The emperor was so pleased that he kept Li Bai at court so that he could assist with foreign affairs. He was promoted to royal secretary at the fifth rank, whose principal duty was to write decrees and summarize petitions. In practice Li Bai didn't do much of those either, and yet the new position gave him an opportunity to witness political proceedings in the top circle. His presence at court made some of the ministers wary, and they began to view him as a potential rival and a troublemaker. Li Linfu and Gao Lishi in particular both hated him and were determined to make his life difficult. Bai, however, was buoyant with illusions and even believed himself to be one of the indispensable courtiers at the center of power. He was no longer just an academic fellow but a real official with a respectable rank and a handsome salary. He should be able to save enough to buy a house within a year and then bring his children to the capital.

But soon a secret smear campaign was launched against Bai. In addition to Gao Lishi and Li Linfu, others in power also regarded him as unstable. His constant drunken state gave the impression that he was incapable of steady work, so top officials would dismiss him when a consequential issue was at hand. They didn't want him to meddle with administrative affairs, and so although Bai would go to court for audiences, his voice was rarely heard. It was well known that Emperor Xuanzong loved Bai's talent and swift literary imagination, and these officials feared that he might earn more favors from the emperor at the expense of their own advancement. Gradually Bai came to feel the sting of envy and malice. "Although His Majesty loves what is beautiful / The jealousy in the palace can still kill you," he says in a poem titled "Song of a Jade Flask." He became frustrated at every turn and began to lose heart.

One morning Bai arrived at Grand Bright Palace to listen to officials as they presented petitions and to the emperor as he issued decrees. To his surprise, His Majesty declared his intent to start a war against Tufan (modern Tibet), which had posed a threat to China in recent decades. The emperor ordered Wang Zhongsi, who was the marshal of the Tang army and also the commander of the Western Regions, to organize an attack on a small town in Tufan known as Stone Fort.

Wang, a stalwart man in his late thirties, was from a family of military officers and had successfully fought several battles against Turks and Tibetans. The instant he heard the imperial decree, his face darkened. Several officials voiced their support for the war and a few junior generals even volunteered to depart with Marshal Wang the next spring. But to everyone's amazement, Wang stepped forward and spoke to the emperor, saying, "My father fought and fell in the battleground for our country. I was raised here, in the capital, and since my childhood I have been bathed in Your Majesty's love and kindness. You gave me the name 'Zhongsi,' so I never dare to forget my family's hatred for the barbarians and the royal bounties you have bestowed on me. Even the successful battles I have fought are far from enough to repay your benevolence. Since you granted me the high position of the marshal, I have pondered my former deeds and have come to believe that attacks and killing are not the best way to serve our country. I would like to follow the model of the great general Li Guang in the Han dynasty, who stayed at the border to stabilize the region. If the barbarians leave us alone, we will leave them alone. If they come to attack, we will be ready to repel them. In that way we will surely succeed and stabilize the hundreds of miles of our frontier. If we make constant war, we waste a great amount of manpower and resources. That could damage the foundation of our country. . . . I am afraid that is not a wise approach, so I am begging Your Majesty to keep peace for now and wait for an opportune time if we have to fight. Please think twice, my Lord."[2]

Bai was deeply touched by Marshal Wang's candid words. He had always felt uneasy about the warfare waged in the western regions; because he had once lived there and had known the tribal peoples, he couldn't view them as enemies deserving to be destroyed. (Unlike other writers of his time, in his writings, he never used the word "savages" [*man*] to refer to those tribesmen.) As he was about to step forward in support of Marshal Wang, he saw the emperor's face drop, so Bai paused. Then Chancellor Li Linfu began to criticize Marshal Wang, claiming he had let the emperor down. Other courtiers and officers also joined the debate. Most supported the expedition, but Wang argued that Stone Fort had no strategic value—it was not worth thousands of soldiers' lives, to say nothing of the civilians who would lose their homes. Li Bai was about to condemn the hawks, but his friend Cui Zongzhi (the handsome man "like a jade tree in the breeze") held him back and whispered not to act rashly. Zongzhi had been Bai's loyal friend since their first meeting in Jiang Prefecture eighteen years before, and Bai trusted him.

Finally Marshal Wang ran out of patience, lowered himself to his knees, and said to the emperor, "Every year we start an expedition and recruit young men for war. There are not many young men left in our central land. Everywhere you encounter widows and orphans. I am not afraid of death, but I don't want to exchange tens of thousands of lives for my own glorious position. Please cancel your decree, Your Majesty, and stop those who only want personal gains at the cost of others' lives. If you do so, our country will be blessed and all the common people will be blessed."[3] Wang then knocked his head hard on the stone floor again and again; his forehead became smeared with blood. The emperor looked upset, but he valued the marshal's bravery and ability—and, having seen him grow up, was personally fond of him—so he only stood and dismissed the audience.

Still restless that night, Li Bai set about composing a petition in support of Marshal Wang. He sat at his desk wielding his brush. As he was writing, his friend Zongzhi stopped by and urged him not to become involved in such a matter—the emperor could very well be furious at Marshal Wang and might take it out on someone less essential to him. To Zongzhi, whose family had served the court for generations, the emperor was no longer the ambitious and conscientious sovereign dedicated to his country's security and prosperity. Look what was going on in the palace. Every day there were dances and ball games and other frivolities. The emperor was already nearly sixty, but was careless about his health and wasted his vitality, indulging in women, wine, decadent music, and elixirs of life, dreaming of immortality. He was completely under the spell of Lady Yang, that Fox Spirit. Keep in mind, Zongshi warned, she must still hate Bai's guts and was surely prepared to pounce on him at any moment. To speak truth to the royal couple now could only incur their wrath against him.

So Bai abandoned his half-written petition. He felt more isolated than before, afraid that all his enemies would join hands in reducing and ruining him. Moreover, he knew that his advocate He Zhizhang, frail and already eighty-four years old, was considering retirement back to his home village on the seacoast. The eight "drinking immortals" would not revel together any longer, and Bai often drank alone, sitting moodily in the moonlight. When drunk, he would dance around the yard by himself, regarding the moon as a companion. "When I sing, the moon will waver, / When I dance, my shadows will be scattered," as he said in "Drinking Alone in the Moonlight." He began to care less about attending the audience at court. He was not indispensable at all, he soon realized, and no one paid heed to his absence.

He remembered Husi, his farmer friend living in the southern outskirts of Chang'an, near Zhongnan Mountain, and went to visit the man one day in the early spring. When Bai arrived, Husi was sowing millet but stopped to receive him heartily, like in the old days. They both marveled at each other's gray hairs. Husi's cottage was even quieter than before—his children had grown and no longer lived with him. The two friends chatted over Husi's home-brewed wine. For the first time since coming to the capital, Bai enjoyed a moment of peace. Husi was a good, patient listener and relished the anecdotes Bai told him about the palace. They also talked about Daoism. Husi knew the *Tao Te Ching* and *Chuang Tzu* quite well and, as before, mentioned that fortune and misfortune were often indistinguishable and one should take them with equanimity. Bai agreed, and shared with Husi his disappointment in the capital, which he had once viewed as a heavenly place where he could realize his political ambition. Now he felt completely out of place. They talked deep into the night.

This visit made Bai see that he did not belong to Chang'an and cemented his resolve to resign. He walked all the way back to the city, carrying a pannier of medicinal herbs, as he always did when he went out to the countryside. This was an old habit he had learned from his teacher Zhao Rui, and he would gather herbs whenever he was in the wilderness.

But before Bai submitted his request for resignation, he did something extraordinary, something that would save his life later on. One day, he joined a group of officials in an excursion to the north of Chang'an. Passing a small town, he saw a convict cart carrying a caged criminal with a narrow placard planted behind his head, followed by a group of troops armed with flat swords. By all appearances they were on their way to an execution ground. The criminal, strapping with a broad back, looked to be a junior officer. His eyes shone with defiance. Bai, who was well read in physiognomy, was struck by the man's thick bone structure and square face.

He went up to speak to the leader of the troops and learned that the convict was Guo Ziyi, an assistant officer under General Geshu Han. Geshu was from a Turgesh tribe, in which his ancestors had been chiefs for generations, but he served China and had become a general in the Tang army under the command of Marshal Wang Zhongsi. The leader of the detail told Bai that Guo Ziyi's troops had accidentally burned a large quantity of army provisions and numerous tents in the barracks, so Guo had been sentenced to death. Bai turned to speak with Guo, who answered his questions clearly and calmly like the officer that he was. Guo also said he had obtained his position via excelling in the military-service tournament.

Bai, as a court official, told the leader of the troops to halt and wait for him to return. He went to their headquarters to see General Geshu and attempted to convince him of his prediction that Guo could become an extraordinary officer. Geshu, who knew of Li Bai and admired his poetry, received him right away, but he could not make an exception and release Guo Ziyi because of the larger need to keep discipline among his men. Only the emperor could pardon such an offender. Bai implored him to at least postpone the execution, to which General Geshu agreed.

As soon as Bai returned to Chang'an, he drafted a petition to appeal to the emperor for Guo Ziyi's life, writing that Guo might well become an exceptional warrior and could be very useful for the dynasty. His Majesty, despite all the slander against Li Bai, still cherished his talent and learning, so he agreed to grant Guo Ziyi a pardon. Guo was released and remained in service. A decade later, he became a major commander of the Tang army, confronting the rebel forces from the northeast and helping the royal family restore the shattered empire. Although no one could know this at the time, by saving Guo's life, Bai had performed a great service to the central government.

Most Li Bai chronologies state that in the late spring of 744 he submitted to the emperor his request for resignation. Knowing that Bai's presence would make Lady Yang unhappy and many others nervous, His Majesty approved it without the usual formality of urging him to stay. Although he admired Bai's talent, he also feared that Bai, who got drunk so frequently, might divulge the court's secrets and cause damage to the reputation of the royal family—it was better to let him leave and keep the palace in peace. His Majesty gave Bai a good amount of gold (more than a hundred ounces) as severance pay. In addition, Bai received the title of "Carefree Scholar." Although this was a nominal honor, Bai alone was granted such a title, which allowed him to consume wine free of charge and to receive a gift of money at every county and prefecture on his way home.

As he was leaving the capital, Bai donned a Daoist cloak and hat, outwardly showing that he was no longer concerned with politics and would exist only in the religious order from now on. To some extent this was also a form of self-protection, because Bai knew that his political enemies could hound him wherever he went and even have him eliminated if they believed he still posed a threat. By wearing Daoist garb, he meant to demonstrate that he was no longer a rival of theirs. His enemies were happy to see him leave Chang'an, whereas his friends rode with him for many miles before turning back to the city.

In total, he had served at court for less than two years.

16

THE MEETING OF TWO STARS

Ashamed of his failure in the capital ("like a flying dragon that falls out of the sky," in his own words), Li Bai didn't return to his family directly and instead started a new period of wandering. Ultimately he wished to be inducted into the Daoist society by a master, but for the time being he would travel and see friends. His first stop was Luoyang, of which he had happy memories from the time he had spent in the city with his good friend Yuan Yan. Although Yan no longer lived there, Li Bai's arrival caused a stir in the local literary community, and several old friends of his began organizing a dinner party to welcome him. They had learned of his resignation, which was becoming news in literary circles all over the country.

On the eastern periphery of Luoyang was a village called Renfeng Hamlet, the home of another great poet, Du Fu. Thirty-three years old, eleven years Li Bai's junior, Du Fu at the time was still unknown. Nine years earlier he had taken the civil-service examination but hadn't passed. Like Li Bai, he traveled the country in search of a post, but without success—he had remained jobless and quite poor. He had recently married, however, and loved his wife. The couple had first made their home in another village about twenty-five miles east of Luoyang, but they had moved to stay with his aunt (who loved him as if he were her own child), and to be closer to the city so that he could enter its literary circle.

His aunt had died of illness the year before, but her husband had insisted that the young couple stay with him. Du Fu was originally from an affluent family that for generations had produced officials and scholars. His clan had deep roots in Henan, in the central area of China; his grandfather, a noted poet and calligrapher, had been the mayor of Luoyang and his father a county magistrate, but Du Fu's own career had stalled. He was excited to hear of Li Bai's arrival in Luoyang. In his mind Bai was an august figure, not only because of his splendid verses and his role as an unofficial poet laureate, but also because of his fearlessness in confronting the servile, wicked top officials in Chang'an. Naturally, Du Fu felt nervous about meeting Li Bai in person. Would Bai greet him as a fellow poet? Would Bai, who hadn't given a damn about the powerful men at court, look down on him? Would his own eagerness make Li Bai consider him a sycophant of sorts? Du Fu couldn't stop wondering.

Nonetheless, he decided to go to Luoyang and attend the party held in Bai's honor. Du Fu did have a growing literary reputation to lean on, with a handful of poems well received by other poets and men of letters. The previous year the essayist Li Yong and the poet Wang Han had written him to express their admiration for his poetry. This was the same Li Yong who had never responded to Li Bai's request for an official recommendation two decades before when he had governed Yu Prefecture back in Sichuan (though few people knew of this incident). So Du Fu reasoned that he should not feel too diffident in front of Li Bai.

The party, held in a fancy restaurant downtown, its front door hung with large lanterns, was attended by dozens of guests. Du Fu was surprised to find Bai wearing a black gown made of hemp cloth and a white headscarf of the same fabric—they were the typical garments of a Daoist hermit, plain and unworldly. The banquet was so noisy that Li Bai could only exchange a few words with Du Fu. But Bai was polite and even said he admired Du Fu's poem

"Gazing Afar from Mount Tai." Du Fu was delighted—at heart he knew that was his masterpiece.

The next day he called on Li Bai at his inn. Bai was more clearheaded than the previous night and even mentioned the two lines by Du Fu: "I should ascend the summit, / Below which all mountains will appear smaller." Du Fu was flattered and moved. The two men talked and talked, each about the frustrations and difficulties they had encountered over the years. Du Fu had gone through a similar pattern to that of Li Bai's early years and shared his disgust at the notorious courtiers Li Linfu and Gao Lishi and their like. Although he had never met them in person, Du Fu knew how they had blocked the way of young scholars not backed by them and how, if their own men did not pass the exam, they would lie to the emperor, saying none of the examinees was exceptional this year and there was no need to appoint anyone, just to save positions for their men. Now, as he and Bai talked, Du Fu felt that the distance between them was closing. They also discussed the art of poetry. Du Fu worshiped Li Bai's imagination and energy, bold and unstoppable like an overflowing river. Li Bai in turn was impressed by Du Fu's learning and swift perception and was pleased to hear that Du Fu's grandfather was the well-known poet Du Shenyan.

Although they admired each other, their approaches to poetry were quite different. Li Bai's lines are fresh and supple but also full of iron whereas Du Fu's are neat, tightly wrought, and somewhat austere. Unlike the Daoist Bai, Du Fu was a Confucianist, his imagination and moral vision confined within the social and dynastic order, his mind occupied by the empire and history. As the two men continued to converse, Bai appeared worried about his safety and mentioned several times that since he was a Daoist, his enemies in the capital could hardly harm him anymore. He and Du Fu disliked the noisy gatherings in Luoyang and wished they could have spent some quiet days together, but both were called by other plans. In the future, it might be possible to reunite: Du Fu was going to Kaifeng in the fall to pay his respects at his maternal grandmother's grave and have an epitaph carved on a stone for her, and Li Bai was fond of Kaifeng's Liang Park. But for now Bai needed to find a Daoist master in the north who could recommend him for the fellowship induction. The two of them agreed to meet in the Kaifeng area in a few months.

Although neither of them could have known it, this meeting of the two great poets was a monumental event in Chinese literature. Over the centuries, scholars and writers have speculated about this occasion—their paths would go on to cross repeatedly for another six months, then diverge. Poet Wen Yiduo (1899–1946), a graduate of the School of the Art Institute of Chicago, describes the event as "the sun and the moon meeting in the clear sky," "a sign of heavenly blessing, worshiped by people on earth."[1] Though hyperbolic, Wen's words illustrate the magnificence of that encounter to the Chinese poets who would come after them.

Despite the age difference between Li Bai and Du Fu, the congeniality initiated their lifelong friendship. Du Fu was deeply attached to Li Bai, even in awe of him, perhaps because his own father had died long before, or because Bai possessed a free spirit more commonly expected in a younger romantic poet. Du Fu firmly believed that Bai's poetry would "last forever and surpass others'." In total, although they met only three times, all within a single year, Du Fu wrote fifteen poems for Li Bai. He even composed two poems about his dreams of Bai. He celebrated Li Bai's art and lamented his fate with lines like these: "Ah, Bai's poetry has no peer. / With a floating manner he thinks how to stand out"; "His brush starts to inscribe, arousing wind and rain, / And his poems can make ghosts and gods weep"; "Your gift is too great for you to succeed / While your virtues are too noble for others to share." By comparison, Li Bai—likely due in part to his Daoist mentality—was more understated in his affections. He did compose several poems for his younger friend, but the verses are not as deep-felt as Du Fu's for him. In "Teasing Du Fu," he writes:

飯顆山前逢杜甫　頭戴笠子日卓午
借問別來太瘦生　總為從前作詩苦

《戲贈杜甫》

At the top of Fanke Mountain I run into Du Fu,
He dons a straw hat in the vertical sunbeams.
I ask him why he's thinner than we last met.
He says he's been working hard on his poems.

Indeed, unlike Li Bai, who was a master of ease and spontaneity, Du Fu always labored over his poetry. He made himself a principle of composition: "After drafting a new poem, I must keep humming it. / If the lines don't surprise, I will revise them as long as I'm alive." Their arts reflected their personalities—one free-spirited and unbound, the other prudent and disciplined.

When Li Bai and Du Fu arrived in Kaifeng in the fall, they were joined by another poet, Gao Shi (704–765), who lived nearby. Gao Shi was known for his robust poetry about frontier life, especially the hardship of the soldiers' lives and the suffering and bitterness of the peasants. He wrote in an esoteric, masculine style that distinguished him from his contemporaries. Li Bai didn't seem to admire the formality of Gao's verses, but he liked the manly confidence of his work and also respected his swordsmanship. Gao Shi was gallant, dignified, clearheaded. One of his poems, written for a musician friend and titled "Farewell to Dong Da," was quite popular as a song: "Yellow clouds shade the white sun for hundreds of miles / While the north wind is blowing away geese with flying snow. / Do not worry about having no friends on the way. /

Under heaven who doesn't recognize your name?" Gao Shi seemed to adore Li Bai, both for his original poetic style and his defiant acts in the capital. He wrote, "Duke Li has an innate grandeur. / He's strapping with a straight back. / His mind wanders through different worlds / While his robe and hat fit the current fashion here."[2] It is interesting that Gao Shi viewed Bai's Daoist garb as something fashionable. Li Bai empathized with Gao Shi, sharing his pain and frustration. Both came from modest backgrounds— Bai's father was a merchant and Gao Shi's father a peasant. In his childhood, Shi had even gone begging in villages and towns. Neither of them had been able to access the civil-service examination and had had to bumble around seeking opportunities, though by now Gao Shi, like Bai, seemed to have lost his interest in an official career. Ironically, he would go on to hold a position in the central government higher than any other Tang poet and would embody the pinnacle of a literary man's political success.

The three poets rode to Liang Park on horseback. There they composed poems for the occasion and recited other verses they had written recently. The immense park held many historic sites and abounded with wild animals. After wandering the area, they rode to Chang Prefecture to hunt in Da-ze Marshland. Whenever Li Bai shot down a goose, he would celebrate, kicking his heels in a little jig. By comparison, Gao Shi was a more skilled hunter, patient and cool, and didn't show much excitement over his kills. Bai was impressed to find Du Fu a capable archer, able to shoot accurately even while riding. Once Bai became so carried away when landing a goose that he rode after the wounded bird for miles until his horse galloped into a neighboring town. Du Fu and Gao Shi, afraid he might get lost, caught up and found him already drunk in a wineshop.

Despite Li Bai's carefree exterior, Du Fu gradually came to sense his pain and agitation. At night, he heard Bai sigh and even shout in his dreams. Bai was troubled by his memories of the palace and worried that his powerful enemies would be after him. In his poem "For Li Bai," Du Fu addresses him directly: "Every day you drink and sing with abandon. / You show all defiance and spunk, but for whose sake?" He felt for his friend and worried about Bai's mental state. Nevertheless, the three poets had a grand time, which Du Fu remembered fondly and described in his poem "Expressing What Is on My Mind":

憶與高李輩　論交入酒壚
兩公壯藻思　得我色敷腴
氣酣登吹臺　懷古視平蕪
芒碭雲一去　雁鶩空相呼

《遣怀》

I remember being with Gao Shi and Li Bai.
We went into a tavern to converse nonstop.
They both had exuberant thoughts
That made me flush with happiness.
Still hung over, we went up a legendary terrace,
Where we thought about ancient times
And gazed at the vast grassland.
When the old clouds wandered away
Geese and ducks were still crying.

After the three men had roamed the lands of Liang and Song (modern Henan Province), Du Fu and Gao Shi parted ways with Li Bai, though they would later meet him in Yangzhou, where Bai's home was. The three of them planned to spend more time together in the Lu area before the cold weather set in. Having said farewell to his friends, Li Bai went north to make arrangements for his Daoist induction.

LIFE IN TRANSITION

The following year—from the winter of 744 to the spring of 746—has often been skipped or sparingly depicted by Li Bai's biographers, mainly because few written records of his life from this period have survived. However, 745 seems to have been a crucial year for Bai and is deserving of more attention.

Shangqiu, Henan, where Li Bai, Du Fu, and Gao Shi had just parted ways, was less than two hundred miles from Bai's family home in Yanzhou, Shandong. Bai could have made a trip to see his children in just a handful of days, but instead he traveled to Hebei to request help from a Daoist master for his induction. The master, Gai Huan, agreed to recommend him and wrote a letter on his behalf to Grand Master Gao Rugui in Jinan, the head of the Daoist society in the Qi region who was in charge of the induction there. Li Bai had known Gai Huan for some years and was delighted that he was willing to be his endorser, which was required for the induction. Master Gao Rugui then planned the schedule for Bai's induction and agreed to guide him through the process, which would be elaborate and arduous. Why didn't Bai go home to see his children first? Why was he so tardy in returning to his family? We can only surmise that he must have held deep trust in the woman of Lu and understood that his children were in safe, caring hands.

After visiting Hebei, Bai finally returned to Yanzhou to join his family. By this time his pockets were well lined with the cash given him by the emperor and by prefectures and counties along the way. He also brought with him plenty of gifts. His daughter, Pingyang, and son, Boqin, were thrilled to see their father return as a rich man. By now, his pageboy Dansha and his wife had left to start their own household elsewhere, and so they were no longer with the Li family.

Soon Du Fu and Gao Shi arrived, and the three poets resumed their drinking and sightseeing. Together they visited Stone-Gate Mountain twenty miles north of Confucius's hometown, Qufu. Eventually they reached Jinan, the city of one hundred springs, where Li Bai was to have his Daoist induction. The ceremony was long, complex, and physically challenging. Many inductees did not make it through the process, and so Du Fu and Gao Shi wanted to be there to support their friend.

During the ceremony, the inductees were required to stay for seven days on different levels of a terrace constructed for the occasion, eating only meager vegetarian meals, most of the time with their hands tied behind them. In addition to reciting scriptures and chanting incantations, they had to remain on their knees and were not permitted to stand until the end of the day, when they could take a quick towel bath on the spot.

If an inductee went through the induction successfully, he would become a member of the Daoist society, fully recognized as a holy man who no longer held any earthly attachment and was no longer subject to suffering or grief. By the custom of the time, neither the powerful nor the rich could harm such a man, because he existed in the religious order and posed no threat to anyone. For Li Bai, the induction was a way to escape his enemies, enter a domain of peace and security, and start another life.

Now, after four days' arduous training and instruction, the last and hardest part of the induction began. Led by his master, Li Bai joined dozens of other inductees on the terrace, surrounded by

ropes and yellow banners. The master wore a long black cloak and
raised a rapier to direct the disciples, who appeared like criminals
on their knees with their hands tied behind their backs. After reciting Daoist mantras and lines from the *Tao Te Ching*, they were
ordered to move around the terrace. The routine was repeated
several times a day. The first two days went by without incident,
though by the end of the second day Li Bai was already pale and
exhausted and a little delirious. From the third day on, the inductees, one after another, began to faint, some passing out from sun-
stroke. Many became too depleted to remain on their knees any
longer and were carried away into the tents pitched in a pine wood
nearby. Strong-willed, Li Bai managed to keep himself from los-
ing his mind and balance. His friends weren't permitted to go up
the terrace to help him, and he had to endure the fatigue, pain,
hunger, thirst, and scorching sun alone. Dehydrated yet drenched
in sweat, he couldn't help groaning when he chanted incantations
with the remaining inductees. The master, donning a black skull-
cap, ascended the terrace more often to encourage them to bear
with the final part of the ceremony. Drums, cymbals, and gongs
boomed and clashed and clanged more frequently now. From time
to time Bai hallucinated, his vision blurred, but he managed to
stay on his knees to the very end.

When the master called him to receive the certificate, Bai was
already in a state of semiconsciousness and hardly able to get on
his feet. He couldn't hear clearly the instructions the master told
him. But they were the same words that every new member was to
repeat after the leader: "All Daoist fellows must regard the Dao as
Father, the divine as Mother, the emptiness as Teacher, Nature as
Friend. . . . You must be careful with your words, moderate with
food, more diligent in physical training, abstain from all desires
so that you can preserve the purity of your complexion and let
your strong body last forever."[1] Two young disciples supported
Bai, holding his arms, as the master handed him the certificate,

a piece of white silk inscribed with words. Bai could no longer lift his hands, so one of the young men helped him, tying the silk around his upper arm.

Now Bai had become a Daoist fellow. For the newly inducted, this was a turning point in their lives. For some, such an induction also meant practical gains in the future. An inducted Daoist was exempt from taxes and corvées and could obtain wealth and recognition from believers. His livelihood was secured. Of course, Bai was much more earnest than other inductees and sincerely aspired to a spiritual ascent. He would not exploit the system, which the central government had tried to take control of lest too many men get inducted and become tax evaders.

After the induction, he slept for days to recuperate. Some scholars believe that Bai, who was already forty-four, never fully recovered from that tormenting ceremony. Still, he was happy about his success, which he felt enabled him to finally turn a new page in his life and become more independent.

It happened that Jinan City's vice mayor, Li Zhifang, was a friend of Du Fu's and Gao Shi's. He had just erected a large bridge in a nearby suburb and was preparing to hold a days-long celebration. An admirer of Li Bai, he invited the three poets, along with other local literary figures, to the party and banquet. Among the guests was Li Yong, Zhifang's uncle, who had refused to help Li Bai back in Sichuan more than two decades before. At the time, Li Yong had been impressed by the energy and audacity of Bai's writing but unnerved by the young man's arrogance and wild vision. Now Li Yong was an old man with white hair and bleary eyes, but he knew so much about Li Bai—his contempt for the machinations of court officials, his resignation from the Imperial Academy, and above all his extraordinary poetry—that he approached the poet and bowed deeply. He loved Bai for his arrogance and irreverence, which he, as a man of letters, felt he could share at heart.

Bai recognized him and immediately returned the bow. They struck up a conversation, reminiscing about their previous meeting. Li Yong said he still had the poems Bai had presented to him back in Yu Prefecture. A little sheepish, he went on to say that Bai's reproach about his mistreatment of him had turned out to be justified. They both tipped back their heads and laughed. Bai in turn admitted that he had been too brash back then. Then he added that he hadn't changed much. They both laughed again. Li Yong told Bai that the two of them had common enemies at court: Zhang Ji and Li Linfu. Because they had disparaged him, Li Yong had been appointed to a remote prefecture, even though he was very senior and should have been promoted to the rank of chief minister long before. He combed his thin hair with his fingers and said he was too old now to care about positions and fame.

Bai was still weak from the seven-day induction and quickly became drunk at the party. Du Fu and Gao Shi took him back to the inn where they were all staying and kept him resting in bed. Gao Shi had some local friends, so he went out to see them during the day and then decided to head south and wander around the Chu region. Du Fu and Li Bai would stay for a while longer. At the mayor's party they had met a local squire named Fan Shi, whose village was near Jinan City. Fan had invited the two poets to come and visit his home, so Li Bai and Du Fu decided to call on him.

They were unfamiliar with the roads and had to climb hills and cross valleys as they continued northeast. At one point Li Bai fell into a bush and emerged covered with burrs, his hat lost, irretrievable. He tried to brush off the burrs but couldn't, so Du Fu began to help pick them off. Bai stopped him and said they shouldn't bother about the burrs. In this state the two men barged into Fan Shi's farmhouse unannounced, and it took the host a while to recognize them. Then he broke into laughter and ordered his servants to cook a chicken, a duck, and cured pork with vegetables from his garden and to pour the sorghum liquor he himself had made. In his front yard was a large flat stone, on which Bai stretched out, barefoot and waggling his toes. The three men chatted and soon began to chant poems of their own and of the ancient poets. Toward evening both Li Bai and Du Fu became tipsy.

That night Li Bai and Du Fu slept in the same bed, sharing a large thin quilt, their feet entangled. In a corner of the room a coil of wormwood burned slowly to repel mosquitoes. Outside the window, a waning crescent moon hung above the treetops as insects trilled in the distance. Li Bai and Du Fu slept soundly until cockcrow. They stayed at Fan Shi's home for more than ten days and slept the same way every night.

Because they shared one quilt, some have surmised there might have been a homosexual relationship between them. The American poet Carolyn Kizer even dramatizes this episode in a poem she wrote in the voice of Du Fu:

> *My lord, how beautifully you write!*
> *May I sleep with you tonight?*
> *Till I flag, or when you wilt,*
> *We'll roll up drunken in one quilt.*
>
> *In our poems, we forbear*
> *To write of kleenex or long hair*
> *And how the one may fuck the other.*
> *We're serious artists, aren't we, brother?*
>
> "TU FU TO LI PO"

In fact, it is unlikely that there was any erotic element to their relationship. Up until recent decades, it was common for Chinese friends of the same sex to share a bed and a quilt without any carnal inclination, especially in cold weather when it was better to sleep together to keep warm. Actually, even in our time such a practice isn't unusual. The current top Chinese leaders Xi Jinping and Wang Qishan once shared a bed and a quilt in the Shaanxi countryside. This episode in the two politicians' lives is often mentioned by the Chinese media as proof of their long friendship. For his part, Du Fu was very proud of such an experience, writing, "Li Bai throws out many great lines, / Which show how prodigious his gift is. / I too am a guest in Shandong / And love him like a brother. / When we are drunk, we share a quilt in the autumn night, / And we also walk around hand in hand during the day."[2]

Before they left the village, they each presented the host with a poem written for him. Afterward they spent a few more days together, visiting sites near Li Bai's home in Yanzhou. Before Du Fu, as planned, left for the capital to take the civil-service examination again, Li Bai threw a farewell party for him. He also wrote these lines, depicting the two friends climbing a mountain near Bai's home:

醉別復幾日　登臨遍池臺
何時石門路　重有金樽開
秋波落泗水　海色明徂徠
飛蓬各自遠　且盡手中杯

《魯郡東石門送杜二甫》

Only a few days are left,
So together we climb up to face the endless pools.
When will we get on the stone path again
Toward the gate up on the mountain
And raise our cups up there?
The autumn waves spread on the Si River,

An ocean view brightens Julai Mountain.
Like tumbling weeds, we will go separate ways,
So for now let us drain our cups.

"SEEING DU FU OFF IN EASTERN LU PREFECTURE"

Li Bai cherished Du Fu as a devoted friend, though the younger man was still an obscure poet, his poetry known only to a small circle of readers, and would remain so all his life. Bai could tell that this might be their final meeting. Du Fu too seemed to sense that their paths might not cross again. The few months he had spent with Bai affected him profoundly—it was an unforgettable time in his life, which he would recall fondly time and again. Even in his last years he would dream of Li Bai, who had died by then, and would compose poems about him as if the light shed by Bai had never left him.

Their friendship did not affect Bai as deeply; Du Fu seemed to leave his thoughts once they had parted company. In spite of his gregariousness, Li Bai was at his core a loner, a solitary figure in Chinese poetry, like a blazing star whose light also comes from a deep indifference to the world below.

Now, what should Bai do with the money he had brought back from the capital? His partner, the woman of Lu, must have urged him not to squander the gold on drinks and parties. So when it was warm enough in the spring, he had their house renovated and bought some farmland, which was added to the land allocated to him by the local government. For centuries the government issued land to individuals, each receiving several acres, as a way to keep the land productive so that taxes could be levied. We do not know how many acres Li Bai owned, but it must have been a good number. The land was meant to be the basis of his property so that it could support his family when he went on the road again.

Bai also built a bar of his own, which he named the First Wine

House Under Heaven. In spite of its striking name, the place was modest, with just a few tables in the main room, but it sat on a slope that commanded a full vista of the landscape. One could see the nearby Si River and the faraway Wen, which flowed like a ribbon flickering in the wind. Mount Tai also loomed in the distance to the northeast.

In addition to hosting friends and relatives in the place, Bai sometimes lived there. In his own words, he wished he could be "always drunk without the need to sober up." His failure in the capital still tormented him—he knew that his political career had no clear way forward, so he wanted to invest his energy and talent in another, more spiritual path. Daoism, as the state religion, dominated the land: all over China, Daoist shrines had been built, and the emperor himself was psychologically addicted to the so-called pills of immortality.

Li Bai soon resumed his practice of making the elixir of life, which he believed would enable him to ascend to the world of divinity and live forever. He celebrated this illusion in his poetry. "If I come by the pills for immortality / I will fly away to the divine world" ("Visiting Mount Tai" [4]); "If I grow wings / I'd lounge in the sphere of paradise forever" ("Gazing up on Heavenly Terrace at Dawn"). The elixir was intended not only to prolong physical life, but also to produce fleeting moments of spiritual transcendence.

Throughout his adult life, Bai had taken such pills regularly, even becoming addicted to them, but now he wished to produce them himself. It was a complex process, and an expensive one. The pills were made from many precious materials: gold, silver, pearl, bright jade, mica, cinnabar. At a late stage of the firing in a special stove, costly medicinal herbs also needed to be added: wolfberries, lilyturf, red celery, sealwort, caterpillar fungus. The equipment required was elaborate and extensive: stoves, kilns, fine sieves, jade knives, earthen cauldrons, iron pots, grindstones, mirrors, cooking vessels, brass basins, bamboo pots. What's more, there was no way to evaluate the quality of the product. Some graded the pills by their color and glossiness, but there was no empirical basis for such an assessment. Far from extending his life, Li Bai's regular consumption of the pills might well have ruined his health. His drinking, too, may have harmed him even apart from the alcohol itself—most wine containers in ancient China were made of alloys, which usually were heavy with lead.[3]

Despite everything, however, Li Bai persisted in making the elixir and even styled himself as a master of the alchemic art. He often experienced hallucinations induced by the pills, which were believed to be a sign of their potency. He searched for minerals and herbs deep in the mountains. When he began the firing, he would sit in front of the stove for many days. He rarely produced the desired quality product, though he always obtained the most expensive honey available to make the pills glossy. After the minerals were fired and reduced to a whitish powder, he would sample the result and then suffer diarrhea and palpitation. Nonetheless, he never gave up. He resolved "to make the elixir of life and shun the world for good" ("Ancient Songs 5").

The use of the pills was prevalent among Tang poets, many of whom developed addictions to the pills and even died from them. The poet Bai Juyi meditated on such "magical pills," reasoning, "Red sand is cheap like dirt. / Why should it be burned into pills?" In his poem "Thinking of My Old Friends," he laments the deaths of his fellow poets who had become obsessed with pills of immortality, which at the time most people still believed to be beneficial to their health: "Han Yu, eating sulfur, / Once ill, could not recover. / Yuan Zhen burned stones / But died before he was old. / Du Mu got the secret recipes of the panacea / And would no longer touch any meat." In fact, five emperors in the Tang dynasty died of poisoning from the pills. Thereafter, more and more people began to see their poisonous nature, and they gradually went out of fashion.

We cannot say how accomplished Li Bai was as a maker of the elixir, but he must have learned a good deal from his Daoist friends such as Yuan Danqiu, who were master makers of the pills and possessed knowledge of alchemy.

During this period, Li Bai also wrote a long treatise on his beliefs, titled *Book of the Dao,* but the work is lost and we know nothing about its contents. Even if we had it now, few might be able to understand his imaginative thoughts.[4]

18

ON THE ROAD AGAIN

The immortality pills and the drinking caused Li Bai to become ill in the summer of 746. For several months he was bedridden and often coughed violently. During the fall he often had fantastic dreams: in them, he wandered to distant places and even to the celestial spheres, where he encountered deities and witnessed splendid views of heaven. He recorded his visions in the poem "Singing of My Visit to Mount Tianlao in My Dreams." The poem, one of his most celebrated longer pieces, presents the majestic hills and grand architectural constructions on the celestial mountain and his tours through its landscape. The poet describes himself as a divine visionary who belongs to the heavenly space and is welcomed by deities. These verses are meant to demonstrate his yearning to transcend worldly existence and strife. Li Bai was still tormented by his resignation in the capital and struggled to accept it. The last few lines of the poem express this inner struggle:

世間行樂亦如此　古來萬事東流水
別君去兮何時還　且放白鹿青崖間　須行即騎訪名山
安能摧眉折腰事權貴　使我不得開心顏

《夢遊天姥吟留別》

Human happiness is similar to those dreams.
Since ancient times
Everything has been like the flowing water
That will never return.
Friends, I am leaving now,
But when will I come back?
For now I've sent the white stag in the green mountain.
When I travel, I will ride it to legendary hills.
How could I drop my eyes and bow
To the rich and powerful,
Not letting myself smile and laugh at will!

Li Bai told his friends about his desire to travel, but they urged him to wait until he was fully recuperated—at least until the spring. His family tried to dissuade him as well, but to no avail. By now his estate was somewhat substantial, with many acres of farmland and at least two houses, but he didn't feel attached to his properties. He wanted to visit the sites haunted by recluses and holy men. He longed to wander in unworldly lands like a semi-deity, a *xian*.

Realizing that Bai could not be persuaded to stay, or even to delay his journey, his friends threw a farewell dinner party for him. At the gathering he presented them with "Singing of My Visit to Mount Tianlao in My Dreams," which he signed "As a Keepsake." Then he set out, despite the cold weather and his frail health.

He headed south. His first stop was Suiyang, a town in Liang Park in Henan, where he and his friend Cen Xun had once planned to meet. It was snowing heavily when he arrived, and he soon learned that Cen Xun was preparing to depart for Minggao Mountain, more than two hundred miles to the west. Tired of the government job that he had taken two years before, he longed to become a recluse in the mountain. He had just sold most of his belongings and was working to wrap up his affairs so that he could get to Minggao Mountain before the end of the year.

Although Bai's arrival took him by surprise, Cen Xun was over-joyed to see him. The two friends went to a tavern, where over dinner they vented their anger and despair. Bai composed a long poem for Cen Xun. The verses lament the harsh landscape of his friend's destination, symbolizing the danger and hardship of the political life that Cen Xun was about to leave behind. Bai had never been to Minggao Mountain, but he described it imagina-tively in his poem. In the second half, "Song of Minggao Moun-tain, Seeing Cen Xun Off," Bai stacks up analogies that evoke the ugliness of the official arena: "Chickens swarm together to grab food / While a phoenix has to stand away and alone. / Earthworms dare to laugh at dragons / And fish eyes can pass for pearls." Bai shared his friend's desire to have cranes as his companions as he wandered hills and waters.

From Suiyang he traveled farther south, mostly by boat, and soon arrived at the city of Yangzhou. It was mid-March now—spring in the air, orioles warbling, white viburnum flowers scat-tered on shrubs like butterflies—but the charm and warmth of the place didn't cheer him. He purposely avoided others. His return to Yangzhou must have been deeply emotional: this was where, two decades before, he had been stranded, sick and penniless, and his friend Meng Rong had him nursed back to health. At that time—despite his poverty, homesickness, and obscurity—Bai had been full of lofty spirit and aspirations, believing he would grow into a literary and political giant. It was here, lying in his sickbed, that he had composed "Reflection in a Quiet Night," the masterpiece that had made him famous. Now he was staying in an inn alone, exhausted and ashamed. Yet he couldn't help writing once more about this city, which occupied a singular place in his memory. In the verses he produced, "Farewell to My Friends in Guangling (Yangzhou)," he remembered the joy and adventure that he and his friends had once found here. They all believed that Bai would rise high enough to reach the palace. Indeed he had. But what now? As he wrote, "I rode a tiger but dared not dismount / And soared with a dragon that suddenly fell out of the sky."

He had now become clear about the purpose of this trip. These days his thoughts often turned to his onetime mentor at court, He Zhizhang. Bai knew that the old poet had retired to his hometown, Kuaiji (modern Shaoxing); he wanted to go see him, but he would travel at his own pace and let the journey ahead unfold naturally.

Soon he arrived in Nanjing and spent the entire spring there. Although very fond of the city, he again avoided others and kept to himself. When he had first come to Nanjing twenty-one years before, he had written a slew of songs for singers and dancers. This body of work had founded his reputation as a poet who celebrated good wine and pretty courtesans. Now, at age forty-six, he no longer cared about female charms or lighthearted songs. Instead, on the bank of the Yangtze he strolled alone for a long while and composed a solemn poem:

鳳凰臺上鳳凰遊　鳳去臺空江自流
吳宮花草埋幽徑　晉代衣冠成古丘
三山半落青天外　二水中分白鷺洲
總爲浮雲能蔽日　長安不見使人愁

《登金陵鳳凰臺》

On the Phoenix Terrace phoenixes once roamed,
But now the birds are gone
And only an empty terrace spreads on the flowing river.
Grass and flowers cover the silent paths at the Wu Palace
While the crowns and gowns of the Ji dynasty
Are all buried in their ancient graves.

Three hills stand beyond the clear sky
As a band of water divides the Isle of White Heron.
Hovering clouds can always block the sun
And the absence of Chang'an gives me grief.

"ASCENDING THE PHOENIX TERRACE IN JINLING"

This poem, written in regulated verse with seven-character lines, is one of Li Bai's best. The restrictive form was not generally one of his strengths, but this is an extraordinary exception. With this poem, he had now produced a masterpiece in every poetic form of his time. Two decades before, Bai had been so awestruck by Cui Hao's regulated poem on the wall of Yellow Crane Tower that he declined to write anything there himself, knowing he would only suffer by comparison. But now he had grown into a poet capable of excelling in any form. The poem is as good as Cui Hao's, even if there are still traces of influence (its ending is clearly derived from Cui Hao's closing couplet). Some even consider it superior to Cui Hao's, though others have pointed out minor defects in its versification. In spirit, however, the poem is stronger and deeper than Cui's—"the clouds" and "the sun" (Son of Heaven) allude to the political situation in Chang'an, adding a historical dimension that Cui's verses lack. Bai was aware of the transient nature of dynastic splendor and glory, embodied here by the deserted Wu Palace and the interred Ji gowns and crowns. Far away from court, Li Bai would no longer be able to return to the political heart of the country, and such a loss filled him with anguish. The last line shows his longing for the capital, which had never left his mind ever since he had resigned. Yet by now his art had deepened with maturity—his poetry was beginning to possess a kind of gravity absent from his early work. Despite his continued desire to soar to the heights of political power and even into a celestial world, his art was becoming more earthbound, more rooted in reality.

All the chronologies of Li Bai's poems agree that in the summer of 747 he arrived at Yunyang (present-day Danyang, Jiangsu), a town east of Nanjing, where he would visit Heng Mountain. Outside the town, on the canal, he came upon a group of laborers pulling a barge loaded with an enormous rock, quarried as a treasure stone and an article of tribute. The sun was scorching, and sweat glistened on the backs of the men. Even cicadas in the treetops sounded tired and thirsty. As the men trudged past him with the barge, they broke into a work song. Bai had seen such trackers— boat pullers—many times before along the Yangtze, but had never paid much attention to them, let alone been moved to sing of their plight. But now, standing on the canal's bank and gazing at those struggling men with bent shoulders and shaved heads that could make their sweating more endurable, his eyes misted over. His heart ached for them, and he composed this poem:

雲陽上征去　兩岸饒商賈
吳牛喘月時　拖船一何苦
水濁不可飲　壺漿半成土
一唱都護歌　心摧淚如雨
萬人系磐石　無由達江滸
君看石芒碭　掩淚悲千古

《丁都護歌》

Going up north from the town of Yunyang,
I've seen many rich merchants on the riverbanks.
In the Wu land even buffalos pant hard in the dog days.
Look, how hard the laborers are pulling a barge.
The muddy water is undrinkable,
Every kettle half filled with mud after being boiled.
From far away comes the work song the men are chanting.
It breaks my heart, my tears flowing.

Thousands of men quarry huge stones,
But they can hardly ship them to the riverside.
Look at the giant stones scattered around—
The endless sorrow makes me weep.

"SONG OF DINGDUHU"

This is another one of his masterpieces and marks a new development in his art. Beginning in 747, Li Bai's poetry began to register more of the dark aspects of common people's lives, as though he was becoming a bard of the land. However unhappy he himself may have been, he couldn't stop singing, and his songs echoed the bitterness and suffering of the people at the bottom of society. As a result, the following years saw the peak of his poetic art. His voice grew deeper and more resonant as he produced verses full of gravity and significance. He was no longer a romantic poet only capable of making popular songs: more and more his art spoke of his country and time.

Finally he arrived at Kuaiji, where he planned to see his old mentor; but to his dismay, he learned that He Zhizhang had passed away three years before. The old poet's two-story house was half-deserted now, though lotus flowers still bloomed in the limpid pond and willows still wavered in the breeze. At the sight of the flowers that Zhizhang must have loved so much, remembering the happy times they had spent together in the capital, both of them drinking with abandon, Bai became overwhelmed. How he loved that old man! He went to pay his respects at Zhizhang's grave under a large cypress. Later, drinking alone in the town, he wrote two short poems in memory of his beloved friend.

Bai proceeded east to the coast, but didn't reach the seaside. Instead, he climbed Tiantai Mountain, which the ancients had regarded as divine and which Li Bai believed to be a place free of earthly cares. This was a mountain he had often dreamed of. In fact, before setting out on the road at the end of 746, he had written in his poems that he wished to see this very mountain, the land inhabited by gods and spirits. Now he was here, but the place was far from what he had imagined—he found no deities but some coolies on the steep trail carrying goods with shoulder poles and bamboo baskets. Still, he loved the sight of the towering, gnarled pine trees standing along the trail that led to the summit. The view of an august temple moved him; the sound of a babbling brook and the sight of stone bridges over streams and gulches lifted his spirit. Without delay he climbed up to the summit. There he was struck by the magnitude of the view: the misty ocean in the east, the clouds in the west shading a chain of hills. This indeed was the so-called Peng-lai Land of *Xian,* but where were the deities? Bai knew that kings and emperors had visited this mountain in search of a paradise on earth, but none of them had ascended into the divine order as they earnestly pursued immortality—all met their ends in tombs built of earth and stones. Now as he gazed out at the vista, he felt somehow let down. His yearning to discover an ethereal domain had just been a fixture of fantasy. Pain and misery still stirred in his chest, sinking deeper into his being. He descended the mountain disillusioned.

He composed a poem about this experience. In it he talks about his inability to escape the dark, ugly world and find the celestial place that he dreamed of. He asks, "Don't you see the palaces and tombs have become ashes and dirt, / Which only shepherds come to scale? / Robbers and thieves snatched away the treasures, / But when did deities ever do something about it?" ("Climbing up a High Mountain and from Its Top Gazing at the Sea Far Away"). His mind was unable to let go of what he had witnessed in the capital, the center of evil in many eyes. He felt trapped, grounded on earth.

According to most of the Li Bai chronologies, in the spring of 748 he returned again to Nanjing, a city he loved, home to a vibrant literary scene. But his arrival was quiet and hardly noticed by others. He spent a good deal of time with a friend in the city who was known as Wang Twelve. Wang's full name and life have remained a mystery, but we do know that through this man Bai gradually learned about the numerous abuses of power that had occurred in recent years. The central government had manufactured many baseless cases against people, including some of Bai's friends, falsely accusing them of misdeeds or crimes and destroying their lives. There was his friend at the palace, Cui Zongzhi, the handsome man "like a jade tree in the breeze," who at first had been promoted for his role as a lead singer in the celebration of the canal that reached the capital (the waterway was vital for transporting grain). But within two years Cui's superior was unjustly charged with collaborating with foreign powers and thrown into prison. Everyone who had been involved in the celebration, down to the boat rowers, was seized and punished. Many were tortured to death; some committed suicide by swallowing poison. Thanks to his inconsequential post, Cui was merely banished to a small county south of Dongting Lake.

Then there was the tragedy of Li Yong, the older man whom Li Bai had met and befriended at the dinner party in Jinan after his Daoist induction. Because of Li Yong's fame as an essayist and his seniority in government administration, he was regarded as a rival by Li Linfu, the primary chancellor to the emperor (and an enemy of Bai's as well). Li Yong, as the governor of Beihai Prefecture, was fond of luxuries and somewhat careless in handling administrative affairs. Whenever possible, he would spend his time hunting in the wilderness or partaking in dinner parties. But he was unaware that his enemies were monitoring him, reporting his small misconducts to the evil powers at the emperor's side. Soon he was accused of spreading rumors against the royal family and disparaging the policies instituted by the central government. Li Linfu dispatched two lackeys to Beihai Prefecture, where they interrogated

Li Yong in the courthouse. The old man was outraged and protested openly even as they had him flogged with sticks. He cursed them until they beat him to death in front of his subordinates. A few of his colleagues were also implicated in the case, and they too were eliminated—killed or driven to suicide.

What shocked Li Bai most was the case of Marshal Wang Zhongsi, a loyal, peace-loving man whom Bai had held in high esteem. Bai remembered how at court Wang had opposed the emperor's plan to send an expeditionary army to Tufan to capture Stone Fort, believing that a site of such little strategic value was not worth sacrificing thousands of soldiers. But the emperor coveted the vast land west of the fort, which stretched north to the side of Qinghai Lake, and believed the small town could be a significant factor in future negotiations with Tufan. Because His Majesty was fond of Marshal Wang he didn't openly show his displeasure, but Li Linfu could read the emperor's intentions and later commenced the expedition himself. The court ordered Marshal Wang to lead the campaign. His troops fought bravely but suffered heavy casualties and were ultimately unable to take the stronghold, which was protected by high cliffs and steep gorges. Wang's failure enraged the emperor, who ordered him executed, but his assistant commander, Vice Marshal Geshu Han, managed to save Wang's life and resume the attack. For three months the Chinese soldiers charged up the fortress and finally took the town. To their horror, they found a mere four hundred defenders, who had surrendered only because they had run out of food and reinforcements. But this small number of troops had inflicted more than sixty thousand casualties on the Chinese army. A catastrophe, not a victory! Such an outcome shocked the whole of China, though nobody would dare to voice their discontent openly. Marshal Wang's warning about the cost in lives turned out to be true.

Nonetheless, Wang was thrown into jail and suffered interrogations and tortures. Then he was banished to Hanyang, where he soon died. Unlike most of the men of letters at the time, such as Wang Wei and Gao Shi, who praised the "victory," Li Bai was blunt about this disaster and even condemned Geshu Han, a man he had once admired. In a poem, he urged others, "Please don't learn from Geshu, who carried a sword and marched through Qinghai, / Attacking Stone Fort to earn a purple robe for himself" ("In Reply to Wang Twelve in a Cold Night While Drinking Alone"). The purple robe was a garment for Tang officials whose ranks were higher than the third. Bai here points out that Geshu sacrificed his troops for his own gain.

He was so incensed by the court's self-destructive actions that he composed the following poem in the form of a folk song:

去年戰桑乾源　今年戰蔥河道
洗兵條支海上波　放馬天山雪中草
萬里長征戰　三軍盡衰老
匈奴以殺戮爲耕作　古來唯見白骨黃沙田
秦家築城避胡處　漢家還有烽火然
烽火然不息　征戰無已時
野戰格鬥死　敗馬號鳴向天悲
烏鳶啄人腸　銜飛上掛枯樹枝
士卒塗草莽　將軍空爾爲
乃知兵者是兇器　聖人不得已而用之

《戰城南》

Last year we fought at the source of the Sanggan,
This year we are fighting along the Chong River.
We've washed our weapons on the waves of Lake Balkhash
And grazed our horses at Tianshan Mountain covered in snow.
Fighting thousands of miles west of home,
All the troops have grown feeble and old.
The Huns take killing as their livelihood

And since ancient times there have been only
Yellow deserts growing white bones.
The Qin people built the Great Wall against the barbarians,
On which the Han men lit beacons of war.
The fire hasn't stopped burning
As war has continued ever since.
Soldiers fell on battlegrounds
Where riderless horses neighed piteously to the sky.
Crows pulled out human guts
And hung them up on leafless branches.
Soldiers' blood spilt on wild grass,
Yet generals could gain nothing at all.
Please understand that war is a lethal thing,
Which the wise will not use unless they must.

"ZHAN CHENGNAN"

The last two lines are quoted from the *Tao Te Ching*. Although they sound somewhat intrusive, a bit dissonant from the verse's collective voice, they carry a message that was of primary importance to Li Bai. The geographic names are all places northwest of the frontier and give the impression of endless battlefields.

Li Bai couldn't contain his anger at China's military actions and spoke plainly for the soldiers. This was something new in his poetry, which by now had shed all the lightness and decadent touches of his early work. His voice had grown deeper, more resonant, and more emotional as his art became starker and more truthful.

Wang Twelve also told Bai of the fate of his poet friend Wang Changling, who, though exiled to the southern hinterland, had managed to return to the capital a few years before. The reason for his new banishment was vague—it was said only that he had been "careless about his demeanor," implying that he had offended someone powerful at court. Hearing that his friend had left for a small remote county in Longbiao (modern Hongjiang, Hunan), Bai wrote a short poem for his friend: "When poplars drop their catkins and cuckoos begin to sing, / I've heard you pass five streams to reach Longbiao. / I'm sending you my sorrowful heart through the bright moon, / Which flows with the wind to west of Yelang" ("On Hearing Wang Changling Demoted to Longbiao"). Li Bai couldn't know that years later, he himself would go the same way, banished to Yelang. There was no way for him to foresee that his own misfortune would be greater than his friend's; what he does in the poem is assure Changling that their friendship, pure like the bright moon, will outlast the hard times.

Stunned by the news of his friends' deaths and exiles, Bai tried to remain detached. He felt helpless, as he confessed to Wang Twelve: "I compose poems and essays at the north window, / But ten thousand words are not worth one cup of water" ("In Reply to Wang Twelve in a Cold Night While Drinking Alone"). So he boated on rivers and lakes, wearing his Daoist gown inside out so that people might not recognize him. He joined young men in hunting rabbits with hawks. He spent more time drinking and playing games with new friends in taverns and restaurants. But in the end, he couldn't keep his grief and anger at bay. He wrote satirical poems mocking corrupt officials and condemning them in various voices. He never signed his name to any verse that criticized the central government or the emperor. Nevertheless, people knew that the poems were Li Bai's.

NEW MARRIAGE

During his stay in Nanjing, Li Bai missed his children in Shandong. He often talked about them, and whenever a friend was traveling north, he would ask him to make an excursion to Yanzhou to see how his family was managing. A small number of his poems about his children have survived. One of the best-known is in the epistolary form and titled "To My Two Young Children in East Lu" (reproduced in part on pages 138–139 of this book). As we have seen, this poem is one of our primary sources of information on his daughter, Pingyang, and his son, Boqin. In it Bai tells us he has been away from his family for three years. This time—the duration of his absence from home—is mentioned in several other poems from this period. In "Seeing Xiao Thirty-First Off for Central Lu, Also About My Young Son Boqin," Li Bai asks his northbound friend to go to his home and see how his son is faring. Toward the end of the poem, he writes, "My home is nestled against Sandy Hill, / And it breaks my heart not having seen it for three years. / When you arrive you can recognize my son Boqin, / Who is old enough to drive a little carriage pulled by a white sheep." He loved Boqin, Little Bright Moon, who must have been quite young at that time, seven or eight. Bai had high hopes for him; the son loved his father too. Many years later, Li Hua, an uncle of Bai's who composed the poet's epitaph, praised Boqin: "[He is] steadfast in character and eloquent in debate. As his virtues continue to grow, he will surely achieve great fame." In fact, Boqin ended up taking a path completely different from his father's, leading a quiet life as a clerk in a salt station, though he did marry and have children.

We should keep in mind that during Bai's absence, the woman of Lu stayed with his children, caring for them and managing his estate. Her devotion to the family allowed Li Bai to sojourn in the south for years. The woman also had her own child with Li Bai, a much younger son called Poli, of whom we know very little. "Poli" was an exotic name, associated with Bai's native land in the western region beyond the border, and is a phonetic transcription of the Chinese word *boli,* meaning "glass." A treasure mostly from Persia, glass was highly valued in China at the time. The ancient historian Shen Yue (441–513), in his *Biography of Prince Liangsi,* records that during the reign of Emperor Songwen (407–453), a merchant brought back from Central Asia a large cube of glass one and a half feet long and wide, weighing more than forty pounds. When Emperor Songwen asked the price, the merchant's reply was a million strings of cash. Songwen consulted his courtiers, who believed that they couldn't pay such a price even if they emptied the royal treasury. Shen Yue states, "The whole country could not tell how valuable it was, and naturally no one would consider making an offer."[1] In fact, China had made glass at least a millennium before Li Bai's time, though on a very small scale, mainly in the form of marbles, necklace beads, and chess pieces, but it remained rare and precious until the eighteenth century when the technology of glass production from the West finally made inroads into China. Artisans began to make small glass containers like snuff bottles and vases. Such products were considered artwork, and glass was still a sought-after material similar to jade.

By giving his son such a name, Li Bai must have intended him to have a bright and transparent character, as the boy's nickname Tianran (Natural) indicated as well. There is also a second meaning to "Poli": the Poli Mountain in the western land that produced legendary horses, "divine steeds" said to be able to run three hundred miles a day. In either sense, precious glass or a great horse, "Poli" was associated with the land of Bai's birth.[2]

The poems about his children from this period do not mention Poli, however, because the boy was born out of wedlock. The culture of the time maintained a strict distinction between children born in a marriage and those born outside it. Their fathers usually would not mix them, just as Li Bai omits Poli when speaking of Pingyang and Boqin in his verses. This does not mean he ignored Poli; in fact, we might argue that Bai loved him no less than his older son. Seven years later, during the An Lushan rebellion, Li Bai expresses deep concern for Poli in a poem: "I am grieved over my son in northern Shandong, / And am separated from my old wife trapped south of Nanchang. / The whole family is scattered in wild grass / Unable to help each other in the calamity" ("Angry Words Submitted to Official Wei"). The poem was written in 757 when Bai was in prison and when Boqin was already in central Anhui, rescued from Shandong by Bai's disciple Wu E. The "son in northern Shandong" refers to Poli, who must have been with his mother, the woman of Lu.[3] Bai doesn't mention her in the poem; apparently she had left him and their partnership after more than a decade, perhaps because she could see no future for herself with him (Bai had by then remarried and so would never marry her). At most she could become his concubine, and Li Bai might not even give her such a role if it would upset his bride. Indeed, in the poem he worries about his new wife instead, who was somewhere south of Nanchang, unable to join him because of the war. But though the boy's mother might no longer be Bai's concern, he does think of Poli. Since Poli was too young to leave his mother, both mother and son vanished from Bai's life. That must have broken his heart.

Bai would not marry the woman of Lu mainly because of her humble and uneducated origins. His new wife, Miss Zong, was from an aristocratic family. Li Bai married her around 750 when he went to Kaifeng and revisited Liang Park. We don't know her personal name, so we can refer to her only by her family name. The Zongs had once been wealthy and powerful. Miss Zong's grandfather Zong Chu-ke had served as a chancellor at the Tang court three times (demoted and reinstated twice), though his work had been unremarkable and he had often become entangled in political intrigues. When the current Emperor Xuanzong had been only a prince and rebelled against the faction headed by Queen Wei, he'd had Chancellor Zong executed, together with the queen and her other collaborators. The family's reputation was tarnished by Zong Chu-ke's misconduct: taking bribes, using public funds to construct his own residence, ruthlessly wiping out his political rivals by having them killed or dismissed. In general, men of good repute would avoid marrying into such a family, but this didn't deter Li Bai. He loved his bride and even bragged about her aristocratic background. In a poem written for her, he says in her voice, "My family had a chancellor three times, / But we lost power and retreated to western Qin. / In our household there is still an old band, / Though the tunes they play sadden our new neighbors" ("For My Wife"). Throughout his life, Bai seemed strongly drawn to aristocracy and wealth, considering that his first wife was also from a fallen chancellor's family. As with his previous marriage, when he married Miss Zong he married into her family, unbothered by the stigma of the arrangement. He acted on his own terms.

However, it would be simplistic to say that Li Bai was a snob. There was genuine attraction and love between him and Miss Zong, who was a bright woman with an independent spirit. Above all, they shared the same religious faith. She was in fact more cultivated than Bai in Daoism and practiced it with great devotion, completely detached from fame, power, and other worldly pursuits. Her detachment made her more attractive to Bai. Legend holds that before they met, Miss Zong loved Li Bai's poem "Song in the Liangfu Tune," which he had inscribed on a wall in a restaurant, and so she bought the wall to prevent the poem from being erased. When Li Bai heard of this young woman who showed such attachment to his work, his interest was piqued. Although the story is most likely apocryphal, it might explain how Miss Zong became a loving wife to Bai and why he trusted her and was attached to her. While his first wife's family, the Xus, had hoped that Bai would achieve a high rank and resurrect the declining family, the Zongs did not expect anything from him. Miss Zong, at least twenty years Bai's junior, valued his talent and poetry, as did her brother Zong Jing.

Li Bai's love for his wife was also manifested in his respect for Miss Zong's Daoist master, Li Tengkong. Tengkong was the daughter of Bai's enemy Li Linfu, but unlike her father, she rejected the political machinations of Chang'an and practiced Daoism in Mount Lu for decades, eventually becoming a master respected by her fellow Daoists and beloved by the locals. She often treated the sick and helped the needy; many people depended on her services. The two women were very close, likely in part because they both came from the families of chancellors and were disillusioned with the world of power and wealth. Bai admired Tengkong and harbored no trace of resentment toward her, even encouraging his wife to study under her guidance. He once accompanied Miss Zong on a visit to Li Tengkong deep in the mountain. On the way, he composed two poems, one of them celebrating Tengkong:

君尋騰空子　應到碧山家
水春雲母碓　風掃石楠花
若愛幽居好　相邀弄紫霞。。。

《送內尋廬山女道士李騰空》

If you look for Master Tengkong
You should go to her cottage in the green mountain.
She is ladling water for making the elixir of life
While a breeze sways heather flowers nearby.
If you like her remote quiet dwelling,
You should stay here, caressing purple clouds with her.

"ACCOMPANYING MY WIFE TO LOOK FOR
MASTER LI TENGKONG IN MOUNT LU"

Li Bai's attitude toward Tengkong indicates that he valued another kind of existence in the religious order, one that could transcend social strife and hatred and violence. In fact, his love for his wife grew partly from her devoted pursuit of such an existence. Throughout his life, Bai had struggled to achieve religious transcendence, rarely able to enter and stay in the heavenly space. Miss Zong was more successful in this pursuit.

Because of her unusual spiritual strength, his wife might have gotten along well with Pingyang, though we are not certain if they ever met. Li Bai wrote to his friend Yuan Danqiu that both his daughter and his wife loved religious life: "My humble wife is fond of riding a phoenix / While my delicate daughter loves flying cranes" ("Inscribed at Hermit Yuan Danqiu's Residence in Mount Song"). Although in 750 Bai had remarried and founded a new household, his children still remained far away in Shandong. Why didn't they join him in his new home in Henan? The unusual circumstances of his marriage prevented such a reunion—he lacked his own home and income, though he had two houses and farmland in Shandong. Clearly Bai was at a disadvantage. Miss Zong's younger brother Zong Jing, who was a dear friend of Bai's, must have played a significant role in bringing Bai and his sister together, but Bai was still married into the household, so he didn't command the authority normally accorded a husband. In fact, his wife's younger sister stayed with the newlyweds, indicating that the family remained unchanged by the marriage and that Bai had to adapt to the Zongs. By custom, an unmarried daughter stayed with her parents, not her sister, but apparently Miss Zong's home remained the same and she could still let her younger sister stay with her and Bai. This explains why Bai didn't bring his children to Henan, although he missed them terribly.[4]

Despite his new marriage, which was based on mutual love, he still found it difficult to adapt to his wife's household, accustomed as he was to life on the road. In a way, we can say that his home was the road and the essence of his being existed in his endless wanderings. He would set out time and again in spite of his wife's objections, as though he was doomed to remain a guest in this world.

20

ON THE NORTHEASTERN FRONTIER

In the fall of 751, Li Bai received a letter from his old friend Yuan Danqiu. Danqiu had recently built a hermitage at Rock-Gate Mountain near Nanyang, a town in southwestern Henan. In the letter, he described the tranquility and beauty of his new surroundings and invited Li Bai to come and enjoy his new home with him. Bai decided to go, having stayed with the Zongs long enough that he was beginning to feel restless again. His friend's invitation rekindled his wanderlust.

Danqiu's cottage sat in the middle of a clearing on a gentle slope, beyond which birdcalls and monkeys' cries echoed deep in the mountain. It was even more secluded than his former dwelling at Mount Song. Li Bai loved this new place. He and Danqiu climbed nearby hills every morning. On their climbs they were often surrounded by patches of mist as if they were moving through clouds, their clothes damp from the moisture of the air. At night they would sit in front of the cottage to enjoy a cool breeze and the bright moon. Bai was so fond of this place that he began to tell Danqiu that he hoped to move here and live an eremitic life like his. Danqiu would tease him, replying that Bai had always talked about such a wish but could never act on it. He knew that Bai was a drifter by nature and couldn't settle down in one place for long. Bai laughed and admitted that nobody knew him better than Danqiu.

Now that Bai was again a married man, Danqiu pointed out, even if he wanted to settle in a mountain he would have to persuade his wife to come with him. But Bai was certain that she would love such a life. She was devoted to her Daoist practice; her family had seen great vicissitudes of power and fortune in recent decades and was unwilling to be involved in politics again. In a way, her faith was why she had been willing to marry Bai, an idle drifter but a Daoist fellow. By now her family's estates were nearly gone—only a few dilapidated eateries and wine houses were left in the area of Liang Park—so she often thought of moving. If her brother Zong Jing hadn't urged her to stay on, she might have left long before.

Seeing the earnestness of Bai's plan, Danqiu began to join him in looking for a site where Bai and his wife might build a house. They decided on a spot within a stone's throw of Danqiu's cottage, and Bai cleared the grass and bushes to make it look like a lot. They made sure that no one owned the land, which could be used. At the moment, Bai didn't have the money for building materials, but once his wife agreed to come, she could sell her family's properties back in Liang Park.

However, within a month Bai's mind began to wander again. He couldn't stop mulling over a letter he had received from his friend He Chang-hao. Chang-hao had been a poor scholar who had failed the civil-service examination, and Bai had given him money several times to keep him from cold and starvation. Later the young man went to the northeast and joined the staff of the military commander of Youzhou. He served as a junior counselor in the headquarters there. His letter to Li Bai was full of exuberance and showed he was doing well on the frontier. He wrote to Bai, "In arms and letters, you are ten times more capable than I am. If you come to this region, surely you will find a suitable post! Even though you might be reluctant to serve in the military, it will do no harm if you just come this way for fun."[1]

Chang-hao's words rang in Li Bai's mind. They reminded him that he was not just a poet—he was skilled with the sword and well versed in military strategies, knowing *The Art of War* by heart. He should be able to go into military service. Why not drop the brush and pick up the sword? It might not be too late to join the army and accomplish something extraordinary. He was not yet fifty-one. It would be silly to stay home, live to a ripe old age, and die like an everyman. He shouldn't lead a long quiet life that might turn out to be meaningless. Again his political aspirations overrode his Daoist detachment, and he couldn't stop imagining a military career.

In addition to his desire to serve the country, which had always formed a partial justification for his political ambition, there was another motivation now: he wanted to deserve his bride. Miss Zong was young and pretty and from a renowned family; he was a vagrant without prospects. "My hair is mostly white / But I have accomplished nothing," he reproaches himself in a poem ("Good-bye to Magistrate Liu in Xihe"). This sense of unworthiness had tormented him ever since he had resigned from court. Now he hoped he could do something that would restore his reputation and make him worthy of his young wife. This might be his last endeavor, he reasoned. He would become an old man soon.

Li Bai knew that You Prefecture (northeast of modern Beijing), where Chang-hao was stationed, was under An Lushan's control and might not be safe to visit. An Lushan (703–757) was a for- eigner, of Sogdian and Göktürk extraction, and his parents died when he was a young boy. Later his tribe broke up and he became a vagrant. He wandered to the region inhabited by the Chinese. He was clever and bold and strong, and was adopted by a general, whose family name was An. In time An Lushan rose through the ranks to become a general himself. He was nearly illiterate but extremely insolent and calculating and perceptive. The emperor liked him and gave him important military commands—three major circuits were under his control, which was unprecedented in China. He had a complicated and intimate relationship with Lady Yang. At one point he became her sworn brother, at another her adopted son, even though he was sixteen years her senior. It was whispered that they had been lovers. The emperor even made him a prince, which meant he belonged to the royal family and could enjoy all its privileges.

Li Bai had heard so much of this notorious man that he felt uneasy entering his territory. On the other hand, he reasoned, An Lushan must be very capable, a linchpin of the empire, loyal to the emperor and court. Otherwise he wouldn't have been made a prince, the very first foreign man in the dynasty to achieve such a position. It was reported that An knew six foreign languages and was able to deal with the northeastern tribes. He weighed over 350 pounds but could dance "like a swift wind." A massive tree tends to attract more lightning bolts, Bai reassured himself. Many people must have been jealous of An Lushan. It would not hurt if Bai went northeast and took a look at the place with his own eyes.

Intuitively he knew this might be his last chance to join the military. He had no option but to try his luck with An Lushan's army: An commanded half of the Tang forces. The other half, under Marshal Geshu's charge, stayed in the western regions, where they engaged the tribes from Central Asia. That was where Li Bai's family had come from, and Bai could not imagine fighting those peoples. So the only place he could pursue military service was the northeast. Once he was clear about this, he wrote his reply to his friend He Chang-hao. The letter is a poem that expresses his depressed state of mind and his desire to come to the northeastern frontier:

有时忽惆怅　匡坐至夜分
平明空啸咤　思欲解世纷
心随长风去　吹散万里云

羞作济南生　九十诵古文
不然拂剑起　沙漠收奇勋
老死阡陌间　何因扬清芬
夫子今管乐　英才冠三军
终与同出处　岂将沮溺群

《赠何七判官昌浩》

Sometimes suddenly I feel sad for no reason,
Sitting up alone deep into midnight.
In daylight I shout uselessly to the sky,
Unable to sort out the world's mess.
My heart would like to fly away with the long wind
To scatter the clouds of a thousand miles.
I'll be ashamed of becoming another Jinan,
Who at age ninety still pored over classics.
It will be better to rise with my sword
And fight in the desert to do miraculous feats.
If I died in my homestead and fields,
How could I earn and spread my name?
You are as capable as those statesmen of old,
Your talent towering over the army you serve.
I would like to fight together with you
To avoid an end like the ancient hermits.

"FOR JUDGE HE CHANG-HAO"

Without telling Danqiu, Bai sent the letter to Chang-hao. He then took leave of his friend and returned to Liang Park. When he told his wife about his plan, she was vehemently against it. Miss Zong abhorred politics and wanted her husband to stay clear of the army in the northeast. She had heard a great deal about An Lushan and believed he was an evil man who could bring trouble and even destruction to the country. If Li Bai went to the northeast, he could be in danger. She knew that her husband tended to act impulsively regardless of consequences. What she desired was a peaceful, ordinary life that Bai and she could share together, every day similar to the one before.

Bai, who had not expected such a strong objection from his wife, fell into silence. But Miss Zong, knowing that her husband wouldn't change his mind so easily, continued to talk about An Lushan as a dangerous man and the northeast as a potential battle-ground if the tribal forces came to attack. However, the more she warned Bai, the more intrigued he became. He emphasized that because of the potential trouble brewing there, he felt all the more called upon to investigate and find out the truth. He didn't want to stay home like a coward; he was thinking of the country and the fate of common people.

Husband and wife argued for months, until she caved in. The next summer she prepared winter clothes for Bai and saw him off with tears in her eyes.

Li Bai chronologies all place his departure in the early summer of 752. Riding a sturdy horse, he planned to cover the four hundred miles to the northeast in less than a month. But once on the road, he could not suppress his agitation. At a ferry on the Yellow River, he even shed a few tears, as though he was on a mission that might decide his fate. After crossing the river, he traveled at his leisure but hesitantly, often stopping along the way. From time to time he would be given a welcome party, thrown by admirers of his poetry and legendary personality. If he ran into a friend, he would stay a few days to enjoy the hospitality. As a result, his original plan was completely altered. Not until early October did he finally arrive at the city of Ji, where the military headquarters of Youzhou were located.

He Chang-hao was ecstatic at his arrival. He put him up in the barracks and took him to dinner, at which roast venison and pheasant and fat, juicy mushrooms were served. But Chang-hao also looked a little ill at ease. He explained to Bai that Commander An Lushan had just left with a group of top officers for the capital and, as usual, might not return until the next spring. For Bai, this was bad timing indeed. His disappointment, however, was minimal, and he even felt a bit relieved, considering he wouldn't have to meet the top commander in person right away; he accepted his friend's advice to stay for the time being and tour the region. He would simply enjoy himself for now; he could not decide yet whether to wait for Commander An to return.

It was already deep in the fall, chilly in the evenings. In the morning, hoarfrost glazed the boundless yellow grassland. It was customary at this time of year to gather fuel and prepare foods for the winter, but An Lushan's troops were still active in training and battle exercises, as though about to engage hostile forces on the front. The smoke of beacon fires continued to rise from hilltops in the distance. Bai often saw messengers galloping to the staff at the headquarters, as if the chief commander were still there. He was impressed and thought that An Lushan must be a very capable general, his army well disciplined and ready to fight invaders.

Inspired by the sight of the military activities, Bai began to practice swordsmanship on his own, reasoning that he should make himself useful in case he might take part in a battle. He would also ride out with He Chang-hao to hunt in the wilderness. Bai was a good archer and once shot down a hawk in flight. The soldiers were impressed, and he told them that the great general Li Guang had been his ancestor. His claim implied that both arms and letters ran in his blood, for there had been highly literary men in the royal clan as well. The sight of the valiant troops moved him, and he wrote poems praising the soldiers and the power of the frontier army. In one of them, he even imagined the victory these men were to win: "They will sweep away the chieftains' troops / And scatter the wild tribes. / Then the news of victory will reach His Majesty / So these triumphant men can return to the capital"

("Out of 'Song of North Ji'"). Clearly, his attitudes toward the northeastern tribes and the western tribes were markedly different.

One day, at noon, Bai passed by a large tailor shop. At its front door stood two guards holding wolf-tooth clubs, combat weapons with a long handle and steel spikes on the top end. Perhaps this shop made military uniforms, he guessed. But as he passed the entrance, he saw piles of silk and brocade gowns within, and on a long table hundreds of official hats were stacked up in lines. There were also bundles of colored sashes, like those worn by civilian officials. Bai wondered why the shop was producing official garments at this time of the year—it was already early winter, the rivers almost iced over. He asked a worker who happened to step out into the street. The man shook his head and said he didn't know, though a shadow of a smile crossed his face. Bai left and gave no more thought to the encounter.

One morning as Bai was perusing a volume of military maps loaned to him by Chang-hao, a junior officer named Cui Du came to see him. The husky young man was in a way an old friend of Bai's. His father was Cui Zongzhi, the elegant man "like a jade tree in the breeze," who had been banished. A decade back when Bai had been in Chang'an and visited the Cuis, he had met Cui Du, then a boy in his early teens. Bai had taught him how to play chess and strum the lute, how to kick a feathered shuttlecock, and how to inscribe a few characters in cursive script, a fluid style of calligraphy. Now Bai was delighted to recognize Cui Du, calling him "my nephew." Who could have imagined such an encounter on the front! They were both amazed. The young man called him Uncle Bai.

Bai complimented Cui Du on his uniform and his position in the army, but at this the young man's face clouded over. He explained that after he had failed the civil-service examination three times, he had decided to give up his books and join the army instead. He had been in this region for nearly four years, serving as a junior staff officer in the headquarters of Ying Prefecture, which was also under An Lushan's command. Bai praised him again, saying he had made the right choice and would have a brilliant career. Besides, he looked so strapping and handsome like his father. But Cui Du shook his head and whispered with a wink that they should go somewhere else so they could speak more freely.

Together they rode out of town and toward an ancient terrace built of granite. Once there, they sat on a stone step and talked some more. The young man said that An Lushan was a complete fraud and had been the cause of numerous military clashes with the tribal forces beyond the border. An provoked hostility without hesitation and, under the guise of friendship, had blatantly betrayed China's foreign neighbors time and again. He had once invited several heads of tribes to dine with him, but after enough wine was consumed, An had the chieftains arrested and sent to the capital so that he could claim rewards and promotions from court. That was how he had become the military commander of three key circuits and gotten half of China's army in his clutches. Cui Du had been observing An Lushan for a long time. He had concluded that the man was loyal only to himself and was preparing to invade the central land to seize the throne. All the incessant drill and training here was a façade—the army was still recruiting men and had to get them ready for battle. In short, An Lushan would march inland sooner or later.

Bai was shocked, and a gust of fear seized him. Now he understood why the tailor shop in town was making official garments. A new government was in the offing, and there would be numerous official appointments in need of gowns and caps. Bai told this to Cui Du, who only shook his head and smiled, saying everyone here knew that. Bai wondered if he should go to Chang'an and report An Lushan's plot to court. No, no, that couldn't be done, Cui Du told him. Over the years there had been some brave, loyal men who had gone to the capital to expose An Lushan, but without exception they had been sent back to An with their hands and feet in irons. The emperor trusted An Lushan so deeply that he wouldn't hear any words against him—he'd had the informers dispatched back to be handled by An Lushan himself. Those poor souls had all been executed publicly. Two had even been tied to stakes and skinned alive. There was no way to make the emperor see the truth.

The more Li Bai and Cui Du talked, the more heartbroken they became. In the end they embraced each other and fell on the stone steps weeping. Bai realized that the emperor was too dense and stubborn to redress the dire situation. If An Lushan's army marched inland, the dynasty would be finished.

Bai and Cui Du decided to leave as soon as possible, but knew they must not go together. Within a few days the young man obtained a home-visiting leave, which enabled him to flee the dangerous region for good. Bai happened to receive a letter from his wife, informing him that she was ill, so he said farewell to He Chang-hao and headed home without delay.

21

MOVING TO THE SOUTH

As he journeyed homeward, Li Bai often ran into friends, some of whom were officials with connections to court. From them he learned more about the political intrigues in the palace and the dire prospects facing the country. Chancellor Li Linfu had recently died, and Yang Guozhong, a distant cousin of Lady Yang's, had been appointed to the position of chief chancellor. In spite of his duplicity and cruelty, Li Linfu had been a capable man—good at maintaining discipline, balancing the power of factions, and managing royal affairs—so An Lushan had been obedient to him. But Yang Guozhong was more like An himself: coarse and nearly illiterate. He and An had never gotten along. Moreover, An was now the most powerful man outside the capital; he would not regard Yang as his equal, though Yang stayed at court and could easily disparage him in front of the emperor.

Worse still, An suspected that Yang Guozhong had only claimed to be a cousin of Lady Yang's and that there might be no blood relationship between them at all. So, following Yang Guozhong's own trick, An Lushan had shamelessly knelt in front of Lady Yang, calling her Mother (she was only in her twenties). Though astounded and flummoxed, she was persuaded by the emperor to accept such a son. "Just for the fun of it," His Majesty was reported to tell her. Thereafter, An Lushan began doing everything he could to win Lady Yang's favor. Whenever he returned to the capital, he would bring rare products and treasures from the northeast. In his own words, he was simply doing his best to fulfill his filial duty to her. Despite being a big fat man with his belly touching his knees, An Lushan was extremely nimble when he danced, and his jigs often thrilled Lady Yang. Gradually he became as close to the royal couple as if he were a member of the family. Once Lady Yang even bathed him personally, calling him "my big son." These intimate incidents, of course, displeased Yang Guozhong, who attempted to disparage An Lushan at every opportunity. As a result, hostility continued to mount between the two men; surely great trouble lay ahead.

The more Bai heard about the maneuvers and plots at court, the more depressed he became. When he was drunk, he would lament loudly that he was useless, unable to deter An Lushan. His ravings unsettled his friends, who feared that Bai's words might reach An's ears. An had always been ruthless in annihilating his rivals and opponents; the devious man had agents throughout the country gathering intelligence for him. Nonetheless, whenever Bai encountered people from the capital, he would urge them not to associate with An Lushan. Some officials followed his advice and began to avoid the man so as to protect themselves. By chance, in Kaifeng City Bai ran into Zhang Ji, the man who had once deceived him by sending him to Princess Yuzhen's villa in Zhong-nan Mountain. He urged Ji to have no further dealings with An Lushan. Though a deceitful man himself, Zhang Ji was astonished by what Bai told him about the events in the northeast, and promised to avoid An Lushan. Bai calculated that Ji might pass the message on to his wife, a princess, who in turn might tell the emperor, or at least some members of the royal family, about the impending coup. We are unsure if the information ever reached His Majesty, but we know that Ji listened to Bai and managed to distance himself from the general.

To Bai's relief, he found his wife recovered when he returned home. He told her his discoveries in the northeast. Husband and wife talked at length about the catastrophic prospects ahead. If war broke out, what would they do to survive? The rebels would surely come this way to attack Luoyang, the East Capital, and capture it as a major victory in their invasion of the central land. Bai and his wife realized they should avoid the major cities. They would be safer secluding themselves in a remote town or mountain. In a poem, Li Bai speculates on this imminent predicament: "People in Qin ask one another: / Where should we go? / Go to the Peach Blossom Garden, / Where a thousand years pass without being noticed" ("Guest Zheng Enters the West Gorge"). The lines refer to the fable by Tao Yuanming, in which a utopian village has been insulated from the outside world and its inhabitants, unaware of the dynastic changes, are protected from the destruction of historical violence. Bai and his wife longed for such a haven.

Then Bai received a letter from Li Zhao, a distant cousin who was mayor of Xuan Town in east Anhui. Zhao invited Bai to come and spend some time in his small city. He described the place elaborately to entice Bai. He wrote that since ancient times Xuan Prefecture had been a renowned region: that it had rich soil and an abundant water supply, that it combined the advantages of both land and water, that it had gathered the cultural essence of different areas and times (even in small streets and alleys, in teahouses and taverns, songs and music and opera were performed every day), that Xuan Town sat against Lingyang Mountain, protected by two rivers, and that, more amazingly, during the Nanqi dynasty (479–502), the poet Xie Tiao had been in charge of the city and built his residence on top of Lingyang Mountain. His house and tower still stood there, attracting poets and scholars who wished to witness the beauty of the landscape below. Xie Tiao (464–499) had been one of Li Bai's literary heroes throughout his life. Bai admired him for his natural yet rigorous poetic style and for his detachment from political affairs, despite his aristocratic origins and the official positions he had held. Li Zhao invited Bai to come enjoy his city and share the literary spirit of Xie Tiao. He was sure that Bai would find the place peaceful and would be inspired to write while he was there. The invitation seemed to Bai like an exciting opportunity, and he showed his wife the letter. Together the couple talked about what to do.

They decided that Bai should go to Xuan Town and see how he liked it. If the place was safe and peaceful, the rest of the family should follow him there. Though this seemed to be a natural decision, it meant that Bai would have to give up his dream of "pacifying the country and helping the common people," as he declares in his poem "For Official Cai Xiong." He had even thought of returning to the capital to do such work; he had expressed his wish to go there and personally report An Lushan's plot to the central government, but his wife had dissuaded him. She was aware of the compromise he was making, but she was eager to keep him far from the political arena. From now on, he had better live as a Daoist like herself. This he wasn't sure he could do, but he agreed to try his best to walk the path of faith and build a haven for himself and his family. He told his wife that once he found a good place in Xuan Town, he would come back to fetch her. Meanwhile, she should sell her family's eateries and wine houses, which would be drastically devalued once rebellion broke out.

In the early summer he packed his bags, put on his Daoist outfit, and set out on the road. Xuan Town was more than three hundred miles to the south and he would travel by land. As before, along the way he encountered friends and acquaintances who kept him company and enticed him to stay as long as possible, taking him to noted sites and giving parties in his honor. Some would go out of their way to introduce others to him, clearly proud to have him as a friend. Bai enjoyed the festive gatherings, which made him feel honored. If a host was particularly considerate and generous, he often stayed a little longer. As a result, his progress south was unhurried.

In mid-fall he arrived at a place called Hengjiang Ferry on the Yangtze. The river as a whole flows from west to east, but at the foot of Mount Lu it turns northeast for more than a hundred miles, then swerves again to the south of Wuhu, running north all the way to Nanjing. Hengjiang Ferry was a spot north of Wuhu used by people for crossing the river. The water there was rapid and rough, and sometimes the ferry closed because of foul weather. When Li Bai arrived, it was windy and the river was roiling, impossible to cross, so he stayed at a nearby inn. Rain continued to fall over the next few days. Whenever there was a pause in the downpour, Bai would put on a cone hat made of bamboo skin and walk along the riverbank to gaze at the water. In the distance, waves rolled and surged, as if the river were an ocean partly enveloped in fog. He went to see the man in charge of the ferry and asked about the operating schedule, but was told that it would take several days for the boat to run again. The man said that because a storm was rising on the sea, more roaring winds and raging waves would be coming this way. His words made Bai reflective, reminding him of the larger situation of the country and of his life. His troubles had always seemed to be caused by something far away, beyond his control, and he felt that indeed a violent political storm was approaching.

Having nothing to do at the inn, he wrote a series of poems titled "Six Songs at Hengjiang Ferry." Together they carry a considerable amount of allegorical resonance and express Bai's disillusion and despair. They go as follows:

一

人道橫江好　儂道橫江惡
一風三日吹倒山　白浪高於瓦官閣

二

海潮南去過潯陽　　牛渚由來險馬當
橫江欲渡風波惡　　一水牽愁萬里長

三

橫江西望阻西秦　　漢水東連揚子津
白浪如山那可渡　　狂風愁殺峭帆人

四

海神來過惡風回　　浪打天門石壁開
浙江八月何如此　　濤似連山噴雪來

五

橫江館前津吏迎　　向余東指海雲生
郎今欲渡緣何事　　如此風波不可行

六

月暈天風霧不開　　海鯨東蹙百川回
驚波一起三山動　　公無渡河歸去來

《橫江詞》

1

People all say Hengjiang Ferry is a good spot,
But I say it is quite awful actually.
The wind blows for three days and can topple hills,
Huge whitecaps higher than a palace's tiled roof.

2

The ocean tides are coming all the way to Jiujiang,
So Niu-chu and Ma-dang are too perilous to sail through.
The roiling waves stop people at Hengjiang Ferry,
Where the river runs like a long flow of sorrow.

3

All I can do is gaze at the mountain in the west,
Then watch the Yangtze flowing east into the Chu land.
How can you cross over with white waves like hills?
The stormy wind makes men feckless under high sails.

4

As soon as the ocean tides pass, the wild wind arrives,
Waves smashing the cliffs of Heaven's Gate.
Even Zhejiang is like this in the eighth month—
The waves are rolling over like mountains of snow.

5

The official in charge of the ferry points east,
Saying more clouds are gathering there.
"Mr. Li, why are you so eager to cross over?
You can't go against such wind and waves!"

6

The moon is blurred by the wind and fog
While whales charge up and swerve around.
The huge waves leap and shake the mountains.
You mustn't cross and had better turn back.

The time here would have been September, which by the lunar calendar is August, already mid-fall in that area. That is why the fourth poem says "the eighth month."

After several days' delay, Li Bai finally crossed the Yangtze and continued south. He arrived at Xuan Town when the leaves were turning yellow and red. Although it was already deep fall, the climate was dry and warm. The striking landscape reminded him of his home region in northern Sichuan. The Wan Brook just east of the town was shallow and limpid and resembled the Jian River outside his home village, Qinglian. Even the birdcalls, made by cuckoos and orioles, sounded familiar, bringing back childhood memories. As his cousin Li Zhao had written in his letter, the town was peaceful and charming and full of historic sites. Zhao was a good host and did his best to make Bai comfortable. As the mayor, he hoped that Li Bai would settle in the city permanently so that the great poet could become a cultural presence. Bai began to feel at ease and even at home there.

Bai enjoyed visiting the historic sites with the new friends he'd made, and if the weather was bad, he would stay in his study reading Daoist texts. He mixed well with the locals. Not far from where he lived was a wine house named Deep Spring, which offered wine brewed by its owner, Old Ji. Li Bai soon started to frequent the place and got to know Old Ji well, who allowed him to get wine on credit. In fact, from time to time various local men settled Bai's wine debts with Old Ji because Bai had written poems or short essays for them. He enjoyed sitting in the shop, which had a handful of tables, and chatting with others. The locals were impressed by his words, especially when he was tipsy and raving with abandon. Never had they met such a loquacious man, who often talked as if in tongues. Above all, Bai loved the wine Old Ji made. Most times when he was done drinking in the shop, he would bring a jar of Deep Spring back to his lodgings. The warmth of the local people was comfortable, but still he was unsure if he could live here for good.

To his cousin Zhao, Bai seemed content, though he still wouldn't say if he had decided to move his family here and settle down. Every day Bai strolled around the town and its vicinity. He would also hike up a knoll called Jingting Hill and sit on top of it alone for as long as he could. Once, while on the hilltop, he heard someone piping a tune in the woods. The music sounded familiar; he remembered having heard it many times in Chang'an, though this tune was not exactly the same. Its robust exotic melody reminded him of "The Tune of Charging out of the Front," a popular song performed in the capital at the time. As he listened, tears trickled down his cheeks. He composed a poem capturing the nostalgic moment:

胡人吹玉笛　　一半是秦聲
十月吳山曉　　梅花落敬亭
愁聞出塞曲　　淚滿逐臣纓
卻望長安道　　空懷戀主情

　《觀胡人吹笛》

A man from the west blows the jade pipe—
Most tunes are from the land of Qin.
The mountains in Wu are clear in October
As plum blossoms are dropping at Jingting Hill.
In grief I hear the music of "Charging out of the Front,"
Tears soaking the ribbons of my hat.
Again I gaze at the way to Chang'an,
Full of useless feelings for my Lord.

"LISTENING TO A MAN FROM THE WEST BLOW THE JADE PIPE"

Peaceful and pleasant as the town was, Bai felt restless: the capital, the political center, still exerted a hold on him. He longed to return to Chang'an, to the emperor's side. Yet he had genuine feelings for this place, especially Jingting Hill, which often gave him peace of mind and allowed him to enjoy a stretch of solitude. Occasionally the spot also brought him a sense of detachment and tranquility. He began to regard Jingting Hill itself as a companion of sorts. He wrote a short poem about the knoll, which became one of his finest works: "All birds have flown high and disappeared / While a lone cloud is floating away idly. / We two keep looking at each other, never bored— / Only Jingting Hill and I can do this"

("Sitting Alone on Jingting Hill"). The last two lines personify the knoll as a soul mate, and.they also show, though only momentarily, Bai's predilection for nature and for staying above earthly strife. He loved the hill so much that he boasted of setting up a home there, as he declared in a poem to his banished friend Cui Zongzhi: "My home is at the foot of Jingting Hill / So I can follow what Xie Tiao described. / Hundreds of years have passed between him and me, / But his style is fresh like yesterday's. / I climb up this hill to get near the moon / And looking down, I see green hills around the town" ("A Letter to Cui Chengfu about My Climbing Jingting Hill"). The home Bai referred to might have been a temporary residence or a future one he had in mind. Although he longed for the capital, he had also been considering how to move his family here.

Sometimes when he grew restless, he would go and visit villages and county seats near Xuan Town. After winter had passed, he often set out alone. The vice magistrate of Nanling County was a friend, so Bai went there to see him. The official received him enthusiastically. Together they visited Five Pine Mountain and the copper mine owned by the government. Bai also went to Qipu and Qingyang towns, where the locals were hospitable and accompanied him on his sightseeing. Then Bai arrived at Jing County; its magistrate, Wang Lun, was a cheerful scholar and a lover of poetry. He had been a fan of Li Bai's for a long time, so Bai's arrival was a great event for him. Lun invited Bai to spend a few days in a scenic village called Peace Blossom Pond; together the two of them had a festive time there. Bai got drunk every evening, but Lun remained sober so that he could be an attentive host. Three days later, when Bai was departing and about to board a boat, a band of villagers, invited by Wang Lun, suddenly arrived and began to perform a folk dance called Ta-ge in Bai's honor. They sang, waved their arms, and clapped their hands while their feet tapped the sandy bank, smiling at Bai happily. Their performance was a way to say farewell to him. Bai was so touched that he composed a poem on the spot:

李白乘舟將欲行　　忽聞岸上踏歌聲
桃花潭水深千尺　　不及汪倫送我情

《贈汪倫》

I, Li Bai, get on a boat, about to leave—
Suddenly I hear Ta-ge performed on the bank.
The water of Peach Blossom Pond is a thousand feet deep,
But it's nothing compared to Wang Lun's feelings for me.

"FOR WANG LUN"

Despite the good times that Bai found in Xuan Town and its vicinity, he was yearning to hear news about the capital. Here he felt isolated and even bereft. He couldn't stop lamenting this isolation and even declared his grief so immense that his hair had grown "white and three thousand feet long."

Fortunately, a distant uncle of his, Li Hua, was passing through Xuan Town on an official journey to the southeast. Li Hua was an inspector of the eighth rank. Though only a petty official, he was noted for his literary writings, and being from the capital, he was well connected and well informed. When he traveled, local officials treated him respectfully. Bai was excited about the older man's arrival and accompanied him to scenic sites in and outside Xuan Town. Li Hua brought news of the palace, all of which was dismal. Chancellor Yang Guozhong had become very hawkish in handling foreign affairs and had started expeditions at random. Two years earlier, he had dispatched an army to attack Nanzhao Kingdom (part of modern Yunnan Province, Burma, Laos, and Vietnam). The Chinese troops reached the Hei-er River but were defeated roundly. Yang covered up the loss and dispatched another army, which was again destroyed by Nanzhao's forces. In total, the Chinese suffered nearly two hundred thousand casualties. Even more outrageously, it was whispered among officials who had inside information that this war had been sparked by a love affair between the queen of Nanzhao and a local Chinese governor, who had attempted to blackmail her husband and had been ruthless in collecting levies. The king of Nanzhao was so outraged that he launched an attack at the local government, killed the governor, and seized almost the entire Yunnan region, causing war to break out.

The Tang court was not aware of the true cause—the whole of China was ignorant of it, all believing that Nanzhao Kingdom must be punished for its aggression. Although Nanzhao sent emissaries to China in pursuit of peace, the Tang court would not accept a truce. But the Chinese army lost one battle after another, and many more troops were killed by disease. Eventually the military had to give up the expedition. The Tang emperor, unaware of the cause of the war and the magnitude of the catastrophe, only sought pleasure with total abandon—the palace was filled with endless parties and entertainments. The siblings of Lady Yang all received major appointments and titles, and top officials competed to consume delicacies of land and sea. Common people, meanwhile, lived in deplorable conditions: in recent years a severe famine, caused by heavy rains and floods and then by locusts, had struck the central land, and the price of grain had risen tens of times. Many starved to death, and bodies littered the streets in every city Li Hua had visited. Even cannibalism had occurred in some far-off regions.

Li Hua himself, though a royal inspector, could hardly do anything to curb the misdeeds and wrongdoings of local officials. He knew it was useless to expose them, so he had grown a bit jaded.

Whenever he tried to dig into a case, he would find the involvements of the higher-level governments and senior officials in the capital. He attempted to be conscientious and even made bold to report a number of cases to court, but it was clear his honest efforts might only bring trouble to himself. He couldn't help but feel a demotion or banishment looming over his head. In short, the dynasty was already rotten to the core.

Bai recited some of his recent verses to his uncle. The older man praised the new work and was particularly fond of the one titled "Battling South of the Town," which Li Hua believed was a masterpiece. Bai also composed a poem for Li Hua, which became another of his signature works:

棄我去者　昨日之日不可留
亂我心者　今日之日多煩憂
長風萬里送秋雁　對此可以酣高樓
蓬萊文章建安骨　中間小謝又清發
俱懷逸興壯思飛　欲上青天攬明月
抽刀斷水水更流　舉杯消愁愁更愁
人生在世不稱意　明朝散髮弄扁舟

《宣州謝朓樓餞別校書叔雲》

Yesterday, having left me, couldn't be pressed to stay.
Today, still disturbing me, makes me more upset.
The long wind is sending the autumn geese far away,
And viewing them from this high tower, we should drink more.
Your essays are fresh and strong like those of the Han dynasty
While my poetry resembles Xie Tiao's in vigor and beauty.
We both have lofty spirit, thinking of soaring
To the sky to grab hold of the clear moon.
I draw my sword to cut water, which won't stop flowing,
And I raise my cup to douse my sorrow, which grows stronger.

Ah, life is such a sad thing that tomorrow
I will undo my hair and sail away in a little boat.

"SONG FOR ACCOMPANYING UNCLE HUA ON XIE TIAO'S TOWER"

Li Hua's visit convinced Bai that he must not remain isolated for too long and should have more frequent contact with the outside world. So he began to travel north to Wuhu, where he could take a boat up and down the Yangtze, visiting cities that were more culturally active.

Yet Xuan Town had become his base. By now he had been there for more than a year but still hadn't yet brought his family over. He must have realized that he needed to live in a city on the Yangtze so he could travel more easily and have more contact with other places, such as Nanjing and Yangzhou. Despite his intermittent longing to retreat into wild mountains and waters, he acted as though he were still eagerly waiting for an opportunity to return to court. He could not abandon the dream of getting back to the capital and restarting his political career. What made him hesitate to go there was An Lushan, who might launch his army inland anytime. Bai had to avoid the capital for now.

AN UNEXPECTED GUEST

Li Hua left with Bai a critical poetry anthology, *The Essence of Mountains and Rivers,* which was compiled by Yin Fan and had recently become available at bookshops in the capital. Bookshops were very small at the time, usually each having just two or three shelves or stands in a shed or room. In some cases, a bookshop was just an open-air stand. Yin Fan was a literary scholar and a retired official, and his anthology, two volumes altogether, would become one of the most influential among the dozens that appeared in the Tang dynasty. Even today the book is still valuable for scholars in their study of Tang poetry, mainly because it offers a perspective on how poets were received by their contemporaries. Li Bai was pleased to find himself among the twenty-four included poets (many of whom were friends of his such as Meng Haoran, Cui Guofu, and Gao Shi), but was disconcerted to see that his thirteen poems were outnumbered by those of poets like Wang Wei (fifteen poems), Wang Changling (sixteen), and Chang Jian (a minor poet who had been allocated fourteen poems). Did this mean they were more famous than him? He was certain that he was one of the most popular among the poets in the anthology, but Yin Fan must have had his own agenda to push, promoting the poets he liked and setting his own criteria. There was no justification for including only six poems by Meng Haoran, a major poet by any standard. Worse still, in the commentary Yin remarked on Li Bai's work with reservations, saying, "Like his personality lacking in restraint, his style is self-indulgent but extraordinary." Although most of Bai's thirteen poems were indeed his masterpieces, the editor's comments irritated him. He tried to dismiss them from his mind. It was true that his genius was beyond the traditional boundaries of poetic art, and a pedant like Yin Fan must only be capable of assessing decorous rules, metrical patterns, and technical finesse. By no means should he take the editor's words seriously.

Bai noticed that his friend Du Fu was not in the anthology at all, though he was far superior to most of the included poets. (In fact, some of them would fade into oblivion. Later Yin Fan added another volume to the original two and again left out Du Fu.) Although the editor had shown a certain amount of integrity by not including many poets who were high-ranking officials, Du Fu was, like Li Bai, radically different from the court poets, and his originality must have been difficult for Yin Fan to appreciate.

From his uncle Li Bai had learned that Du Fu was still in the capital but had been unsuccessful in his efforts to seek office. Bai didn't like this aspect of Du Fu, who seemed to him to follow the conventional way too earnestly and was much more Confucian than Bai. The man was a little prim, a paragon of virtue. Why had he put so much effort into the civil-service examination? With his talent and intelligence, he could excel through other ways. Bai knew that two years prior, at an imperial ceremony, Du Fu had composed three poetic essays (rhapsodies) that pleased the emperor greatly, but his opportunity for an appointment was time and again subverted by devious courtiers, some of whom even lied to the emperor, saying there was no qualified examinee in all of China for an important post that needed to be filled. The worst part was that His Majesty believed these lies. The system was so corrupt that it was understandable that Du Fu couldn't succeed in his efforts. In his lifetime only one anthology contained his poems, and his work remained unknown until nearly half a century later when mid-Tang poets rediscovered him and began to mention him in the same breath as Li Bai. Some even considered Du Fu a greater poet than Bai. The poet Zhang Ji (767–830), of the younger generation, often hand-copied Du Fu's poems, burned them, and then drank the ashes, hoping that the remnants might inspire his own poetry.

After Li Hua had left, Bai began to travel along the Yangtze extensively, mainly to the cities on the river, though he used Xuan Town as a retreat of sorts. He thrived on the social life of the cities; he must have been eager to keep in touch with the outside world and above all to maintain his audience and sustain his fame. His nature didn't allow him to live in isolation for long—he needed engagement and recognition.

One summer day, while Bai was staying in Yangzhou, a young man came to call on him. The visitor, named Wei Hao, was a devoted fan of his poetry. He told Bai how he had been searching for his whereabouts and had finally found him. First he had gone to east Shandong, where he met Bai's son Boqin and the woman of Lu. She told him that Bai was in Liang Park with his new wife. Hao then went to Henan, where Bai's wife told him her husband was in the south, though she was no longer sure of his exact location. So Hao journeyed to the land of Wu, traveling from city to city—Hangzhou, Wenzhou (by sea), Nanjing, and many other places—hoping to pick up Bai's tracks. At last he got word that Bai was in Yangzhou, so he had come here without delay. All told, Wei Hao had traveled more than a thousand miles in search of Li Bai. On hearing this, Bai observed the visitor more carefully: he looked trustworthy, a bit insouciant, and somewhat distracted, probably thanks to this miraculous meeting he had dreamed of for so long.

As their conversation continued, Bai learned that Hao loved the ancient writers and also wrote poetry himself. The two men shared a common taste and spirit. Bai was impressed by the young man's sincerity and touched by his love for his poems, some of which he could recite. So he let Hao stay with him. They wandered together as a pair; their sojourns to nearby towns and cities and to mountains and rivers brought Bai much joy. Though there were more than twenty years between them, Bai treated Wei Hao as a younger brother and a kindred spirit. Hao wrote about their friendship in a poem: "One old man and one young man / Keep looking at each other like brothers." Li Bai also wrote about his young friend: "Being together with you gives me boundless joy." Wei's words provide for us vivid physical descriptions of Bai: "His eyes were piercingly bright while his mouth opened like a hungry tiger's. He often tied a sash around him, which gave him a casual but elegant manner. Because he had been inducted into the Daoist society in Qi, he wore a black embroidered hat."[1]

Bai wrote a poem about Wei Hao, which consists of 120 lines and is the only one Bai wrote about the man that has survived. It lists the places Hao had visited in search of him and gives an account of the delightful trips they made together. Bai describes Hao with great affection: "You wore a Japanese gown / With an air of detachment from earthly cares. / In May you came and we chatted tirelessly, / And I realized you were not a madman at all. / Then our joy in being together / Spread all over the streams and rocks where we lingered" ("Seeing Wei Hao, Hermit of Wang Wu, Returning to His Retreat"). Hao's gown was an exotic garment, made of imported fabric given him by Chao Heng (698–770), a Japanese man serving as an official in the Tang government.

Chao's original name was Abe no Nakamaro; he had come to China at the age of nineteen as part of a cultural mission of young Japanese students. His was the eighth such mission that his country had dispatched to China. Its members were to learn crafts and study arts and various branches of knowledge so that they could bring back to Japan the achievements of the Chinese civilization. Nakamaro studied classics and literature, which in a few years he learned so well that he passed the civil-service examination at the first attempt. While most of his fellow students returned to Japan and became experts in various fields, Nakamaro stayed in China and took an administrative position with the seventh rank, quite high for a beginner. Later he was promoted to collator of texts in the Imperial Library, the same post that the great poet Bai Juyi would take half a century later.[2] Nakamaro was a kind, sincere man who befriended many literary figures, including Li Bai, Wang Wei, and Chu Guangxi (700–760). He also became a friend and official companion of Prince Yi, the emperor's twelfth son. In 753, the year before Wei Hao found Li Bai in person, Nakamaro obtained approval from the Tang court to return to Japan. He set sail from Ningbo, but soon his ship encountered a storm and was thrown off course, landing on the coast of Vietnam. Word came back to China that he had drowned in the ocean.

Li Bai was heartbroken upon hearing of his friend's death and wrote this poem in memory of him: "My Japanese friend, Sir Chao, left the capital, / A lone ship sailing toward the celestial islands. / Like a bright moon he sank into the gray sea / And left white clouds and sorrow over the green mountains." But to everyone's surprise, Nakamaro had in fact survived the shipwreck and managed to return to China in 755. When he saw Li Bai's poem mourning his death, he was so moved that he wrote a poem in response:

卅年長安住　歸不到蓬壺
一片望鄉情　盡付水天處
魂兮歸來了　感君痛苦吾
我更為君哭　不得長安住

《望鄉》

After living in Chang'an for thirty years,
I sailed back to the celestial islands but without success.

All my homesickness was thrown away
On the water that spread to the end of the sky.
My soul and myself now are back,
Touched by your pain over my disappearance.
I too weep, but for your sake—
You can no longer stay in Chang'an.

"LOOKING HOMEWARD"

Bai and Hao must have reminisced together about their remarkable Japanese friend. Hao's wearing of the gown showed how much he cherished his friendship with Nakamaro.

Hao was especially grateful that Bai didn't view him as a fool as others often did because he tended to appear arrogant and off balance. In fact, Bai trusted Hao and saw a bright future awaiting him. He told Hao, "Surely you will make a great name for yourself in our country. When that happens, don't forget this old man and my son Little Bright Moon." He gave Wei Hao all the manuscripts he had with him and asked his friend to edit a book of his collected writings.

Wei Hao would go on to live up to Li Bai's expectations, passing the civil-service examination and becoming an official. After Bai died, Hao did compile his collected works; this compilation, unfortunately, has been lost, but Wei's preface has remained. It is an essential source of biographical information on Li Bai and offers an intimate look at the great poet. From it, we know that Bai told Wei he had been summoned to the capital by the emperor in 742 not because of his poetry but because, as an accomplished Daoist fellow, he was recommended to His Majesty by Princess Yuzhen. This could be a boast, as Bai's heart had never really left the palace and he might have felt attracted to the princess. He always longed to join the royal family as a way to justify his extraordinariness, and also to eclipse his humble origins. However, the biographical information the preface provides on his family's origin and migration and his personal life is congruent with other sources and has become the basis of Li Bai scholarship.

The Tang poets had many loyal fans like Wei Hao; indeed, they were part of the poetic culture. In Jing Prefecture, a street policeman named Ge Qing was so devoted to Bai Juyi that he tattooed more than thirty of Juyi's poems on his body, as well as drawings inspired by his verses. People called him "Bai Juyi's Walking Poems and Pictures." Jia Dao (779–843) had a fan named Li Dong who cast a small brass statue of Jia so that he could carry it with him and pray to it a thousand times a day. Li Bai must have had many other dedicated fans and disciples as well. One of them, Wu E, would risk his own life to help Bai rescue his family.

23

ESCAPING FROM THE REBELS

I n November 755, An Lushan, after repeated provocations by Chancellor Yang Guozhong, launched his rebellion against the central government. His army assembled in Hebei and swiftly marched inland. His men were well trained, his generals loyal and capable, and they took one prefecture after another as they advanced. The two hundred thousand troops were simply unstoppable.

Li Bai was in Nanjing when the news of the rebellion came. War refugees had begun to appear on the Yangtze, crossing the river and fleeing farther south, and Bai worried about his wife in Henan and his son Boqin in Shandong. His disciple of many years, Wu E, came to Nanjing from the coastal area to ensure that Bai was safe. On hearing about his family's predicament, Wu E volunteered to go to rescue his son—the rebels would surely seize Shandong soon. Wu E was a knight-errant skilled in martial arts, bold but also coolheaded. Bai was terribly anxious about his family's safety. Without delay he and Wu E started out north together. After a hundred miles or so, they parted ways: Bai headed west to Henan to fetch his wife, while Wu E made for Shandong to look for Boqin. Bai recorded Wu E's adventure in his poem "For Wu Seventeen," composed to express his gratitude to the young man.

Bai found his wife in Liang Park, which the marauding troops had already reached. Unsure if Wu E would succeed in rescuing

Boqin, Bai and his wife decided to join the refugees fleeing south. They headed back toward Nanjing, where, as planned, Bai would wait for Boqin and Wu E. Along the way they encountered bodies scattered on roadsides and saw beggars everywhere. Beacons of war sent up smoke in the distance. Country people abandoned their homes, scrambling for places where the old social order might remain intact. The rebels killed and plundered at random, burning villages and towns. Their savagery terrified people, many of whom fled blindly toward Chang'an: in the public eye, His Majesty still embodied the governing power and the prospect of order and peace. The common people couldn't see how disarrayed the central government truly was. The stunned emperor, by now seventy years old, was too feeble to organize an effective counterattack. He and Lady Yang could not believe that An Lushan, their beloved "son," would make war to topple the dynasty.

In just one month the rebels captured Luoyang City. Then, in January 756, An Lushan established a shadow government in Luoyang and declared himself the emperor of Great Yan, his new dynasty. He would advance west all the way to Chang'an in the name of "clearing the side of His Majesty," which meant eliminating the courtiers he hated. The main corps of his troops moved west along the Yellow River and continued to conquer towns and cities. In desperation, Emperor Xuanzong announced that he would personally lead the imperial army to confront the rebels, but then realized his health was too frail. Instead, he ordered Geshu Han, the grand Turgesh general serving in the Tang army, to march out of their current position at Tong Pass and lead the counterattack. He also ordered Guo Ziyi, commander of the Northern Army (and the very man Li Bai had saved from execution), to attack the rebel forces from the rear.

Marshal Geshu was experienced in military operations and revered by the common people. A popular folk song eulogized him as a great power that alone could stabilize the frontier: "The

Big Dipper hangs high in the sky / And Geshu carries a sword at night. / The barbarians can only watch our horses in the pasture, / Not daring to invade our borderland" ("Song About Geshu"). However, Geshu was old and no longer had the valor and vigor he'd possessed in his prime. He was not optimistic about the present situation. He argued with the emperor, saying that his central army should continue to defend Tong Pass, the last stronghold on the rebels' path to Chang'an, rather than take the offensive. If the rebels breached Tong Pass, there would be no place remaining in which to build a defense line and Chang'an would be completely open to assault. But the emperor refused to listen, so Geshu had no choice but to decamp and head for the enemy. He was ambushed on the way and caught by An Lushan's men, his army routed. He later died in the rebels' prison, an absurd and pathetic end to a glorious career.

When Geshu lost his army, the emperor was still under the illusion that the enemy was far away. Then the beacon smoke rose in the east, the capital was thrown into turmoil, and people were scrambling to flee. A chief counselor offered the emperor an odd piece of advice: he should grant sweeping administrative powers to four of his sons and make them fight to save the shattered empire. Strangely enough, His Majesty accepted the advice: he appointed his third son, Li Heng, as the marshal of the central army overseeing the vast territory north of the Yellow River; his sixteenth son, Li Lin, as the ruler of many southern prefectures; his twenty-first son, Li Qi, as ruler and military commander of several eastern prefectures; and his twenty-sixth son, Li Feng, as ruler of the prefectures around the capital. However, the twenty-first and the twenty-sixth sons would continue to stay at court, ruling their territories from a distance, so their appointments were meaningless. Prince Li Heng, the third son, was already the mainstay in organizing the counterattack forces: he directly commanded generals whose troops were engaging the rebels competently, including Guo Ziyi in the northeast and Li Guangbi in central China. His brother, Li Lin, Prince Yong, had also been resisting the rebels, building defenses along the Yangtze while occupying the fertile Wu land. The emperor's decree stated clearly that all four princes had the right to levy taxes, appoint officials, and raise armies within their territories. This meant they would become actual rulers. The emperor did not foresee the unintended consequences of this decree, which would divide the empire.

As the rebels approached the capital, the court decided to flee. The common people were terrified and implored the emperor to unite all the forces to defend Chang'an. His Majesty was too feeble to do that personally, so he allowed Prince Li Heng to take charge of the imperial army and try to stabilize the situation. He then granted his throne to Li Heng, who refused to accept it. Instead, the prince led the army north to engage the rebels. But once he arrived at Lingwu (near modern Yinchuan), Prince Li Heng, urged by his counselors and supported by the populace, declared himself Emperor Suzong. His father, desperate in flight, had no option but to abdicate and accept the title of the so-called Grand Emperor— from now on he would be a mere nominal sovereign.

Escorted by a contingent of royal guards, the emperor and his court began their flight to Sichuan. The next afternoon the exhausted retinue stopped to have lunch at a courier station called Ma Wei Po, but after the break, the soldiers refused to continue. They killed Chancellor Yang Guozhong, who had been viewed as one of the main causes of the calamity. They then demanded that the emperor get rid of Lady Yang, another evil figure in their eyes. By now her three sisters, all wives of high officials, had already been killed by the outraged troops. The emperor was trembling from fear but refused to condemn his beloved consort to death. Gao Lishi, the head eunuch, urged him to yield to the soldiers' demand so as to save his life, the dynasty, and the empire. Still the emperor refused. The commander of the guards came to appeal to him again and again. Finally His Majesty granted Lady Yang a piece of white silk, with which she hanged herself on a pear tree.

She was thirty-seven, at the prime of her beauty, and was buried at Ma Wei Po. Her tomb is still there: the site has been constructed like a small exquisite temple, which draws visitors and tourists. Controversy continues to surround her death: some believe a maid had hanged herself in place of Lady Yang. Rumor even says she didn't die at Ma Wei Po and eventually sneaked out of China and settled in Japan. Today there are Japanese who claim to be her descendants.

Soon Prince Li Heng, with the help of capable generals, managed to contain the rebels. Now the new emperor, he ordered his brother Prince Yong, who occupied the vast land south of the Yangtze, to come to Sichuan to see their father. But Prince Yong, nervous about intrigues at court, disobeyed the order and instead began to raise a large army to defend his land. He attacked prefectures whose governors were loyal to the court, and cast out of his territory those officials newly appointed by the central government. Prince Yong believed that with abundant resources he could establish his own state south of the Yangtze—such a kingdom had appeared several times in history. But the populace regarded his older brother as the true emperor; their father had already approved Li Heng's ascension to the throne.

Meanwhile, Li Bai and his wife were seeking safety. They had originally planned to go to Nanjing to avoid the rebels—the city was defended by Prince Yong's forces, and its river might deter the enemy. But soon they realized An Lushan's troops had been occupying places north of the Yangtze and might advance farther south as well. The Lis decided to go in a different direction. They boarded a boat and sailed west up the river without a clear destination. They stopped wherever Bai encountered a friend in a town or city. From his friends Bai learned what had happened on the battlegrounds and that the court was in flight. He was heartbroken, still in shock, and often had difficulty breathing properly. He wished he could do something to help the country, but for now he had to find a safe place for his wife and himself.

The couple finally stopped at Jiujiang and went up into Mount Lu, believing that the rebels were unlikely to reach such an isolated place. Indeed, the rebellious forces were slowing down and becoming less aggressive, as An Lushan grew content in Luoyang. The following months were somewhat stable for Bai and his wife, though he was often depressed, still in disbelief that the empire could be shattered overnight. It looked like they might have to spend the winter at the mountain. Miss Zong took comfort knowing that her master, Li Tengkong, also lived on Mount Lu, though many miles away.

It is recorded by all Li Bai chronologies that at the beginning of 757, Wei Zichun, an acquaintance of Bai's from Chang'an, came up the mountain to visit Bai and asked him to join Prince Yong's camp. Wei now was the prince's right-hand man, a top adviser, and represented his master on this visit. Bai was delighted to learn that Yong's forces were already in Jiujiang and that the prince knew his whereabouts and was inviting him to help defeat the foreign rebels. Yong planned to found a new government in Nanjing, which would rule the entire Yangtze delta. All night Li Bai and Wei Zichun talked excitedly about plans to advance north to destroy An Lushan's rear base and save the country.

Bai neglected the fact that Prince Li Heng had already ascended the throne, dreaming only of how he might help Prince Yong found a new dynasty. His political vision was anachronistic, based primarily on the books he had studied. Despite his scant experience in the state's affairs, he believed that at long last an opportunity for glory was presenting itself and that soon he would become a major statesman under Prince Yong.

He wished to leave the mountain with Wei Zichun at once, but his wife stopped him, saying that the Spring Festival was approaching, families were supposed to be together on the holiday, and he couldn't leave home now. After Wei had departed, Bai and his wife argued back and forth. She believed it would be too risky for Bai to join Prince Yong's camp and that politics was too treacherous an area for her husband to step into. Furthermore, there was already a new sovereign and Bai could not support a prince who was staking a rival claim against Emperor Suzong. She wanted him to stay home and foster the peace and quiet needed for their Daoist cultivation. Bai did not oppose her overtly, but felt miserable and even guilty for not contributing his efforts to help save the country. He didn't make the distinction between Emperor Suzong and Prince Yong, seeing them as equally legitimate members of the family that ruled China, both exercising authority granted them by their father. In his mind, by joining Prince Yong he would be serving the court and the royal clan. Soon he resumed the debate with his wife, saying they ought to put the country's interests before their own, that this would be his way of expressing his fealty to the royal family.

Immediately after the Spring Festival, Wei Zichun came up the mountain again. He presented to Li Bai a case of gold, five hundred pieces, and a letter personally written by Prince Yong inviting him to come to Jiujiang and join his staff. Bai was pleased about the money and again wished to go down the mountain with Wei. Again his wife dissuaded him, saying it would be inauspicious for him to leave home before the holiday season was over, which lasted fifteen days after the festival. She argued hard with Bai and became so upset that she burst into tears. After Wei left with his footmen, Bai and his wife talked late into the night. Finally both agreed that Bai should go and take a look. If Prince Yong didn't treat him well, he should return immediately.

Bai and his wife didn't know that just a few days earlier, An

Lushan had been murdered by his own servant, a eunuch he had raised and trusted. His death halted the momentum of the rebel forces. It also meant that the court would now begin to reunify the country and eliminate any elements that stood to breach the nation. This was the popular sentiment at the moment too. Prince Yong now was viewed by Emperor Suzong, and by many people, as a rebel who must be subdued. Indeed, for months the prince had been busy recruiting troops and the support of public figures but had not succeeded in finding anyone willing to join his camp. Li Bai, completely ignorant of the complexity of the political situation, was the only public figure who expressed support for him.

As soon as the holiday season ended, Wei Zichun came up Mount Lu again. This time he brought with him four men carrying an exquisite sedan chair, which Wei said was the very vehicle used by Prince Yong himself. Wei told Bai that this was his third visit to the mountain: Bai must leave with him or he, Wei, would be unable to go back and face his master. So Bai put on new clothes and a felt hat. He was in such exalted spirits that he wrote three poems for his wife, the second of which said, "As I am leaving, my better half grabs my robe, / Asking when I will be back from the west. / I joke that when I return wearing a gold seal, / Do not refuse to leave your weaving wheel to see me" ("Leaving for the Front and Bidding Goodbye to My Wife"). But she could not share his buoyant mood and turned into their inner room, struggling to hold back her tears.

Wei Zichun was puzzled by Bai's poem and asked him why he expected his wife to be unwilling to see him if he came home as a major official. Bai explained she was such an accomplished Daoist that she viewed high positions as an earthly attachment, a kind of vulgarity. On the way down to Jiujiang, Bai also composed a poem for Wei, which ended with these lines: "At last I can pacify the country. / After the success I'll head for the five lakes" ("For Counselor Wei Zichun"). Having gone through decades of frustration and disappointment, Bai was still the same man who dreamed of becoming a great statesman and a legendary recluse.

In Jiujiang, the sight of Prince Yong's large fleet pitched Bai into ecstasy. On the flagship, a banquet was prepared in his honor. The prince and his advisers and generals all partook in the feast. The last flotilla had just arrived, drumbeats rising and falling among the ships, horns sounding frequently. At the feast, as fifes and mandolins began to play, a group of girls started to dance. Although the prince did not appoint Bai as an officer or official—everything indicated that the poet was merely a cultural decoration in Prince Yong's camp—Bai was in raptures and couldn't stop talking loudly about his political aspirations. He even called the fleet "the royal force" and Prince Yong "the Son of Heaven," completely convinced that he was helping the royal family save the dynasty. He composed a poem at the banquet praising the prince as the savior of the people in the central land.

Afterward, Bai continued to write a series of poems titled "Songs of Prince Yong Marching East," which consisted of eleven works. They all eulogized the rebellious prince: Bai called him "My Divine Lord" and "My Virtuous Sovereign." He even wrote that the prince's forces would fight all the way to Chang'an to pay homage to the Son of Heaven. These praises and hyperboles were inconsistent and disordered—and would later serve as evidence of Bai's crime.

As Prince Yong's army moved east to engage Emperor Suzong's forces, Bai was confident that his new master's infantry and navy would prevail. It happened that Gao Shi, who was Li Bai's poet friend, was serving on the opposing side in the camp of Suzong as a military commander and the emperor's chief counselor. This was the man who had spent several months with Li Bai and Du Fu in Henan and Shandong twelve years before. Quite a few times the three poets had even shared a large quilt in the same bed so that they could keep warm. At that time, although Bai was already well known and Gao Li and Du Fu were obscure, Bai had treated them as genuine friends. Now Li Bai and Gao Shi, each serving their own masters, had to face each other as enemies. Unlike Gao Shi, a man of political acumen and military skills, Bai was foolish, consumed by delusion, unaware of the implacable animosity between the new emperor and Prince Yong.

Prince Yong had no experience in governing a country or commanding a large army. Even before his men engaged the enemy near Nanjing, his army had collapsed and been destroyed by Emperor Suzong's forces. His ships were burned and sunk, and none of his generals were able to stop their soldiers from deserting. The prince himself fled southwest toward Jiujiang but was wounded, caught, and then killed by troops led by a local official. Li Bai managed to run from the battlefield and desperately headed south. But before he could reach Mount Lu, he was captured and put in a jailhouse outside Jiujiang. He became a criminal condemned by the public.

24

IMPRISONMENT

Li Bai was hallucinatory and raved in prison for days. Even after he had calmed down, his hands still shook, but he worked furiously on a petition. He believed he had been unjustly arrested. Between his bouts of writing, he read a volume of *Records of the Grand Historian* by Sima Qian (154–90 BC), attempting to find strength in the stories of heroic historical figures. His wife had managed to deliver a few books to him and he was allowed to keep them in jail. At the same time, he felt remorseful for having incidentally gotten entangled in the politics of court. He had become a joke and a criminal in the public opinion, though he did not believe he was guilty. Sometimes he would raise his head and shout out his complaints, but the guards ignored him.

One day in late March a young man named Zhang Mengxiong came to see Bai. Zhang was a fan of Bai's and told him that he was going to Yangzhou to join the army led by Gao Shi. He also told Bai that General Ji Guangshen was now serving on Gao Shi's staff. Bai was amazed: Guangshen had been Prince Yong's major officer and should have been punished, if not executed, but it seemed he was safe and even had a high position in the army of the former enemy. Meanwhile, Bai had landed in prison with an uncertain fate. It was likely that he would be exiled.

The more Bai thought about this, the more convinced he became that he deserved more lenience: he had never fought against the emperor's army and had joined Prince Yong's camp for less than a month. So he decided to appeal to Gao Shi for help. Gao was a military commander of two circuits, a major power in Emperor Suzong's government. He was the only poet in the Tang dynasty to have reached such an important position, though later he would fall from the pinnacle of his career. Bai felt uncomfortable appealing to Gao Shi openly, so he wrote a poem instead and asked Zhang Mengxiong to deliver it to Gao Shi personally in Yangzhou. The poem praises Gao Shi for his victory over Prince Yong's army and expresses Bai's remorse and emotional turmoil. The last four lines state, "I don't have much bitterness, / Though everything, good or bad, was destroyed. / What can I say trapped in such a situation? / All I can do is shed my tears" ("Goodbye to Scholar Zhang Who Is Leaving for Inspector Gao's Camp"). Bai hoped that his old friend would see his plight and offer his help. At the same time, he could not afford to complain openly—if Gao Shi turned against him, the poem could be used as evidence of his hatred for the court—so his language is rather bland and hesitant.

Zhang Mengxiong delivered the poem to Gao Shi, but the latter remained reticent about it. About a month later, Zhang sent a poetic note to Bai, which informed him, "It's a pity that you're not Ji Guangshen, / Having no power or troops. / A man of books is worthless like dirt / And had better not expect any help."[1] Evidently Zhang had made no progress with Gao Shi and reported the bad news to Bai, who was devastated by his old friend's silence. Meanwhile, at his wife's insistence, he completed the petition he had written on his own behalf, proclaiming his innocence. Miss Zong began to present it to powerful people, attempting to find a way to get him out of prison. She paid bribes to men in key positions, spending all the gold Bai had received from Prince Yong. She went to Gao Shi to beg for his help, but the man would not receive her (and still would not respond to Bai's poem). Clearly, Gao feared being implicated in Bai's case.

It might be unfair to judge Gao Shi too harshly: he had been generous to his other friends and even had provided for the impoverished Du Fu, building him a cottage and arranging for his family to receive foodstuffs. Yet his refusal to help Li Bai remains a stain on his character: to this day, Li Bai's fans condemn him for having betrayed the great poet. They tend to neglect the fact that Li Bai was the only public figure who aligned himself with Prince Yong—all other noted literary men, including Du Fu, supported Emperor Suzong. Viewed through this lens, Bai was a national disgrace, a criminal who had worked against the country's unification, which had become a popular mandate.

However, there were other friends of Bai's who worked to get him out of jail. Among them were Cui Huan and Song Ruosi, both high officials who were well connected in the central government. When Bai's wife learned that Song's father and Bai had been close friends during their time in the capital, she went to Song with Bai's petition. He agreed to do his best to help. Song was an assistant director of the Royal Censorate and had been traveling with three thousand troops under his command to review criminal cases in the southern prefectures. Through Song Ruosi, Bai's wife also secured the assistance of Cui Huan. The two officials had heard that Emperor Suzong had wept on learning about his brother's death. His Majesty flew into a rage, blaming the local official who had had Prince Yong killed without first bringing him to the court. The emperor stripped the official of his post and announced that he would be "unsuitable for employment for the rest of his life." In fact, this was just a show on the part of the emperor to mask his own guilt—without the order from His Majesty, no one would have dared to put the prince to the sword. Yet by seizing this moment when the emperor appeared to forgive his brother, Cui Huan and Song Ruosi managed to put in a good word for Li Bai and have him released from prison. Bai stayed on Song's staff as a civilian adviser, where he was safe and could recuperate.

In the fall, the court finally returned to Chang'an. Throughout China people celebrated what appeared to be the restoration of the imperial reign. But the victory was dubious and even shameful: the emperor had not been able to take back the capital with the Chinese army alone. Instead, he had borrowed tens of thousands of troops from the Uighur State and let them attack the defending rebels. The Tang court made a pact with the Uighurs to divide the spoils: "When the capital is recaptured, all the land and people of high classes shall belong to the Tang government, whereas gold, silver, fabrics, women, and servants all shall go to the Uighurs." This agreement also applied to Luoyang. As a result, the foreign troops sacked both cities and inflicted tremendous destruction.[2] Nonetheless, the court wished the whole country to celebrate its return to Chang'an. Even convicts were given better food for a day. Li Bai also became infected by the excitement and wrote ten poems to sing his praises of the event. The series of poems was sent to the palace by his friends, who hoped that they would please the emperor enough that His Majesty would award Bai a position. The country needed an indispensable talent like Li Bai now more than ever, they argued.

Bai also wrote a self-recommendation to Song Ruosi and intended to have it passed on to the emperor. In the letter, he said that as a man who was deeply knowledgeable in the arts and capable of managing civilian affairs, he was still useful to the country. He implored, "Please grant me a post in the capital." Even though already fifty-six, an old man by the standards of the time, Bai kept alive the dream of having a high position near the emperor. He believed that he deserved a reward now that he had been absolved of any misdeed. He also regarded himself as "a supremely cultured man," a great celebrity whose presence could draw all kinds of talent to Chang'an. But although Song Ruosi dutifully dispatched the letter to court, he was unsure that Bai would be allowed to proceed to the capital: they were yet to hear from the emperor about how to handle Li Bai's case, which was actually still pending despite Bai's own conviction of his innocence. Bai was notorious throughout the country; only a few friends remained loyal and sympathetic to him. Du Fu was one of them and wrote several poems lamenting Li Bai's fate. In one poem, he says, "People all want to have him executed, / But my heart alone aches for his gift." In the same poem, Du Fu, trapped in Sichuan himself, summons Li Bai to return to his home region: "The quiet reading place on Kuang Mountain is the same. / Please come back despite your full head of white hair."[3]

Then Bai wrote Song Ruosi a petition in which he suggested that the court move to Nanjing and make it the new capital. Indeed, Nanjing possessed a great cultural heritage and was perfectly situated, sitting in the north of the fertile Wu land, against a mountain to the south and the Yangtze to the north. The city was a natural fortress, Bai argued, a most auspicious place for the new capital. Many dynasties had set up their capitals in Nanjing, so Emperor Suzong should seriously consider moving east. In the petition, Bai spoke eloquently, like a classical state counselor, a role he had always dreamed of for himself. There were many advantages, he argued, in moving the capital to Nanjing, to which many rich families had fled from the north during the rebellion: the land was now the wealthiest area in the country. Bai must also have intended to remind the emperor of his sincerity and concern for the royal family and their dynasty.

In spite of all this, it was unlikely that Bai could have himself fully exonerated of his egregious misdeed, which had in fact arisen from a more deeply rooted cause. Ever since his studies with his teacher Zhao Rui in his youth, Li Bai had been possessed with the spirit of the migrant advisers and knights-errant of the Warring States, ready to seize any opportunity to help a sovereign expand his territory and conquer his neighboring countries. For those ancient statesmen, chaotic times usually presented the optimal moment for such action. Bai's foreign origins also had influenced his blunder—the chieftains of the western tribes often ascended the throne by brute force, heedless of decorum and procedure. We can say that Bai's act was in keeping with the core of his mind-set and character.

Not until the end of 757 did the emperor's reply come. It decreed Li Bai's punishment: "Banish him to Yelang for three years." Yelang was a far-flung county in the southwest, more than a thousand miles away. Everyone was stunned: his wife cried for days and Bai was devastated. Such a banishment, however, was a light punishment compared to what the emperor had originally had in mind for him. His Majesty viewed Li Bai as an accomplice of Prince Yong, which meant that he should have been sentenced to death. But General Guo Ziyi, the officer Bai had saved from execution thirteen years before, implored Emperor Suzong to spare the poet. It is said that Guo was willing to sacrifice his own position in exchange for Bai's life. Guo was a brilliant warrior who had led his army back from the northeast and helped retake Chang'an from the rebels. By now he had become a linchpin of the country, so the emperor relented and showed mercy to Bai.

Zong Jing, Bai's brother-in-law, joined his sister to see Bai off at Sugong Town. They accompanied him south for twenty miles to Jiujiang, where he boarded a boat to sail up the Yangtze. Then sister and brother turned back and returned to Henan. Because of his fame, Bai was treated decently by his guards; his wife had also given them each a piece of jewelry to ensure they would not be rough with him (though he had to wear irons at all times). By rule they were to arrive at Yelang within a year, but an additional clause to the rule also said, "Extension may be allowed for exceptional circumstances." So they let Bai proceed at his own pace—he could stay in a town or port as long as he wanted on their travel up the river—the guards could report that the convict was ill and had to pause from time to time. After a year's imprisonment, Li Bai had indeed grown very frail and bony. He had also aged considerably and now had the gray hair of an old man.

The journey was slow and arduous. Fortunately, they could take breaks on occasion. As on his previous travels, Bai would run into friends in the towns and cities along the river; though in disgrace now, he didn't always meet hospitality as before. Some friends would host him and keep him for days, sometimes even a month. When they reached Jiangxia (modern Wuhan), its governor, Wei Liangzai, who was a friend of Bai's, received him as an honored guest. Liangzai persuaded Bai to stay in his city for two months so that he could recuperate. In August when they arrived at Hanyang, a port town in Hubei, another friend of Bai's from his days in the capital, Zhang Wei, kept him in his home for a whole month. In mid-fall they reached Jiangling, where again friends and local officials hosted Bai for several days. The guards themselves enjoyed the journey to a degree because they were treated to fine dinners and had time to relax.

Not until winter did they enter the Three Gorges. As they traveled up the river, the mountains on both sides grew higher and higher and the hilly landscape turned to rocky walls and cliffs. The waterway narrowed and flowed more rapidly. Bai had traveled this way when he had left Sichuan at the age of twenty-four, but on that journey he had been sailing down the river. Now they were going up against the current, and the boat had to be pulled by trackers. They proceeded so slowly that the pace surprised and frustrated Bai. At Yellow Oxen Mountain, the boat hardly moved at all. Weary and bored, Li Bai wrote this poem:

巫山夾青天　巴水流若茲
巴水忽可盡　青天無到時
三朝上黃牛　三暮行太遲
三朝又三暮　不覺鬢成絲

《上三峽》

Going up the river, we enter Wu Mountain,
Where hills hold the gray sky in between.
The water suddenly seems to end,
Although the sky stretches ahead endlessly.
Three mornings we've gone up the Oxen Gorge
And three evenings we still sail in it.
For three full days we cannot get out of it.
This pace makes my hair grow white and sparse.

"GOING UP THE THREE GORGES"

It took them two months to emerge from the Three Gorges. Not until the early spring did they reach Fengjie, the ancient Baidi Town. From there they would turn south and head down toward Yelang. This was Bai's first time back in his homeland of Sichuan. The dialect was refreshing and comforting to his ears, the food tasted spicier and more peppery, and everything reminded him of his youth. Even the butterflies and dragonflies looked as familiar as if he had met them before. His hometown in the northwest wasn't far away, but he needed to follow his course, trudging south by land. For more than three decades he had dreamed of returning home; now finally he was back in the land of Shu, but only as a criminal. Even if he had been allowed to continue northwest, he wouldn't have let his family and neighbors see him in such a condition. He would only have brought them disgrace and heartbreak. Besides, his parents had died long before.

As Bai was about to depart from Fengjie, suddenly word came that he had been pardoned. No one had expected such wonderful news, and Li Bai was astounded, unable to understand what had happened. In fact, his pardon came from an unlikely and impersonal source. A severe drought had been plaguing the central land, and so the court, in its efforts to combat the natural disaster and unite the country, granted amnesty to all exiled convicts. Bai was ecstatic and believed the pardon signaled the end of his troubles. All the evil chancellors who had once hounded him were dead now, and even the head eunuch, Gao Lishi, had been expelled from the palace. Bai had no more enemies at court. His path to the capital was finally open, he believed, and in all likelihood he could ascend again.

Without delay he boarded a small boat, sailing down the river swiftly. His buoyant mood inspired him to compose a verse, which would become another masterpiece of his:

朝辭白帝彩雲間　千里江陵一日還
兩岸猿聲啼不住　輕舟已過萬重山

《早發白帝城》

In the morning I leave Baidi Town hidden in colored clouds,
Sailing three hundred miles back to Jiangling in a single day.
Before the gibbons on both shores can stop screaming,
My light boat has passed ten thousand hills.

"LEAVING BAIDI TOWN IN THE MORNING"

The beauty and fluidity of these lines is charged with political resonance. The swift boat is unstoppable, no matter how the gibbons leap and clamor. Bai is darting back to the central land. In his mind, this sudden twist of fate foreshadowed his imminent ascent.

He misunderstood the pardon, which stemmed from a general amnesty, believing instead that the emperor had been so impressed by his writings that he had granted him a personal favor of clemency. Therefore he decided not to immediately return to his wife and instead stayed in the region near Dongting Lake, waiting for the new appointment that would bring him back to the capital.

25

DISILLUSION AND THE END

All Li Bai chronologies find him returning to Jiangxia (modern Wuhan) in the spring of 760. Azaleas and cherry flowers were in bloom, swallows darted back and forth, and the streets bustled with activity. The city was in a festive mood: people believed that the rebels had finally been suppressed and that the central government was restoring peace and order throughout the country. Bai too was in good spirits, expecting to be summoned to the capital. Jiangxia was now a political center in the south, home to many high officials. They often invited Bai to their banquets and parties, mainly to impress their guests of honor with the presence of such a well-known artist (though to some people his reputation was tarnished by the stain of treason). But Bai would get drunk and act as if he were a host or one of the honored guests. He composed poems that boasted of his ability and aspiration. On one occasion he compared himself to a great fish trapped in a roadside puddle, dreaming of returning to the ocean. On another, he said he hoped to become a great roc able to soar into the sky. He would dance and perform sword routines for the other guests, but his performances were pale versions of his former abilities. His behavior tended to embarrass his hosts.

Then he composed a long poem titled "Song of the Divine Horse," an allegory that depicts the life of a beautiful celestial steed from a western region. In his youth the horse is full of strength, fast, and handsome, but when he grows old, his feet cannot move as swiftly as before, though he still dreams of drawing his master's carriage through the clouds. Now the horse has been harnessed as a draft animal, transporting salt up hilly roads. How he hopes someone will recognize the great horse within him! Even without his former vigor and speed, he can still serve as a grand symbol up in heaven when a dance is performed at the side of a jade pool where he had often stood before. The poem echoed Bai's own life too well, and as a result, he didn't know to whom he could present it. Bai felt bewildered by such uncertainty: all his life he had given poems as gifts, which had invariably been cherished by the recipients. Now he couldn't think of anyone who might appreciate this poem.

The mayor of Jiangxia, Wei Liangzai, was preparing to depart for a new post. He had done good deeds for the city, so the local powers initiated a project of erecting a monument that would record his virtues and accomplishments. They commissioned Li Bai for the text to be carved on the stone. The mayor was a friend of Bai's, so the poet worked hard on the short essay; later, he even wrote a lengthy poem for Liangzai personally. In the poem he told the departing man, "You are going to ascend to the phoenix pool, / But don't forget the talent of a struggling scholar. . . . / Every night I sigh four or five times, / Worried about our great country" ("For Jiangxia Mayor Wei Liangzai—Memories of the Separation from My Family and the Exile Granted by the Emperor"). He implored Liangzai to recommend him for a post in the capital. Such a request was beyond his friend's ability, so before leaving, Liangzai gave Bai a cane with a jade handle as a gift, which seemed to be the best way he could thank him for his work. Bai realized that again his efforts to return to the capital had gotten nowhere. In spite of the pardon from the emperor, he was still a semi-criminal in many people's eyes and was even viewed as a madman by others.

In the fall, he went to Baling on the southwestern side of

Dongting Lake. It was a small town with a long cultural history, and was frequented by visitors, especially literary figures. There Bai met his poet friend Jia Zhi, who had recently been banished from the capital. Then a distant uncle of Bai's, Li Ye, arrived to visit Baling. Ye was a new exile, too, but had been ordered to a more remote place in the southern borderland and was on his way to his new place and only passing through. The three men talked about the news in Chang'an and the nefarious nature of official life. From his uncle, Bai learned that the rebels were still active in some areas. The emperor had ordered Generals Guo Ziyi and Li Guangbi to move their forces about at random, an order that rendered them unable to fight effectively and thus caused them to lose a major battle to the rebels, incurring tens of thousands of casualties. Bai also learned that An Lushan's follower Shi Siming had again occupied large parts of Hebei and Henan and proclaimed himself the new ruler of Great Yan. The so-called restoration, which had kept officials at all levels busy with celebrations, was in Li Ye's opinion a joke.

Together the three of them went boating on the lake and climbed up Yueyang Tower, where many poets had left their lines inscribed on the walls. It was drizzling and the rain soured their mood. As Bai spent more time with the two men, he saw that neither Jia nor his uncle expected to be called back to the capital despite the fact that some exiles had returned after they served their terms of banishment. Jia was afraid he might have to spend the rest of his life in Baling, which he viewed as a godforsaken town. Bai tried to comfort him, but to no avail. Ye, despite his advanced years, was in a better mood; he didn't seem to care where he might end up, and even claimed that he'd count himself lucky if he didn't live out his final days in poverty. By now Bai was convinced that he himself had no chance of returning to the palace, and that it was silly for him to expect such a favor from the emperor.

Bai departed Baling for Yuzhang (modern Wuchang), where his

wife now lived. But conflict blocked his path: a group of local officials in Rangzhou had rebelled against the central government, and the fighting cut off the roads. So Li Bai wandered in the area east of Dongting Lake. He traveled to a town near Yueyang to see his old friend Cui Zongzhi, who was yet another exile from the capital. To his dismay, he found his friend had died. Zongzhi had been a handsome man with a sonorous singing voice, and the fond memories of him saddened Bai. Zongzhi had left a manuscript of poems, *Lakeside Songs*. Li Bai wrote a preface for it, stating that his friend, a good honest man, had been persecuted to death.

Having met so many exiles, none of whom had returned to the capital, Bai wanted only to go home, join his wife, and live out his life in peace. He waited for the suppression of the new rebels and for the roads to reopen. Not until the spring of 761 did he manage to reach home.

Bai found his wife's hair had grayed considerably. She was aged and pallid, perhaps owing to malnutrition: there had been a famine caused by drought, and most people were living hand to mouth. She was happy to see him back and even pawned some of her jewelry to give him a fine dinner for the reunion. Li Bai was sixty-nine years old now and felt ashamed, still without a regular income to his name. Their remaining properties in Shandong and Henan had been lost in the war, reducing the couple nearly to paupers. Bai's brother-in-law had invited them to join his family again in Liang Park, but they were reluctant to accept the offer because it would be very hard for Zong Jing to support both of them. Jing was a petty official of the ninth rank, hardly able to provide for his own family on his meager salary. Then a letter came from Bai's wife's master, Li Tengkong, summoning her disciple up to Mount Lu. The master had settled in a Daoist convent there and resumed practicing folk medicine and producing the elixir of life.

She wanted Bai's wife to come and help her with war-refugee relief work and to continue their religious cultivation.

Bai agreed to let his wife go and join her master, and even accompanied her up to Mount Lu. He wanted to ensure that she could remain there safely. After seeing her settle in, he headed back. He felt like a homeless man, with very little to return to, so again he struck out on the road, trusting that he could always find food and lodging and even some money along the way. He went to Nanjing, the city he loved. But Nanjing was no longer the same. The war had razed thousands of villages and towns and killed millions of people ("white bones piled up like mountains," as Bai witnessed). Refugees were everywhere, and everything was more expensive now. The prosperity of the south was gone, so the officials were no longer as generous as before in receiving ordinary guests. Worse yet, Bai, as a man with a criminal past, was a problematic presence to many of them. Nevertheless, because of his fame and his former position at the Imperial Academy, he was still invited to parties. He was also commissioned to compose poems and short essays, which earned enough for his keep. He could still afford to drink every day. At the parties and dinners, he often became swept up in the festivities, improvising poems that expressed his bitterness and his aspiration, but people did not respond to his work as they used to. In the public eye he was a bit passé. Brash young men would tease him and even offer him menial jobs, to which he would not debase himself to respond. Whenever he was commissioned to write an essay about an official's deeds and virtues, he would try to attach himself to the official's crew, but he was always paid promptly so that they could wash their hands of him. So whenever he received payment, Bai would only feel humiliated and blame himself for wasting his talent and time. As summer approached and the weather grew hot, his temper grew more irascible, and he often took off his felt hat and brandished it at others or threw it on the table.

In May, both the Grand Emperor Xuanzong and the new emperor died within weeks of each other. The court was in chaos, and different factions began fighting fiercely for the throne. When the courtiers backed by the queen were defeated, they were either executed or imprisoned by the group supported by the eunuchs. Finally a new emperor, Daizong, was enthroned. For the entire summer the country was in disarray, and the rebels continued to resurge in the north. By now Li Bai was no longer interested in what happened at court, but then he heard that General Li Guangbi's army was moving to Henan to take Shangqiu back from the rebels. Bai admired Li Guangbi for the victorious battles he had fought in recent years and for the discipline of his troops. Li Guangbi and Guo Ziyi had become the two great warriors the country now depended on.

Bai and his wife had lived in Shangqiu; it was like their hometown, the site of happy times he had shared with Yuan Danqiu and Du Fu. So he decided to set off north to join General Li's army. Although already sixty years old, Bai still viewed himself as a capable warrior and dreamed of serving as an officer or adviser to Li Guangbi. He redeemed his sword from a pawnshop, bought a spear from a weapon store, attached a scarlet tassel to its head, and donned the brocade robe Emperor Xuanzong had once granted him. He then borrowed an old horse from a friend. Without delay he started out north. By joining the imperial army, he intended to redeem himself. He explains in a lengthy poem, "I want to wipe away my shame / And earn favor and honor with valiant deeds" ("On Hearing General Li March Southeast with a Million Troops, Though a Feeble Man, I Want to Join Him"). He also held a sincere commitment to the nation: he confessed that every night he sighed, worried about his "great country." It was very likely that he had been in touch with General Li Guangbi or had friends in Li's camp who had agreed to help him.[1]

Throughout Li Bai's life, one of his great skills was his ability to forge genuine friendships with so many people. Wherever he went and however dire his circumstances were, he could always find help one way or another. But not even halfway to Henan, he fell ill and his horse collapsed from exhaustion. He lay in an inn for a few days, then gave up the trip. He at last admitted that he was too old to fight as a soldier.

Back in Nanjing, he wondered what to do. Should he go back to Yuzhang, where his wife still had a cottage? He decided not to, certain that she wouldn't return from Mount Lu without her master's permission. From what Bai had seen in his last meeting with Li Tengkong, it was unlikely that the master would allow his wife to leave. The two women were as close as sisters, and his wife was more dedicated to her Daoist practice than ever. His son Boqin was not far away, in Xi Prefecture (Wu E had found Boqin in Shandong and succeeded in bringing him to the south), but Bai was unsure if Boqin could support him. Should he return to his hometown in Sichuan? That was out of the question—the shame and sorrow would break everyone's heart, including his own. Having thought for many days, he decided to go to Dangtu County, where a relative of his, Li Yangbing, was the magistrate. Although there might in fact be no true blood tie between them, Bai had once written a poem for Li Yangbing in which he called him "my uncle," praising him as one of the heroes of their clan and celebrating his calligraphy: "Your brush inscribes words in Zuan style / Shattering clouds and surprising people" ("For My Uncle Yangbing, the Magistrate of Dangtu County"). Indeed, Li Yangbing was one of the great calligraphers in Tang China, perhaps the greatest. He is regarded as "one in a millennium" by later generations.

To Bai's relief, Li Yangbing received him wholeheartedly, as kin. But as soon as Bai settled down in Dangtu, he fell ill—his ribs rotted open and he had to take to his bed. He must have had a chronic thoracic problem, aggravated by his drinking. Yangbing sent for doctors, but the affliction had been festering in Bai for so long that the doctors couldn't cure him. It was already winter, and he stayed in bed day and night.

At the end of 761, Yangbing's appointment expired and he had to return to the capital for a new assignment, so he dispatched men to fetch Bai's wife and son. Boqin came to Dangtu without delay to care for Bai. His wife never arrived; perhaps the messenger hadn't been able to find her secluded dwelling in Mount Lu. Yangbing found Boqin a job at a local salt station and left Bai with all the cash he could gather. He also gave Bai a large bundle of his calligraphy so that the poet might be able to sell some of the pieces if the need arose. Although there was no market for artwork in the wake of the war, the calligraphy would gain value in the future. As a low-ranking official, Yangbing wasn't rich; he simply did whatever he could for Bai.

Having made these arrangements, Yangbing went to Bai to say goodbye. Bai sat up in bed and grabbed Yangbing's hand and held it for a long time. Then he gave him all the poetry manuscripts he had with him. He sensed that his end was coming, so he began to tell Yangbing about his life. He spoke slowly and as concisely as though leaving behind a small autobiography, which could serve as the information needed for an epitaph. Yangbing wrote down his words.

Yangbing promised to have the manuscripts published as one volume and to use Bai's autobiographical account as a part of the preface to the book. He spent three nights editing and polishing his notes. Then he read it out to Li Bai. Bai nodded in approval and closed his eyes. Before leaving, Yangbing assured Bai that his talent would find no match. He was "unrivaled in the last one thousand years" and his work would last forever. It was his great honor and fortune for his life to have crossed with Bai's. The two men bade farewell with tears.

· · ·

To everyone's surprise, when spring came, Bai recovered. With a cane, he could move around on his own, and was invigorated by the news that the rebels had been quelled throughout the country and peace had finally prevailed. He began to go out to enjoy the spring: the birdsong, the leafing trees, the blooming orchids and azaleas, the babbling brooks. The air was filled with the scent of acacia blossoms. Occasionally he joined local farmers for a bowl of wine. He would stay in their adobe houses until dark. When he came home, he was pleased to find his son waiting for him in the front yard to help him into their cottage.

As the spring deepened the color of the grass and trees, he remembered his nephew Li Zhao in Xuan Town, which was a mere fifty miles to the south and for which he always had a soft spot. Although unsure if Zhao was still there, Bai decided to return to the town. He set out, using a walking stick as he plodded along and hitching a ride on an oxcart whenever he could. But when he arrived, he found that Li Zhao had left for another post long before. The new man, who was in charge not only of the town but was also governor of the entire prefecture, was Ji Guangshen— the general who had once served Prince Yong and had then been permitted to return to the emperor's fold in Gao Shi's army. Now Ji Guangshen and his administrative personnel were all based in Xuan Town, while his troops were stationed in nearby counties.

He was pleased to see Bai and treated him to dinner. He had a task for which a talented writer like Bai was needed. A vice governor under Ji Guangshen, one Mr. Liu, had recently done some praise-worthy deeds, which the governor wanted to report to the central government so that Liu could be promoted and rewarded. Li Bai believed that Ji Guangshen was treating him as a friend, so he wrote a long poem in praise of Mr. Liu. Bai imagined that the governor might let him stay somewhere near Jingting Hill, the place he had loved so much. But as soon as he presented the poem to Ji Guang-shen, the governor merely praised the lines and handed him some cash, saying the money was for his expenses on the road. Clearly the official—who shared the same infamous association with Prince Yong—didn't want to be associated with Bai in any significant way.

For decades Bai had been torn between two worlds—the top political circle and the religious order—but had been unable to exist in either one. In his own words, "Trying to be prosperous and divine, / I have simply wasted my life in pursuing both" ("A Long Song"). He imagined each world as its own kind of heaven ("The palaces in Chang'an rise above the ninth heaven / Where I was once a courtier beside the emperor" ["In an Autumn Night and at the East Building in Shan County, Seeing My Cousin Shen Off to Chang'an"]), where he was unable to remain because he was doomed by his love for both. However, Bai's conflicting pursuits stemmed from the same thing: his awareness of his limited life span as a human being. Wealth and fame would maximize his experiences, while Daoism was a way to extend his time on earth. Both of his pursuits produced only pain and loneliness. To dull the misery he resorted to drinking: "The divine world is more hallucinatory now, / So it will be more real to get drunk" ("Imitation of Ancient Poems [3]").

He roamed Xuan Town but couldn't find any of his old friends. He remembered the wine house that used to sell the local brew Deep Spring. He missed that wine, which had a long aftertaste. He found the spot where the shop had once stood, but nothing was left there except for an aspen, which was half a foot thick now. He asked others about the owner, Old Ji, and was told that the man had died of illness a few years before. Remembering how kind and generous the shop owner had been to him, Bai wept and wrote a poem in memory of the wine-maker: "Even in the underworld / Old Ji still brews wine. / But Bai is not down there yet, / So who do you sell it to?" ("Mourning Old Wine-Maker Ji in Xuan Town").

He wandered to Nanling, an area just west of Xuan Town. The friends he'd once had there were all gone, and many of the fields were overgrown with weeds. The war had ruined the countryside as well. Fortunately he came upon a farming family, the Xuns, who let him in for the night. The head of the household, whom Bai had known, was already dead, and only the widow and her son remained. They were happy to see Bai and welcomed him as a guest, but there was no food left in the house and they couldn't provide him with a decent meal, much less a cup of wine. The young man went into a shallow pond down the mountain and gathered wild rice plants. Once the ears of the rice were husked, which was an arduous process, the grains would be edible, but would need to be boiled for a long time. Still, the rice had a smooth texture and tasted much better than wild herbs and grain bran.

As the widow was busy husking the rice, Bai began to talk with her and her son. From them he learned that taxes had not been reduced despite the poor harvest of the past several years, and that many people, unable to pay, had simply abandoned their properties and fled. This news made Bai pensive. If this fertile area was so poor now, what was the rest of the country like?

Once the wild rice was cooked and served on plates, the widow urged Bai to eat, but he was so disheartened that he couldn't muster even a hint of appetite. That night he composed a poem:

我宿五松下　寂寥無所歡
田家秋作苦　鄰女夜春寒
跪進雕胡飯　月光明素盤
令人慚漂母　三謝不能餐

《宿五松山下荀媼家》

In the evening I stop at Five Pine Mountain,
Where the village feels deserted and lonesome.
The peasant families have to work hard.

The woman next door keeps pounding rice in the cold.
My hostess kneels to serve me wild rice,
Moonlight shining on the full white plate.
She makes me feel so unworthy that
I thank her three times and still cannot eat.

"SPENDING THE NIGHT AT WIDOW XUN'S
AT FIVE PINE MOUNTAIN"

This is another Li Bai, one we have rarely encountered. He had once been a man full of contempt, arrogance, and self-righteousness, but here we find him humbled by the hardship and generosity of the poor woman and her son. He had seen all kinds of extravagance in his life, but the offer of a plate of wild rice so overwhelmed him that he seemed not to know how to accept it. Although different from many of his more stylish and sublime poems, this plain verse is also a masterpiece, a unique one that shows Li Bai closer to his self.

Unable to find another person whom he had known in the Xuan Town area, Bai headed back to Dangtu to join his son. This was the end of his wandering; he felt it in his bones. Indeed, this was his last trip, a trip back to his family. We don't know when and how he died. His son buried him in a shabby grave, the public unaware of the disappearance of this great genius. Like a star in the sky, he burned out and vanished soundlessly. But we do know that during his final days he often chanted this poem, which was his last song:

大鵬飛兮振八裔　中天摧兮力不濟
餘風激兮萬世　遊扶桑兮掛左袂
後人得之傳此　仲尼亡兮誰為出涕

《臨終歌》

The great roc has been soaring all over the sky,
But it breaks a wing mid-flight.
Its spirit will inspire a thousand generations,
Though the divine tree in heaven catches its left wing.

People in the future will spread this story,
Yet all saints are dead—who will shed tears for me?

"THE FINAL SONG"

The great roc had been his personal symbol from his youth to his last days. It signified a heavenward journey he had attempted but finally failed. Now he was grounded, unable to take off again.

AFTERWORD

In January 764, a court decree came to Dangtu County. It appointed Li Bai as a counselor to the emperor. It was an honorary title, but still a significant post in the palace. At long last Bai had been summoned to the capital once more: when the new emperor had demanded that officials at all levels recommend talents to court, someone (perhaps also several others) had submitted Li Bai's name. The decree threw the government of Dangtu County into commotion, because no one knew where Li Bai was. By now he had been dead for more than a year.

Li Bai's friend Wei Hao was also unaware of his death. In 763, fulfilling the promise he had made to Bai nine years before, he published a book of the poet's writings, *Collected Works of Academician Li*. In addition to the manuscripts that Li Bai had entrusted him with, Wei Hao added other poems of Bai's that he had come across since 754. In his preface, Wei believes that his friend is still alive: "Li Bai is still writing, and I will leave this project in the hands of my son, who will bring out a new edition of Li Bai's poems." Wei Hao's edition was neglected and soon lost. Not until 1068 was it rediscovered. Around the same time as the appearance of Wei Hao's book, Bai's uncle, Li Yangbing, published his own collection of Bai's poems, *Straw Cottage Collection*. In the preface, Yangbing writes, "Nine out of ten of his poems are lost. What this book contains are mainly the poems written during Bai's last eight years, as well as poems that Bai had got back from others." During his later years, Li Bai asked people to give him copies of the poems he had written for them so that he could collect as many of them as possible. These two collections have formed the basis of his works we have today, which in total are about a thousand poems and essays.[1]

In the decades following Li Bai's death, the public seemed to forget him, but the younger generation of Tang poets cherished and celebrated his poetry. Some even went to visit his grave. Bai Juyi was one of them. In 799 Juyi, twenty-nine years old, arrived in Dangtu to pay homage to Li Bai. He managed to find his grave among the weeds and brambles on a riverside and wrote this poem:

采石江邊李白墳　　繞田無限草連雲
可憐荒壟窮泉骨　　曾有驚天動地文
但是詩人多薄命　　就中淪落不過君

《李白墓》

On the bank of Caishi River is Li Bai's grave
Surrounded by wild grass that stretches to clouds.
How sad that the bones buried deep in here
Used to have writings that startled heaven and moved earth.
Of course, poets are born unlucky souls,
But no one has been as desolate as you.

"AT LI BAI'S GRAVE"

Others were also seeking traces of Li Bai. More than fifty years after his death, Fan Chuan Zheng, a royal inspector, came to Xuan Prefecture, in which Dangtu County lay. Fan had been searching for Li Bai's grave and descendants: he was an admirer of Bai's work and, through the correspondence left behind, had discovered that his father had been friends with the great poet. With the help of Dangtu County's magistrate, Fan located the grave, which was almost invisible among wild grass.

It took three more years for them to find Li Bai's descendants—his granddaughters. One day, two women in their thirties reported to the county's administration. Their clothes were made of coarse fabric, patched but clean and neat. Fan could tell that they were peasant women. They seemed slightly nervous in front of the officials but remained composed. As the magistrate questioned them, they confirmed that Li Bai had been their grandfather and Boqin their father. So the officials invited the women to sit down. Fan explained to them that his own father had been a friend of their grandfather's and that he, Fan, had studied Li Bai's poems and essays since his childhood. Needless to say, he loved their grandfather's writings, and he wished to converse with them.

The two women looked bewildered. They seemed to be illiterate and to have no knowledge of poetry. All they could do was give brief answers to Fan's questions. Their father had died twenty years earlier, and before that he had worked at a salt station. They also had a brother, who had left home to seek his fortune elsewhere long ago. They hadn't heard from him for twelve years.

But how did they make their living now? Fan asked. Then he realized they were both married, and went on to ask about their husbands.

They answered that they had both married peasants and that their families grew crops to support themselves. One of the husbands was named Chen Yuan and the other Liu Quan.

But how did their families manage? the county magistrate put in.

They replied that they just had enough to eat.

The officials all sighed. Fan then asked the two women whether he could do anything to assist them.

They said they hoped that Fan could have their grandfather's grave moved to Green Hill in the south of the county. That was where Li Bai had hoped to be buried; Green Hill was also called

Master Xie's Hill, because Xie Tiao, Bai's literary hero, had once lived there.

Fan agreed to have a new grave built for Li Bai. When he asked if they had any other requests, they demurred.

The county magistrate whispered to the royal inspector for a moment. Then Fan turned to the women and said he could find them each a more suitable husband, since they had married so humbly.

The women were taken aback but regained their composure. They told Fan that their poor marriages had been their lot and were now also their duties, so they could not remarry. If they left their husbands for a more comfortable life, when the time came they would feel too ashamed to face their grandfather underground.

Fan Chuan Zheng complied with their wish. The local government granted their families exemptions from taxes and corvées. Later Fan wrote the text for the stone erected at Li Bai's new grave. In the essay, which is another major source of information on Li Bai, he recorded his meeting with Bai's two granddaughters and stated that although they both were married to poor men and led a hard life, their dignified manner still revealed traces of Li Bai.

NOTES

1. Li Changzhi, *A Biography of Li Bai,* 199.
2. An Qi, *Li Bai Zongheng Tan* (Xi'an: Shanxi People's Press, 1981), 77. In fact, there is a history of this version of Li Bai's death in which he rode a whale returning to the moon. For instance, Guo Xiangnian of the Song dynasty says about Li Bai in his poem "Caishi Ferry," "He rides the whale away and will never return, / Leaving behind his tomb covered by green grass." Li Junmin of the Jin dynasty writes in his "Portrait of Li Taibai," "Bai was banished to the world for some years / Where he became an immortal of wine. / If not because of the moon on Caishi River, / he wouldn't have ridden a whale back to heaven." The contemporary romanticization has continued this conventional legend.

I: ORIGINS

1. Wei Hao, "Preface to *Collected Works of Academician Li.*"
2. Gao Shi, "Farewell to Gentlemen Zhou, Liang, and Li in the Central Song Land."
3. The Tang dynasty's administrative divisions fell into this tri-tier order: circuits—prefectures—counties.
4. Li Bai, "On an Autumn Day, at Jingting Pavilion, Seeing My Nephew Off for Lushan."
5. Li Changzhi, *A Biography of Li Bai,* 144.
6. Zhou Xunchu, *A Critical Biography of Li Bai,* 29.
7. Zhou Xunchu, *The Mystery of the Poet Immortal Li Bai* (Taipei: Commerce Press, 1996), 116
8. *The Tang Law:* Clause 306. Li Bai's wife's grandfather Xu Yushi (?–679) was a chancellor at court, but his eldest son killed a man by accident while hunting. Xu Yushi covered up for his son, and as a result he was imprisoned for three months and then banished to a remote prefecture. Evidently, the Tang dynasty took manslaughter very seriously.
9. Li Changzhi, *The Daoist Poet Li Bai and His Suffering* (Tianjin: Tianjin People's Press, 2018), 18–19.

2: AWAY FROM HOME

1. In Li Bai's essay "To Deputy Prefect Pei of Anzhou."
2. Some people believe that Li Bai was a short man. I agree with those who hold that he was quite tall, because his essay "To Han Jingzhou" says about himself, "Although I'm not seven feet tall / My ambition surpasses ten thousand men's." A foot in his time was a bit shorter than ours, so his "seven feet" should be close to our six feet.

3: BACK IN HIS HOMETOWN

1. Quoted by Jiang Zhi, *Li Bai and the Regional Culture* (Chengdu: Bashu Book House, 2011), 100.
2. Jiang Zhi devoted a whole chapter to Li Bai as a petty bureaucrat in his book *Li Bai and Geographic Places* (Chengdu: Bushu Book House, 2011), 98–106.
3. Ibid., 85.

4: LEAVING SICHUAN

1. Liang Shufeng, "Exploring Li Bai's Reason for Leaving Shu for Wu," *China's Li Bai Studies* (2014): 27–39.
2. Yang Xueshi, "An Inquiry into Li Bai's Burying His Friend," *China's Li Bai Studies* (2009): 128–41.

5: DISSIPATION

1. Stephen Owen, *The Great Age of Chinese Poetry*, 62.
2. Yan Yu (1192?–1245) says in his *Canglang Poetry Talk*, "Among Tang poets' works, Cui Hao's 'Yellow Crane Tower' should be the number one poem in the regulated verse with seven-character lines." Item 46.

6: MARRIAGE

1. Stephen Owen, *The Great Age of Chinese Poetry*, 85.
2. Li Bai, "Letter to Deputy Prefect Pei of Anzhou."
3. I agree with Zhu Chuanzhong's interpretation of this poem. See his *The True Li Bai in the Tang Dynasty (Zhen tang Li Bai)* (Beijing: Tongxin Press, 2015), 49–52.

7: MARRIED LIFE

1. Li Bai, "An Official Reply to Magistrate Meng on Behalf of Shou Mountain."
2. This episode is recorded in An Qi, *Li Bai: A Biography,* 55–57.
3. Guangling was another name for Yangzhou.

8: IN THE CAPITAL

1. Zhou Xunchu, *A Critical Biography of Li Bai,* 165.

9: AWAY FROM THE CAPITAL

1. See Li Bai, "Letter to Han Jingzhou."

11: IN THE SOUTH

1. Quoted in *Shiren Yu Xie,* vol. xii, "Ancient Comments on Various Poets."
2. "Seventeen" here means Wu E is the seventeenth male of his generation in his clan, similar to Li Bai, who was often called "Li Twelve."
3. I adopted the years of Li Bai's children's births as they are indicated by Zhan Ying in his *Chronicle of Li Bai's Writings* (Beijing: People's Publishing House, 1984), which makes good sense to me. See *The Immortal Traces of Tai Bai* (Hefei: Huang Shan Book House, 2010), 146.

13: WOMEN

1. Fan Zhenwei, *Li Bai's Background, Marriages, and Family,* 343.
2. Ibid., 353–54.
3. Fan Zhenwei also believes that Li Bai joined the woman of Lu before he left for Chang'an in 742. Ibid., 354.

14: IN THE CAPITAL AGAIN

1. Guo Moruo, *Du Fu and Li Bai,* 42.
2. Du Fu, "Song of the Eight Divine Drinkers."
3. This episode has many versions and has been disputed among Li Bai scholars. The earliest record states that the emperor deflected Bai's request and Gao Lishi did not actually take off Bai's boots. But all the other later records indicate that Gao actually took off the boots, and Li Bai biographers have treated this episode as an actual incident. Either way, Bai, rash and arrogant, insulted one of the most

powerful men for no reason or cause except for his contempt for him. See Yang Yingying, "The Case of Gao Lishi Taking Off Li Bai's Boots," *China's Li Bai Studies* (2014): 154–68.

4. Stephen Owen, *The Great Age of Chinese Poetry*, 116.

15: POLITICAL INVOLVEMENT

1. The historical records of this episode are brief, but over the centuries it has evolved into a full legend with various versions. Lately a young scholar, Wang Song-lin, published a study of the case, which points out that the foreign emissary was from Balhae, a young country northeast of China, but his answer to how Li Bai learned the primitive language (through his intercourse with scholars and students from Balhae) is not convincing to me, so I have followed a conventional version of the episode here. Wang Song-li's paper "Decoding the Perpetual Mystery of the Fan Script" appears in *Song Liao Academic Journal: Social Sciences* 5 (2001): 28–33.

2. An Qi, *Li Bai: A Biography*, 150.

3. Ibid., 151.

16: THE MEETING OF TWO STARS

1. Quoted by Zhou Xunchu, *A Critical Biography of Li Bai*, 112.

2. See chapter 1, note 2.

17: LIFE IN TRANSITION

1. Wang Huiqin, *A Biography of Li Bai* (Beijing: Jinghua Press, 2002), 227.

2. Du Fu, "Together with Li Twelve, Seeking the Hermitage of Fan Ten."

3. See the very informative article by Tang Dexin, "On Li Bai's Daoist Life and the Cause of His Death," guoxue.com/wk/000621.htm.

4. Li Changzhi, *Daoist Poet Li Bai and His Suffering* (Tianjin: Tianjin People's Press, 2008), 37.

19: NEW MARRIAGE

1. Shen Yue, "Biography of Prince Liangsi," in *Song Shu*.

2. Fan Zhenwei, *Li Bai's Background, Marriages, and Family*, 346–47.

3. Ibid., 348.

4. Zhou Xunchu, *A Critical Biography of Li Bai*, 122–23.

20: ON THE NORTHEASTERN FRONTIER

1.   An Qi, *Li Bai: A Biography,* 185.

22: AN UNEXPECTED GUEST

1.   See chapter 1, note 1.
2.   Arthur Waley, *The Poetry and Career of Li Po,* 60.

24: IMPRISONMENT

1.   An Qi, *Li Bai: A Biography,* 219.
2.   Li Changzhi, *A Biography of Li Bai,* 195, 239.
3.   Du Fu, "Unable to See Him."

25: DISILLUSION AND THE END

1.   Guo Moruo, *Du Fu and Li Bai,* 89.

26: AFTERWORD

1.   Arthur Waley, *The Poetry and Career of Li Po,* 97–98.

SELECTED BIBLIOGRAPHY

An Qi. *Li Bai: A Biography.* Beijing: Culture and Arts Press, 1984.

China's Li Bai Studies. Maanshan: Institute of Li Bai Studies.

Fan Zhenwei. *Li Bai's Background, Marriages, and Family.* Harbin: Heilongjiang People's Press, 2002.

Guo Moruo. *Du Fu and Li Bai.* Beijing: China's Chang'an Press, 2010.

Li Changzhi. *A Biography of Li Bai.* Beijing: East Press, 2010.

Owen, Stephen. *The Great Age of Chinese Poetry: The High Tang.* New Haven, CT: Yale University Press, 1981.

Waley, Arthur. *The Poetry and Career of Li Po.* New York: Macmillan, 1950.

Zhou Xunchu. *A Critical Biography of Li Bai.* Nanjing: Nanjing University Press, 2005.

ACKNOWLEDGMENTS

My heartfelt thanks to LuAnn Walther, Catherine Tung, and Lane Zachary for their support and suggestions and patience; to Pei Yongjun and Jin Yu, who bought the books I needed and brought them out of China for me.

ABOUT THE AUTHOR

Ha Jin left his native China in 1985 to attend Brandeis University. He is the author of eight novels, four story collections, four volumes of poetry, and a book of essays. He has received the National Book Award, two PEN/Faulkner Awards, the PEN/Hemingway Foundation Award, the Asian American Literary Award, and the Flannery O'Connor Award for Short Fiction. In 2014 he was elected to the American Academy of Arts and Letters. He lives in the Boston area and is a professor of English and creative writing at Boston University.

A NOTE ON THE TYPE

This book was set in Adobe Garamond. Designed for the Adobe Corporation by Robert Slimbach, the fonts are based on types first cut by Claude Garamond (c. 1480–1561). Garamond was a pupil of Geoffroy Tory and is believed to have followed the Venetian models, although he introduced a number of important differences, and it is to him that we owe the letter we now know as "old style." He gave to his letters a certain elegance and feeling of movement that won their creator an immediate reputation and the patronage of Francis I of France.

Typeset by Scribe, Philadelphia, Pennsylvania

Printed and bound by Berryville Graphics, Berryville, Virginia

Designed by Iris Weinstein